"The protest 'I have to follow my conscience' often is just a way to shut down conversation. Kathryn Lilla Cox uses the claim to open up a dialog with a rich Catholic history of reflection on conscience, dissent, and scandal. With exceptionally clear writing, extensively documented research, and carefully nuanced analysis, she makes an original contribution to the relational quality of conscience wholly engaged in contemporary living."

> — Edward Vacek, SJ
> Stephen Duffy Chair of Catholic Studies
> Loyola University
> New Orleans, LA

"Dr. Kathryn Lilla Cox's *Water Shaping Stone* is a greatly needed book. For too long, discussions of conscience have been couched in the tired debates of personal autonomy versus compliance to authority. Instead of rehashing the arguments or taking sides in them, Dr. Cox shifts the conversation by considering conscience in light of the Christian call to discipleship. Her perspective speaks to why forming a conscience is important, communities are essential for this process, and the development of the whole person cannot be neglected. This relational approach also leads to an interpretation of dissent and scandal not so much as problematic discord but rather as part of the inevitable and important struggles of a community pursuing faithfulness to Jesus. Dr. Cox's is a rich and significant perspective, one that should make *Water Shaping Stone* the starting point for any future discussions on conscience."

> — Jason King
> Associate Professor of Theology, Saint Vincent College
> Associate Editor, *Journal of Moral Theology*

"Appeals to conscience in the midst of high-profile arguments about hot-button political issues have become more and more common in recent years, and this book found its genesis in helping students and others sort through what conscience is and how it might guide them with respect to such arguments. But Kathryn Lilla Cox is interested in far more than the relationship between faith and politics: instead, she guides her readers step by step, with clear and precise explanations and arguments, into an understanding of conscience that is not simply about particular moral choices but rather deeply rooted in the lifelong work of discipleship. Her insight, compassion, and depth of understanding shine as she argues that conscience, when understood in the context of the call to discipleship, can guide us through the ambiguous, shadowed, uncertain times of our lives, illuminating new possibilities for how we might better follow in the footsteps of Christ."

— Colleen Mary Carpenter, PhD
　Sister Mona Riley Endowed Chair of the Humanities
　Associate Professor of Theology
　Book Review Editor, *Horizons*, The Journal of the College Theology
　　Society
　Saint Catherine University

"This is a timely and superb book that very much needed to be written. Not only that, but its prose is both accessible and academically informed as well as inviting and compelling. Many persons, including Catholics and other Christians, may be conscious of conscience, but in an emaciated way that fails to interface robustly with the moral life or, for those of faith, the call to discipleship. Kathryn Lilla Cox is a conscientious and gracious moral theologian, and we are indebted to her for this graceful contribution to a topic that all too often is either oversimplified or over one's head."

— Tobias Winright
　Maeder Endowed Chair of Health Care Ethics
　Saint Louis University

Water Shaping Stone

Faith, Relationships, and Conscience Formation

Kathryn Lilla Cox

A Michael Glazier Book

LITURGICAL PRESS

Collegeville, Minnesota

www.litpress.org

A Michael Glazier Book published by Liturgical Press

Cover design by Jodi Hendrickson. Cover photo courtesy of Dreamstime.

Interior photos courtesy of Thinkstock.

1	2	3	4	5	6	7	8	9

Library of Congress Cataloging-in-Publication Data

Cox, Kathryn Lilla.
    Water shaping stone : faith, relationships, and conscience formation / Kathryn Lilla Cox.
        pages cm
    ISBN 978-0-8146-8302-6 — ISBN 978-0-8146-8327-9 (ebook)
    1. Conscience—Religious aspects—Catholic Church.   2. Catholic Church—Doctrines.   3. Conscience—Religious aspects—Christianity.   I. Title.
    BJ1278.C66C69   2015
    241'.1—dc23
                                                                          2015017070

Contents

Preface

Sometimes theologians choose the topic about which they research and write. Other times, events happen and research topics are chosen for theologians. The latter is how the seeds that resulted in this book were sown. Conscience as a category of sustained study, reflection, and consideration primarily occurred for me several weeks each fall semester. My students and I read and discussed together John Paul II's encyclical *Veritatis Splendor*, as well as Richard Gula's three chapters on conscience in his book *Reason Informed by Faith*. Then 2012 arrived, an election year, and Minnesota (where I live and work) had two ballot initiatives.

Both initiatives requested changes to the state constitution. The first would have required voters to present valid picture identification when voting. The Minnesota voter identification initiative, along with voter identification initiatives across the country, raised and continues to raise many important ethical questions about race, economic status, and societal power. The second initiative would have written into the state constitution a definition of marriage as between one man and one woman. In 2012, state law already defined marriage as between one man and one woman. The legislature as a body could vote to change any state law, but changes to the state constitution require a populace vote.[1]

While the voter identification ballot initiative was and remains an important moral issue, attention given to the marriage amendment by

---

[1] Therefore, in 2012, advocates for and many opponents of the constitutional changes knew that if the proposals passed any subsequent legislative changes to state law would require a prior vote by Minnesota citizens to change the constitution first. Both proposals to amend the state constitution failed to pass. Subsequently, the Minnesota state legislature in May 2013 passed gender-neutral language regarding marriage, and a bill permitting same-sex marriages in the legal arena. This legal right to marry does not entail the right to a religious marriage ceremony. In other words, the legal or state definition of marriage does not necessarily concur with religious definitions of marriage. After the law changed some religious groups and some denominational churches now facilitate same sex marriages, even as other groups and churches do not.

the media, politicians, and many religious communities leading up to the November 2012 election overshadowed the voter identification initiative. The Minnesota bishops supported the proposed constitutional marriage amendment, and former Minneapolis–St. Paul Archbishop Nienstedt, with the help of donors, spent approximately three quarters of a million dollars putting forward the Roman Catholic teaching on marriage. The Minnesota marriage amendment, church teaching, how to vote one's conscience, the effects of highly charged conversations on families and faith communities, and the desire of some same-sex couples to marry and have their relationships recognized loomed large. As people listened to appeals to "vote their conscience" in Minnesota several factors coalesced, creating confusion regarding what exactly "voting one's conscience" meant. These factors included the voices of bishops in other Christian denominations supporting same-sex marriage, the distinction between religious and legal understandings of marriage, the perceived political advocacy by some Catholic bishops, and competing definitions about what it meant to vote, let alone form, one's conscience.

This was the political and localized ecclesial context throughout 2012, particularly as November approached, that shaped my classroom teaching and my speaking to various groups about conscience and conscience formation. Time and again it was a heartwarming and heartrending privilege to listen as people shared their struggles to live their faith, follow the teachings of their Catholic bishops, and consider how to vote in that fall's election. People were wrestling with the reality of their experiences informed by their faith journeys, realities that at times misaligned with the mandates coming from Catholic bishops or Vatican offices. This wrestling included deep, respectful engagement with Roman Catholic teaching, insights from the depth and breadth of Roman Catholic intellectual life and history, Catholic bishops' statements, the statements of their own religious leaders (many students and people were Christian but not Catholic), and the secular issues of state politics. My 2012 experience researching, presenting, and teaching about conscience in the classroom, along with listening to people's stories and questions and having conversations with several colleagues, resulted in this book's basic structure.

While the 2012 Minnesota election year was the initial backdrop for this book, appeals to conscience are ongoing. Since 2012, appeals to conscience have been raised in relation to the Affordable Health Care Act and, most recently, in early reactions to Pope Francis's newest encyclical,

Laudato Sì (On Care for Our Common Home).[2] Santa Clara University's Markkula Center for Applied Ethics sponsored a series of lectures looking at conscience in relationship to stem cells, cloning, peace and justice, and Snowden and the internet, as well as the moral responsibility of corporations. Taken together, these explorations and appeals to conscience showcase the importance of conscience and its formation in many areas of human life.

Despite conscience's importance and relevance, one difficulty I encountered throughout 2012 in groups and in my classroom was the need to dismantle two competing and false understandings of conscience. The first claimed conscience relied on personal experience, thought, and feeling as the sole arbiter of truth. The second believed conscience meant following a course of action dictated by authority (often understood as bishops or Vatican offices) because of obedience conceived of as following orders while seeing no need for personal responsibility or accountability regarding a decision. These two extreme and erroneous perceptions of conscience pit personal experience and convictions against the teaching and authority of the Magisterium, whereby a person or community must choose one over the other. This false binary framework for considering conscience risks the moral agent's capacity for moral responsibility as well as hiding and gutting the call to discipleship.

An eviscerated notion of discipleship diminishes our ability to conceive our capacity for ongoing conversion and growth as a new being in Christ with the accompanying skills, practices, and virtues as features of a moral life. A centuries-long tradition, theological reflection, and the teaching at Vatican II acknowledges and keeps in dynamic tension the teaching authority of the Magisterium along with the individual/community's requirement to follow their conscience in the context of faith and relationship with God—in other words, discipleship.

The reality that discipleship, moral growth, formation, and right judgments of conscience occur over time—often in fits, starts, regression, renewal, and ongoing illumination—is alluded to in this book's title. Various relationships—and for believers the central relationship with the triune God—shape, form, and correct individual and communal consciences over time. Furthermore, the title carries many scriptural resonances

---

[2] The encyclical is dated May 24, 2015, and was released on June 18, 2015. It can be accessed at w2.vatican.va.

regarding water, heart, and formation that framed the research and writing of the book. Consequently, the title functions metaphorically for discussing conscience grounded in the call to and growth in discipleship. In other words, human moral formation (conscience formation) is an ongoing endeavor.

The first word—*Water*—recalls the many scriptural references to water and all that water symbolically means. Water first appears in Genesis when God separates the water from sky, and we hear about all the life that teems within it. Moses parts the Red Sea and the Hebrew people take the first steps toward freedom passing through the walls of water. Numerous wells mark the places where God meets women and men in sacred and revelatory ways (for example, Hagar and Jacob). The prophets see water rushing down the walls. Water also figures prominently in the New Testament, starting with the baptism of John the Baptist, Jesus' baptism, the calming of the waters, Jesus turning water into wine, and so forth. For Christians, water recalls our own baptism into a communal life of prayer, sacramentality, and relationship with the triune God and the requirement to live that life of faith. In all of these instances, water signifies in some way the movement into new life, celebration, transformation, and encounter with the triune God.

Therefore, for me, water highlights that our consciences are not simply a place within our psyches. Conscience, as a concept, pulls together our cognitive, affective, bodily, and spiritual dimensions. Conscience, while experienced as a judging faculty, also has elements of being a skill and virtue, always pointing toward and illuminating the status of our relationships. It is too facile and simplistic to presume that we can predict what conclusions our conscience will arrive at or truths it will illuminate. Instead, our encounters with the living God, with other human beings, with the created world, and with ourselves begin to elucidate the contours of understanding right, wrong, good, evil, discipleship, and holiness. While often difficult, following one's conscience requires focus on what God is bringing forth, where new life is arising, what is being cleansed or washed away—in short, discerning and responding to where God is acting in our lives. This holds true for individuals, communities, and families.

The second and third words—*Shaping Stone*—stem from scriptural resonances to hearts of stone and time spent near the ocean visiting family, friends, and while on sabbatical. Beaches that form the Long Island Sound or the coast of California have many stones and rocks. The stones are different colors, textures, and sizes, shaped by different types of waves, yet shaped by water nonetheless. The shaping of rock into diverse stones takes time. Gradually pieces of rock break apart, sharp edges wear down, and, with the passage of time far exceeding our life span, the rocks and then stones become grains of sand so tiny by themselves. Yet together they form a textured ground upon which to walk, run, and play. Thus, *Shaping Stone* alludes to the manner in which God works on our hearts of stone. We are resistant, hard-hearted, slow. God, patiently and like the waves of the ocean, continues to wash over us, cleansing, shaping, and contouring us over a lifetime—not immediately, but gradually over the years. Like the stones carried and tossed by waves, we are often picked up, carried elsewhere, or tossed around by others, while always remaining within the water, carried by God, the one in whom we live and move and have our being. Becoming a new being in Christ and faithfully living the covenantal relationship, manifest in our relationship with family, friends, enemies, neighbors, strangers, and the rest of God's creation, remains a slower process than we like to think. As is the ability to discern the Spirit's breath of new life, stirring creative responses to the signs of the times. The same holds true for conscience formation.

The subtitle for this book, *Faith, Relationships, and Conscience Formation*, is an acknowledgment that we are relational and spiritual beings, an insight stemming from the belief that we are *imago Dei, imago* triune God. We do not emerge into the world as actualized, fully free moral agents. Neither do we form ourselves in isolation. We are born into a matrix of relationships and familial, cultural, national, religious histories not initially of our making. Thus, while it could be argued that newborns and children do not share the same hardness of hearts that adults have, nonetheless children are born into a world of sin and grace, initially shaped and formed by the communities into which they arrive. As we grow from newborns into adulthood, we interact with the various persons and forces within these communities. We begin making decisions and judgments regarding our actions, the type of person we wish to be, and how we want to be known. As a result, we add our own story and history to the communal mix, becoming part of the formation process for others.

For better or worse, human beings help shape each other. We do so by ignoring God's grace and self-offer while living out of ego, self-destruction, death, and sin—thus, squashing and killing life, hopes, and dreams in so many ways. We also live by responding to God's grace and self-offer by birthing, nourishing, fostering, and supporting new life, hopes, dreams, and the reign of God. Our lifetime work consists, then, in growing, undergoing conversion, and falling more deeply in love with God, fellow humans, and all God's creation. Our faith and relationships form the matrix within which we develop as moral agents and beings.

May God—the One who created, sustains, and calls us to live more deeply a life of love, mercy, compassion, kindness, and justice—help us to see each other and the world as God sees it. May Jesus Christ be our model and guide for understanding what living a life of service, justice, healing, and relational sacrifice entails. May the Spirit enlighten us in our whole being—mind, body, affections, and spirit—as we seek life-giving Truth and deeper intimacy with the Ground of our being so that we may live more intentionally as witnesses to the triune God's love, faithfulness, mercy, compassion, kindness, and justice.

Acknowledgments

While writing is often done in solitude, the reality is that writing has a communal dimension. Therefore, I would like to acknowledge and thank some of the people who, behind the scenes, provided me with support, encouragement, and feedback in various ways.

My colleagues Mary Forman, OSB, and Kevin Seasoltz, OSB, were instrumental in helping me think about the nascent book found in the presentations I had given on conscience and conscience formation. Thank you.

Hans Christoffersen, who from the moment I approached him with the idea for this book was supportive and encouraging about the project. He has been a model of patience, providing guidance, humor at key points, and conversations when I needed them. Thank you.

To my editor, Lauren L. Murphy, thank you for your patience, laughter, and clarifying questions. It was a joy to work with you on this project.

Many colleagues engaged in conversations about the book in various venues. These conversations were valuable in so many ways: for their encouragement, insights, questions, and clarification of my budding ideas. Several colleagues were generous beyond measure in reading, responding to, and commenting on chapter drafts, in addition to numerous conversations regarding the ideas in this book. Thank you to Erin Lothes Biviano, Julia Harless Brumbaugh, and Kari-Shane Davis Zimmerman.

A heartfelt thank you to Anne E. Patrick, SNJM, for her gift of time discussing her work, her feedback on my interpretations of her work, conversations about conscience in general, and her probing questions. Terrence Tilley and Anthony Godzieba both responded to my questions about their work. I am grateful to these colleagues and any mistaken interpretations of their work remain mine.

A special thank you to Connie DeBiase who read and commented on various drafts of all chapters, providing an insightful keen eye from the perspective of decades of work with the faithful of all stripes.

Thank you to all of the staff at Liturgical Press who helped with the behind-the-scenes work on the book. Your work is beautiful.

Research does not happen without a library and librarians. Thank you to the various librarians at the University of San Diego who aided my research and provided a comfortable place to work during my time in San Diego. David Wuolu and Miranda Novak, librarians at my institution (College of Saint Benedict and Saint John's University), provided much needed assistance navigating e-books, scanned digital copies of older manuscripts, broken URLs, and various other aspects of the online internet research world. Their help and candor was appreciated. Thank you to Grace Ellens and the School of Theology and Seminary for hosting Theology Days. You provide a space for conversation within the church.

Patrick, thank you for your support and sharing in this journey as my partner, spouse, and companion. Your unwavering belief that this writing endeavor is in itself a vocation that serves the people of God sustains and reminds me of God's call and presence in my life. Thank you seems insufficient.

The Benedictine communities of Saint John's Abbey in Collegeville, Minnesota, and Saint Benedict's Monastery in St. Joseph, Minnesota, provided space to present and discuss my early research into and thoughts on conscience. Their engagement with my work, their questions, comments, and insights, were invigorating and provided avenues for further research. I remain grateful.

This book is dedicated to the monastic women of Saint Benedict's Monastery with deep joy, affection, and gratitude for their faithful witness, joyful welcome, listening to God with the ear of their hearts, and the ability to midwife gifts in others.

Introduction

Moral theology's history, like any other theological discipline, is richly complex, filled with pitfalls and life-giving insights for Christian living. Over time various emphases within moral theology have swung, shifted, and coexisted. Therefore, even as moral manuals dominated the era immediately before Vatican II, theological shifts were already under way. Consequently, when the Second Vatican Council called for moral theology's renewal, many postconciliar theologians were poised to ponder not only actions but also the human person (moral agent), questions of being (who am I or who are we becoming), and character (practice and cultivation of virtue).[1] Additionally, ongoing research into moral theology's history reinscribed the value of casuistry while dismantling the misconception that moral theology was a static field.[2]

While the renewal brought forth bountiful fruit, Linda Hogan noted in 2000 that contemporary moral theology is fraught with divisions among

---

[1] An early wave of postconciliar writings and debates addressed moral theology's method and content, the implementation of conciliar directives, and responses to *Humane Vitae*, the papal encyclical published a mere three years after the council ended. More specifically, these early postconciliar debates examined the question of an autonomous ethic as opposed to a faith ethic, considered the status of natural law and the role of Scripture in ethics, and fostered the retrieval of virtue ethics. For some overviews of these debates, see Richard A. McCormick, *Notes on Moral Theology: 1965–1980* (Washington, DC: University Press of America, 1981); Charles E. Curran and Richard A. McCormick, eds., *Readings in Moral Theology, No. 1–8* (New York: Paulist Press, 1979–1983); Paulinus Ikechukwu Odozor, *Moral Theology in an Age of Renewal: A Study of the Catholic Tradition since Vatican II* (South Bend, IN: Notre Dame Press, 2003).

[2] See, for example, Albert Jonsen and Stephen Toulmin, *The Abuse of Casuistry* (Berkeley: University of California Press, 1988); James F. Keenan and Thomas Shannon, eds., *The Context of Casuistry* (Washington, DC: Georgetown University Press, 1995); Charles E. Curran, *The Origins of Moral Theology in the United States: Three Different Approaches* (Washington, DC: Georgetown University Press, 1997); Klaus Demmer, *Shaping the Moral Life: An Approach to Moral Theology*, trans. Roberto Dell'Oro, ed. James Keenan (Washington, DC: Georgetown University Press, 2000); Julia Fleming, *Defending Probabilism: The Moral Theology of Juan Caramuel* (Washington, DC: Georgetown University Press, 2006).

theologians themselves, and between theologians and the Magisterium. She wrote that conscience "figures prominently in popular perceptions and discussions of these academic debates" even as conscience rarely has "sustained analysis."[3] Therefore, Hogan saw the need to "reconstruct a theology of conscience in light of the problems of contemporary Catholic moral theology."[4] Her reconstruction accounts for various understandings of conscience within the intellectual tradition, including church documents. While maintaining the church's role in conscience formation, she argues that the church must educate and nurture in ways that are "respectful of the seriousness with which most people engage in ethical reflection and that is supportive of their conscientiously held beliefs and values."[5] Hogan identifies the need to ask questions that consider how we act on our conscientious decisions rather than continually focusing on the status of church teaching, its authority, and what obedience is due the teaching as foundational concerns for conscience. She provides a road map for this shift premised on a personalist understanding of conscience. Hogan's personalist framework attends to the moral agent and their formation when considering moral action and decision making. Her paradigm considers and respects the lived reality, nuance, and various considerations humans bring to bear on their moral judgments, decisions, and actions. Additionally, Hogan argues for shared general principles and sees value in acknowledging that there is a legitimate plurality of applications and interpretations of norms. Her personalist paradigm also has room to consider and judge both character and action.

So, if Hogan provided a framework and model for considering conscience that aids the moral agent in his or her decision-making process and proposes a way beyond some contemporary methodological issues in moral theology, why another book on conscience? Despite Hogan's work and the work of others, as I experienced in 2012, conscience and its role are still frequently misunderstood and misemployed.

Thus, this reality highlights that even with the vibrancy and renewal of moral theology in the fifty years after the council, renewal work re-

---

[3] Linda Hogan, *Confronting the Truth: Conscience in the Catholic Tradition* (New York/ Mahwah, NJ: Paulist Press, 2000), 1. She discusses the debates throughout the book in more detail.

[4] Ibid., 2.

[5] Ibid., 6–7. Hogan uses the term "church" in a variety of ways, sometimes meaning the Magisterium or the papacy, other times not. A more extensive description of how she uses the term "church" is beyond the scope of this project.

mains indispensable. Charles Curran recently wrote that he sees "the most significant agenda for Catholic moral theology today—[as] the need to develop a moral theology that is truly theological in light of Vatican II."[6] Developing a truly theological moral theology necessitates further examination of the areas already explored in Vatican II's aftermath. Moral theologians must continue working to incorporate more fully into their work theological insights from the areas of Scripture, God, Christology, pneumatology, ecclesiology, discipleship, and so forth. This task is more than one book or person can accomplish.

My purpose is to contribute, however modestly, to the job laid out by Charles Curran "to develop a moral theology that is truly theological in light of Vatican II" by addressing once again conscience and the moral agent's formation. My approach will neither detail nor provide a literature review on conscience. Nor do I try to resolve any tensions inherent within the tradition, including the Vatican II documents themselves and in the various interpretations of conscience after Vatican II. Rather, I lay out a selection of conscience's intellectual and historical patrimony in order to lift up and focus on theological aspects drowned out by the noise when personal autonomy stays pitted against magisterial authority. This means I choose to focus on selected thinkers and ideas, raising up certain resources within the tradition for comprehending conscience's role in our moral lives. The purpose is to provide some perspective on why various views on conscience exist and consider often overlooked or underutilized theological resources on conscience. Furthermore, I point to, as an outgrowth of the Second Vatican Council's call to holiness and engagement with the world, how discipleship enriches and deepens our perceptions regarding conscience's value and role in our moral lives.

The book proceeds in the following fashion. Chapter 1 examines conscience as defined in contemporary Catholic magisterial documents composed in the latter half of the twentieth century: specifically, *Gaudium et Spes*, *Dignitatis Humanae*, the *Catechism*, and *Veritatis Splendor*.

Chapter 2 explores conscience in other sources, starting with biblical understandings of conscience and then the work of theologians Thomas Aquinas, Cardinal John Henry Newman, Bernard Häring, and Anne Patrick. Each theologian was selected for the way he or she illuminates the intellectual tradition informing or stemming from Vatican II's teaching.

---

[6] Charles E. Curran, *The Development of Moral Theology: Five Strands* (Washington, DC: Georgetown University Press, 2013), 284.

Chapter 3 discusses how individual and communal conscience formation is a process for developing moral awareness and ongoing discernment that leads to moral decision making, action, and continual reflection on the validity of judgments. The formation process touches on the role of the church community, Scripture, and prayer ritual in our moral formation, illuminating the complexities of and myriad influences on our formation as moral agents.

Chapter 4 explores the question of what is required of a formed conscience leading to a different judgment than official magisterial pronouncements. Avery Dulles's typology of dissent and criteria for dissenting is analyzed along with the 1968 United States bishops' norms for licit dissent. After identifying that dissent as described and considered in these sources concerns orthodoxy, the possibility of legitimate plurality of practices is briefly explored. The work of Thomas Kopfensteiner on the metaphorical structure of normativity and Anthony Godzieba's work on unity, identity, and difference is employed in considering legitimate plural practices springing from a given norm.

Chapter 5 contemplates the reality of scandal as a possibility stemming from rightful disagreement. Thus, defining scandal becomes crucial, as does distinguishing sociological from theological scandal. Both sociological and theological scandal can result from both action and inaction. Theologically, Christians must grapple with the truth that scandal occurs not only because of sinful behavior but also from graced living. Jesus Christ shows us that discipleship can mean causing scandal because one follows the ways of the living God. Therefore, highlighting that scandal can result from both action and inaction, Christianity must deal with the scandal of the cross. In so doing, Christian discipleship and the scandal of the cross refocus our efforts for understanding the formation of the moral agent (conscience formation). Christian discipleship contextualized by the scandal of the cross should influence, inform, and foster how we view conscience formation, practices, and actions. Any individual or community's claim to live from a well-formed conscience needs to be determined not only by assent to doctrine but also by how well we live the demands of discipleship.

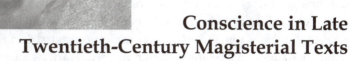

Chapter 1

Conscience in Late
Twentieth-Century Magisterial Texts

Introduction

The Catholic Church's intellectual history regarding conscience contributes to contemporary differences in the understanding and application of conscience. Current tensions surrounding conscience within magisterial documents, as well as among theologians, laity, and the Magisterium, are not unique given the complexity of this history. In this chapter, I examine how the definition and articulation of conscience's function in four specific contemporary Catholic magisterial sources actually contributes to the tensions surrounding conscience. The sources are as follows: the conciliar documents *Gaudium et Spes* and *Dignitatis Humanae*, the *Catechism of the Catholic Church*, and a papal encyclical by John Paul II, *Veritatis Splendor*.[1]

Before proceeding, a word about method in this chapter. Given the ecclesial practice of using prior magisterial texts and statements, Scripture, and other sources when promulgating new ecclesial documents, a chronological analysis of these can be insightful. A chronological study helps identify whether reiteration, reinterpretation, recontextualization,

---

[1] Each of the ecclesial documents has different functions; therefore, when reading and analyzing the ecclesial documents and statements we have to resist the temptation to see them all as carrying equal measure and authority, potentially raising all statements and teaching to the level of infallible, irreformable dogma. For more depth and information on the weight of various magisterial pronouncements, see, for example, Richard R. Gaillardetz, *Teaching with Authority: A Theology of the Magisterium in the Church* (Collegeville, MN: Liturgical Press, A Michael Glazier Book, 1997); Richard R. Gaillardetz, *By What Authority? A Primer on Scripture, the Magisterium, and the Sense of the Faithful* (Collegeville, MN: Liturgical Press, 2003); Francis A. Sullivan, *Creative Fidelity: Weighing and Interpreting Documents of the Magisterium* (Eugene, OR: Wipf and Stock Publishers, 1996).

or renewal of ideas has occurred in the promulgation of new documents. The chronological analysis aids the researcher or reader with this identification by noticing where language or ideas are adopted, dropped, or placed within close proximity to each other. Adaptation, deletion, and placement of ideas within documents shape and inform our contemporary understanding of conscience and its application. As a result, intertextual chronological work can reveal the overlapping and divergent ways new documents utilize authoritative statements that define and interpret conscience. Therefore, remembering that various magisterial documents have distinctive functions, reinterpretation happens, various interpretations can be correct, and new insights emerge remains essential when reading and explaining particular documents on conscience. It is helpful to keep these considerations in mind when studying the effective history of ideas and the Catholic intellectual history starting with four magisterial sources.

This methodological decision for discussing and analyzing *Gaudium et Spes*, *Dignitatis Humanae*, the *Catechism of the Catholic Church*, and *Veritatis Splendor* illustrates how the meaning of a term can shift and change based on context. Both the *Catechism* and *Veritatis Splendor* rely on *Gaudium et Spes* in describing conscience, yet the selective use of textual material subtly shifts the meaning given to conscience in *Gaudium et Spes*.

The discussion and analysis of the four sources proceeds in three major sections. Section 1 briefly introduces hermeneutics since the intertextual work and analysis intended in this chapter is a hermeneutical exercise. Section 2 examines the four documents noted earlier, focusing on an analysis of each document's definition and description of conscience. This analysis includes some brief attention to what other documents or resources are used from the tradition, aiding the assessment of how conscience has been reinterpreted or reappropriated. Section 3 builds on the work done in section 2 by highlighting points of coherence and dissonance between the documents' descriptions of conscience. The points of coherence and dissonance raise additional questions that will be considered in later chapters.

Section 1: Hermeneutics

Hermeneutics as a discipline articulates, studies, and develops various theories of textual interpretation. A text can be a written document, a painting, a sculpture, a musical score, and so forth. Broadly speaking, the field describes the relationship between author and text, the relationship between reader and text, and the effective history of the text's interpretation by individuals and communities. Hermeneutics strives to explain how we engage the potentially myriad interpretations of a text in order to comprehend their meaning within and for a community as sources and frameworks for knowledge. Additionally, hermeneutics aims to illustrate how a text's given meaning shapes and frames the interpretation and comprehension of current or future events or experiences. Thus, texts often have a transcendent quality where they can speak about timeless truths about reality across generations, even as they (texts) require appropriation in new milieus. David Tracy calls these timeless texts classics.[2] The classic text continually reveals or speaks to people even as it contains elements that appear strange or alien to readers in new eras. Further appropriation adds fresh layers of interpretation and possible meaning.

David Tracy argues that this phenomenon occurs because, once the words are written, the author's intention and meaning are no longer in the author's control. Instead, the text is put into a dynamic conversation with the reader. Any textual interpretation and comprehension begins while reading the text because readers bring to any text the constellation of their life experiences, worldview, culture, and other knowledge. This constellation of factors affects how readers interpret, comprehend, and respond to both new and familiar texts.[3] This dynamic interplay between reader and text helps explain why in a book club, Bible study, or art class varied explanations of a book's, Scripture's, or a painting's meaning occur. In fact, you as a reader are already forming opinions, thoughts, and reactions to what you are reading here, informed by your current frameworks, knowledge, and experiences, thus employing the dynamic that the field of hermeneutics explains and explicates.

Experience of God

German theologian Klaus Demmer argues that an experience of God roots all other experiences for the believing moral agent. Believers have an encounter with God that becomes the cornerstone for engaging and

---

[2] David Tracy, *The Analogical Imagination: Christian Theology and the Culture of Pluralism* (New York: Crossroad, 1981).

[3] David Tracy, *Plurality and Ambiguity: Hermeneutics, Religion, and Hope* (Chicago: University of Chicago Press, 1987).

interpreting other experiences within a framework of meaning. According to Demmer, while the individual's unique experience of God shapes her life in myriad ways, "it is the history of God with humanity and of humanity with God, which constitutes the specific object of religious experience."[4] In other words, salvation history is a communal history. Our individual experiences with God, while forming an individual narrative, exist within and are part of a communal narrative, a community's history with God. As Demmer points out, the original shared experience by the original disciples of the life, death, and resurrection of Jesus is centrally important for the Christian community. For Demmer, this original experience includes the anthropological reality that the revelation of God's self in Jesus Christ releases humanity's truth, as understood by Christians. This releasing of humanity's truth reveals our capacity to respond freely to grace—God's self-communication—manifest in human actions, behavior, and interior integrity.[5] Stated slightly differently, experiences of responding to God's self-communication become the crucibles by which believers grow into the possibilities of their freedom.[6] For Demmer, this process of growing into possibilities of freedom through experience is filtered by and interpreted in a faith context. This process, filtration, and interpretation of experience and encounter form the basis for a Christian moral obligation and ultimately lead to norms for action.[7] Thus, experience is not knowledge we collect but a structuring of our life, with the continual process by which we evaluate meaning, our value system, and obligations to God and others manifest in our actions.[8]

---

[4] Klaus Demmer, "Sittlich Handeln aus Erfahrung," *Gregorianum* 59 (1978): 661–90, at 683. All translations from this article are mine.

[5] Klaus Demmer, *Living the Truth: A Theory of Action*, trans. Brian McNeil (Washington, DC: Georgetown University Press, 2010).

[6] Demmer, "Sittlich Handeln aus Erfahrung," 683. Demmer acknowledges the reality that the response to God can be a no, or a turning away from the offer of God's self. A discussion of freedom's complexity is beyond the scope of this text.

[7] Ibid., 683–84.

[8] Ibid., 686. German has two words that can be translated into English as "experience," *das Erlebnis* and *die Erfahrung*. There are nuances between the two terms even though both are translated as "experience." *Die Erfahrung* carries connotations of discovering or knowing about something through living life. For more information on the differences, see *Langenscheidts New College German Dictionary*, ed. Sonia Brough, rev. ed. (New York: Langenscheidt, 1995), s.v. "Erfahrung," 191; s.v. "Erlebnis," 195; Hans-Georg Gadamer, *Truth and Method*, rev. 2nd ed., trans. Joel Weinsheimer and Donald G. Marshall (New York: Continuum, 1995), xiii.

According to Demmer, our experience (*Erfahrung*) is not just data to be added to moral methodology. A dialectical relationship exists between experience and insight. New experiences can result in a changed interpretive framework or perspective, permitting new insights to emerge; with those new insights, new strategies for action can be discovered. This dynamic means Demmer recognizes the reality that moral insight remains grounded in history's developments and conditions.[9] Moral insight—in history and not ahistorical—is both rooted in past experiences and insight and at the same time develops through new experience.[10] Therefore, no pure insight exists since our comprehension of reality, truth, and meaning remains incomplete, always unfolding and revealing what was hidden, potentially opening the human being up to that which goes beyond one's own experience or self.[11] Additionally, experiences themselves are not absolute but always interpreted and understood in light of underlying insights.[12] Experience, while essential to growth in freedom, must be critically appropriated. As Demmer argues, "Experience does not convert mechanically into insight."[13] In other words, experience cannot be put on an assembly line to gain insight. Humans must critically examine and reflect on experience in order to arrive at insight, always mindful that common experiences can yield different moral interpretations or applications—thus the necessity for reflection and critical examination in dialogue.[14]

This brief foray into hermeneutics highlights that knowledge remains partial and incomplete, as does our comprehension or grasp of that knowledge. The theological counterpart is the recognition that God reveals the fullness of truth, yet due to our finitude, our grasp of truth is partial, mediated, and incomplete.[15] This partial, incomplete grasp of truth

---

[9] Demmer, "Sittlich Handeln aus Erfahrung," 661–62. The conditions of history to which Demmer alludes include experience and the known anthropological foundations exerting a moral claim in history, including freedom.

[10] Ibid., 662.

[11] Ibid., 681. In other words, there are experiences that tear the fabric of people's lives, whether positively or negatively, and cannot be reduced to a snapshot of the event. Certain experiences disrupt a worldview, touch us deeply, and require some form of reweaving the fabric of our lives in the attempt to structure a meaningful way to engage the world. Life teaches us that knowledge is more than just facts; knowledge includes practical wisdom, insight.

[12] Ibid., 682.

[13] Ibid., 679–80.

[14] Ibid., 680n49.

[15] Cf. 1 Cor 13:12.

requires ongoing reflection and meditation as we seek a deeper, richer understanding of truth both personally and communally. I would argue that the hermeneutical relationship Demmer perceives between experience and insight helps with reading Vatican II on conscience.

Vatican II documents are the entry point for contemporary understandings of conscience since they provide the theoretical description of conscience and its workings.[16] No one comes to those documents a *tabula rasa*, however. Human beings and communities live the results of conscience's formation, judgment, and effects—author and reader included. Eventually, multiple explications must be considered and placed within an effective history of interpretation, influencing contemporary and future understandings of conscience. The Vatican II documents make use of prior descriptions of conscience while their own definition of conscience permits and requires interaction between objective standards (norms, laws, rules) and subjective engagement (human experience). Any judgment of conscience requires awareness and commitment to truth as

---

[16] Ecclesially, we see a testing of hermeneutical theory as new books are written, theories debated, and new analyses emerge about Vatican II and our ongoing reception and implementation fifty years after the initial event. Questions of meaning, different tropes for understanding the council, and new facts require looking anew at conciliar documents and our own prior comprehension, interpretation, and implementation or lack thereof regarding the council and its effects on theological fields of study. The fiftieth anniversary of Vatican II spanned the years from 2012 to 2015. A plethora of articles, books, commentaries, lectures, and so forth has resulted. These works consider the events of Vatican II itself, who was there, how the documents developed, what the voting results were, among other issues at the council. The analysis of Vatican II also explores events and theological insights that occurred before the council and the effect of those events and insights. Additionally, debates and conversations continue regarding the interpretation of Vatican II. How are we to continue interpreting and appropriating its documents and legacy? How do prior interpretations influence contemporary understandings of the council and its documents? See, for example, the six sets and a series of works celebrating Vatican II published by the Jesuit journal *Theological Studies* from September 2012 to March 2014, now collected and published as *50 Years On: Probing the Riches of Vatican II*, ed. David Schultenover (Collegeville, MN: Liturgical Press, 2015); John W. O'Malley, *What Happened at Vatican II* (Cambridge, MA, and London: The Belknap Press of Harvard University Press, 2008); Massimo Faggioli, *Vatican II: The Battle for Meaning* (New York: Paulist Press, 2012); Kristin Colberg, "The Hermeneutics of Vatican II: Reception, Authority, and the Debate over the Council's Interpretation," *Horizons* 38, no. 2 (September 1, 2011): 230–52; James L. Heft and John O'Malley, eds., *After Vatican II: Trajectories and Hermeneutics* (Grand Rapids, MI, and Cambridge: William B. Eerdmans Publishing Company, 2012); Matthew Lamb and Matthew Levering, eds., *Vatican II: Renewal within Tradition* (Oxford: Oxford University Press, 2008); William Madges, ed., *Vatican II: Forty Years Later* (Maryknoll, NY: Orbis, 2006)

well as the knowledge of the human moral agent (subject) who must live out their commitments, values, and judgments regarding right action. Therefore, the ongoing renewal of moral theology and understanding exactly what the council said about conscience and the effective history of those statements requires turning now to the magisterial documents, starting with *Gaudium et Spes.*

Section 2: Examination of Select Magisterial Documents

General Context

I just finished arguing that experience matters and no author or reader remains uninfluenced by what came before him or her, and this is also true of the council's participants. The conciliar fathers and participants carried with them in various ways effects from political events,[17] ecclesial concerns,[18] papal writings,[19] theological intellectual currents,[20] and historical and societal

---

[17] For example, the French Revolution, the elimination of Papal States in Italy, the Enlightenment, and "liberalism" created upheaval for ecclesial leadership. See O'Malley, *What Happened at Vatican II*, 53–54.

[18] In some intellectual circles within the magisterium there was distrust of certain philosophical schools, the use of the historical method for scriptural exegesis, and other social sciences in the theological endeavor. O'Malley, *What Happened at Vatican II*, 53–92.

[19] Gregory XVI in his 1832 encyclical *Mirari Vos* (On Liberalism and Religious Indifferentism) stated that freedom of conscience for everyone was an "absurd and erroneous proposition." Thirty years later, in 1864, Pius IX published the *Syllabus of Errors*, meant to highlight problems with the current thought and culture seen as threatening Catholicism's place and influence in the world. Leo XIII took a different tack to the concerns regarding modern philosophy, however, when he promulgated *Aeterni Patris* (1879) on the restoration of Christian philosophy. While referencing the great universities of the Middle Ages along with other scholastic theologians, Leo XIII primarily focused on the work of Thomas Aquinas. Theologically the return to Thomism led to various schools of neo-Thomism. See Gerald A. McCool's two books for more details on the neo-Thomism schools of thought: *Nineteenth-Century Scholasticism: The Search for a Unitary Method* (New York: Fordham University Press, 1989); idem, *From Unity to Pluralism: The Internal Evolution of Thomism* (New York: Fordham University Press, 1989). Finally, scriptural studies took a different turn with Pope Pius XII's promulgation of *Divino Afflante Spiritu* in 1943. This encyclical set the stage for Catholic biblical scholarship to utilize the previously suspect historical-critical method of scholarship, leading to new ways of comprehending and assimilating biblical insights.

[20] Some dogmatic theologians were returning to the sources of the early church, the writings of the patristic era. This *ressourcement* laid groundwork for later theological movement. Meanwhile, certain moral theologians sought alternatives to the moral manual. For examples, see Gérard Gilleman, *The Primacy of Charity in Moral Theology*, trans. William F. Ryan and André Vachon (Westminster, MD: Newman Press, 1959); Franz Tillmann, *The*

changes.[21] The various ecclesial, theological, and societal events formed the background canvas and chorus for Vatican II's participants, while their experiences, training, debates, and study became the soil that bore the conciliar fruit of their labor bringing the church into the modern world.

Gaudium et Spes

Pope John XXIII called for the council in 1959. The council's preparatory years occurred between 1959 and 1962. The council itself consisted of four sessions, each ten weeks long, from 1962 to 1965.[22] The Second Vatican Council resulted in sixteen documents promulgated by Pope Paul VI, "in his name and in the name of the council."[23] These sixteen documents are placed into three categories: constitutions, decrees, and declarations. The first, constitutions, carry the most weight and consist of four documents: *Sacrosanctum Concilium* (Constitution on Sacred Liturgy), *Lumen Gentium* (Dogmatic Constitution on the Church), *Dei Verbum* (Dogmatic Constitution on Divine Revelation), and *Gaudium et Spes* (Pastoral Constitution on the Church in the Modern World).

Originally, *Gaudium et Spes* (*GS*) was not on the conciliar agenda. The seeds for it were planted, however, during debates in the first session on the church schema. Cardinal Leo Joseph Suenens distinguished between "the church looking inward (*ad intra*) and the [church] looking outward to the world (*ad extra*)." The role of the church looking outward eventually was captured and put forth in *GS*.[24] *Gaudium et Spes* passed during the

---

Master Calls: A Handbook of Morals for the Layman, trans. Gregory J. Roettger (Baltimore: Helicon Press, 1960); and Bernard Häring, *The Law of Christ*, 3 vols., trans. Edwin Kaiser (Westminster, MD: Newman Press, 1961). For an excellent discussion of their lives and work, see James F. Keenan, *A History of Moral Theology in the Twentieth Century: From Confessing Sins to Liberating Consciences* (New York: Continuum, 2010), 59–110.

[21] O'Malley, *What Happened at Vatican II*, 53–92; David Hollenbach, "Commentary on *Gaudium et Spes*," in *Modern Catholic Social Teaching: Commentaries and Interpretations*, ed. Kenneth R. Himes (Washington, DC: Georgetown University Press, 2005), 267–69. The historical and societal events include, but are not limited to, the Enlightenment, the industrial revolution, the United States Civil War and later the civil rights movement, two world wars, the effects of neocolonialism on the continents of Africa and Asia, and the Cuban Missile Crisis.

[22] For more specific information on the council, see O'Malley, *What Happened at Vatican II*.

[23] Ibid., 333n2. This footnote discusses that Paul VI was the first signatory, and then that all the conciliar fathers signed the documents. Each document had the same prologue.

[24] Ibid., 157–58. For more detail on *GS*'s road to promulgation, see Michael G. Lawler, Todd A. Salzman, and Eileen Burke-Sullivan, eds., *The Church in the Modern World: Gaudium et Spes Then and Now* (Collegeville, MN: Liturgical Press, 2014).

fourth and final session on December 7, 1965, the day before the council closed. As a pastoral rather than a dogmatic constitution, *GS* does not restate doctrine even as it remains grounded in doctrinal principles.[25] Rather, the document seeks to illuminate the solidarity between Christians and all people, to provide guidance for helping people engage the world, live their faith, and show faith's relevance in answering or engaging the questions of the day. As the opening lines read:

> The joys and hopes, the grief and anguish of the people of our time, especially of those who are poor or afflicted, are the joys and hopes, the grief and anguish of the followers of Christ as well. Nothing that is genuinely human fails to find an echo in their hearts. For theirs is a community of people united in Christ and guided by the holy Spirit in their pilgrimage towards the Father's kingdom, bearers of a message of salvation for all of humanity. That is why they cherish a feeling of deep solidarity with the human race and its history. (*GS* 1)[26]

These opening lines indicate that Christians share the same hopes, joys, sorrows, and anguish of all people. Christians belong to the human family and thus are affected by its problems and life-giving endeavors; we are not separate from but integrated into the world. From the perspective of faith, we view the problems and possible solutions "in the light of the Gospel" and have resources and insights to bear on the world's ills (*GS* 3). How does *GS* attend to these issues, and where does conscience fit in?[27]

---

[25] Austin Flannery, ed., *Vatican Council II: The Conciliar and Postconciliar Documents* (Collegeville, MN: Liturgical Press, 2014), 903n1.

[26] While an argument can be made to keep the original translation from the Latin into English, since "man" or "men" could at the time mean all of humanity (female and male) or men in particular, I have chosen to use the gender-inclusive language translation.

[27] Structurally, *Gaudium et Spes* has a preface, an introduction, and two parts. The preface and introduction to *GS* cover paragraphs 1–10. Part 1 has an introduction and four chapters incorporating paragraphs 11–45. Paragraphs 11–39 discuss the human person and develop the theological anthropology undergirding part 2. Paragraphs 40–45 discuss the relationship of the world and the church as well as the faithful who inhabit both spheres. The dynamic learning from each other is briefly acknowledged and sketched before moving to part 2.

Part 2 looks at the issues and problems facing the world and its people, offering response outlines grounded in part 1's theological anthropology. Part 2 has an introduction and five chapters spanning paragraphs 46–93 that consider the following issues: marriage and family, cultural development, economic and social life, the political community (public life and politics), peace, the community of nations, war, and the role of the church/its members in all of these areas. Part 2 provides the contours supporting the argument for connecting personal (individual or even communal) with public, social morality.

Pick up many moral theology books discussing conscience and *Gaudium et Spes* 16 (see below) is cited as the conciliar statement on conscience. While it is valid to use *GS* 16 as the basis for describing conscience, this paragraph is not the only place *GS* speaks about conscience. One danger in focusing on *GS* 16 without considering its textual placement or other descriptions of conscience within *GS* is the risk of proof-texting. Hermeneutically, where the term appears matters since the surrounding discussion affects any definition, comprehension, and interpretation of conscience. Knowing where and how conscience shows up in the document provides additional clues for understanding conscience. For example, comparing the English translation provided by Austin Flannery[28] with the Vatican's English translation[29] reveals slight variations in how the Latin *conscientia* is translated into English. Where variance appears, both usually maintain the sense of the original Latin, *conscientia*. Therefore, I will focus on the twenty-five times both English translations use "conscience" as the translation of *conscientia*.[30]

The term "conscience" shows up in seventeen different paragraphs dispersed almost equally throughout parts 1 (16, 19, 26, 27, 31, 41, 43) and 2 (47, 50, 52, 61, 74, 76, 79, 87), with one mention each in the preface (3) and the introduction (8). Each paragraph uses conscience once, with paragraph 16 being the one exception. Eight of the twenty-five shared references in Flannery's and the Vatican's translations occur in paragraph 16, almost a full third. This simple fact highlights why theologians cite

---

[28] Austin Flannery, ed., *Vatican Council II; The Conciliar and Post Conciliar Documents,* (Collegeville, MN: Liturgical Press, 2014). This is the inclusive-language translation.

[29] The Vatican's translation can be found at http://w2.vatican.va/content/vatican/en.html.

[30] The Latin version of *Gaudium et Spes* uses *conscientia* or a declension of this term thirty-eight times. The Vatican's English translation uses conscience twenty-seven times in the text and once in a footnote. The term "conscience" can be found in the Vatican's English translation in the following paragraphs: 3, 8, 16, 19, 26–27, 31, 41, 43, 47, 50, 52, 61, 73–74, 76, 79, and 87. The other eleven declensions of *conscientia* are usually translated as awareness, or as a sense of responsibility or cooperation. Comparing the Vatican texts with the commonly used translation by Austin Flannery, Flannery uses conscience twenty-five times, corresponding to the Vatican's English translation. Eleven times Flannery's translation of *conscientia* or its declension matches or closely matches the alternative usage in the Vatican's English translation. Thus, thirty-six times the English translations agree. Twice the English translations do not agree with how to translate the Latin. These differences are found in paragraphs 52 and 73. The Vatican's translation uses conscience twice in paragraph 52, where the Flannery translation only uses it once. Flannery does not use conscience in paragraph 73, where the Vatican does. A thank you goes to Mary Forman, OSB, who helped me assess the validity of the translation variations. Any mistakes remain mine.

GS 16 so often when exploring magisterial teaching on conscience or when defining conscience. Nonetheless, the almost even dispersal of the term "conscience" throughout parts 1 and 2 illuminates the reality that any consideration of conscience must grapple with its theological-anthropological significance and its function in prudential and practical judgments regarding responses to the world's problems and concerns as it is used across the document. I turn first to the theological-anthropological implications as outlined in part 1 of *Gaudium et Spes*.

Conscience's first two mentions occur contextually in a brief description of the human being's meaning, purpose, and *telos* in light of current world trends. Humanity remains central in any consideration of the world's concerns, and humans are to be considered "in his or her totality, body and soul, heart and conscience, mind and will" (*GS* 3). The council notes that the world's accomplishments and trends can create imbalances, one of which "occurs between concern for practical effectiveness and the demands of moral conscience; yet another occurs between life in society and the individual's need for reflection and contemplation" (*GS* 8). Using "conscience" here with the adjective "moral" points to the reality that conscience carries with it a requirement to act and respond to events or trends, even as the council does not immediately offer a resolution to the tensions noted. The first two remarks about conscience indicate that, on the one hand, conscience is a dimension of the human being like the body, soul, heart, mind, and will. On the other hand, conscience places demands on us propelling us to consider our communal and relational responsibilities, highlighting that we are not islands. Both ideas are found together along with others in *GS* 16.

Paragraph 16 is also the next time conscience is mentioned. The full paragraph reads:

> Deep within their consciences men and women discover a law which they have not laid upon themselves and which they must obey. Its voice, ever challenging them to love and to do what is good and to avoid evil, tells them inwardly at the right moment: do this, shun that. For they have in their hearts a law inscribed by God. Their dignity rests in observing this law, and by it they will be judged. Their conscience is people's most secret core, and their sanctuary. There they are alone with God whose voice echoes in their depths. By conscience, in a wonderful way, that law is made known which is fulfilled in the love of God and of one's neighbor. Through loyalty to conscience, Christians are joined to others in the search for truth and

for the right solution to so many moral problems which arise both in the life of individuals and from social relationships. Hence, the more a correct conscience prevails, the more do persons and groups turn aside from blind choice and endeavor to conform to the objective standards of moral conduct. Yet it often happens that conscience goes astray through ignorance which it is unable to avoid, without thereby losing its dignity. This cannot be said of the person who takes little trouble to find out what is true and good, or when conscience is gradually almost blinded through the habit of committing sin.[31]

The first thing to notice is that, as in the earlier contexts, conscience exists as part of the human being. While the idea of "deep within" indicates place, conscience is not a place. Rather, the term "conscience" directs our attention inward, to our interiority, and to the reality that within ourselves we recognize that which is both in us and yet comes from outside of us. In our depths, in stillness, conscience is where we meet God, engage God, and find God's law.[32] Additionally, *GS* 16 provides other images describing conscience as a voice calling to us and as a sanctuary. As a voice, conscience calls to us and helps us love, know, and do good while shunning and avoiding evil. As a sanctuary, conscience is where we encounter God, who speaks to us.

Sanctuary is a sacred place, a holy place where we meet God. In architecture, the sanctuary, the innermost core of the church, is often quiet or the space of communal worship. James T. Bretzke argues that the sanctuary of the conscience is the dynamic interplay between understanding what God is asking and our response to the understanding of God's call.[33]

---

[31] There are three biblical citations referenced with this paragraph, Romans 2:15-16; Matthew 22:37-40; and Galatians 5:14. The only other citation in this paragraph is Pius XII's radio message on rightly forming the Christian conscience in youth from 1952. Nevertheless, the love of God and neighbor is a biblical command that can be found in the gospels, Deuteronomy, and Leviticus. See Matt 22:37-40; Luke 10:27; Mark 12:30-31; Deut 6:5; and Lev 19:18.

[32] The term "law" has many nuances beyond the scope of this discussion; however, at a minimum one should keep in mind that scripturally "laws" are found in the Torah. The Torah serves both individuals and the community in fostering a more intimate relationship with God, seeing the world as God sees it, a structure for guiding, imagining, and living into the kingdom of God. Law in this sense is not a minimum requirement but a starting point for cultivating a more just world.

[33] James T. Bretzke, *A Morally Complex World: Engaging Contemporary Moral Theology* (Collegeville, MN: Liturgical Press, 2004), 110, 129. While Bretzke says this of the individual conscience, it holds true for communal or familial discernment as well. What is God calling

Thus, identifying conscience as the sanctuary within us draws attention to the ability to get beyond the surface noise to our deepest selves, the place where God speaks within us. The community captures shared experiences of God's revelation and summons in Scripture, and yet as individuals and communities we must continually reencounter God's summons. God's summons happens in the common sanctuary when we worship together and in the individual sanctuary of our inmost being.

The law that conscience reveals by its voice and by our keeping company with God is charity, the love of both God and neighbor. Our human dignity rests on obeying the law written on our hearts by God, so we are judged by how well we fulfill the law by loving God and neighbor. Who is the neighbor to whom we are obliged by obedience to conscience? Expanding on the list found in Matthew 25:35-40 (the hungry, the sick, the naked, the imprisoned, the stranger), *GS* identifies the neighbor as every human being. More specifically, and giving some examples, *GS* equates our neighbor with the elderly, the abandoned elderly, refugees, immigrants, the child born into circumstances beyond his or her control, the "starving human being who awakens our conscience," those who think differently than us, our enemies, and our persecutors (*GS* 27–28). In other words, this nonexhaustive list requires us to attend to anyone who would shake us out of our complacency. In so doing, we find the areas within communities and ourselves that still need conversion to the reign of God.

Elsewhere, *GS* delineates a list of actions that foster death rather than life, further illuminating and giving substance to the neighbor who is to be loved. Listing actions to be avoided (sin or evil) provides an implicit description of required actions. Engaging in murder, genocide, abortion, euthanasia, mutilation, or torture (physical and mental), by fostering or permitting subhuman living conditions, slavery, prostitution, treatment of persons as "tools for profit rather than free and responsible persons," is deplorable, degrading the human dignity of both sufferer and inflictor (*GS* 27). Therefore, when we individually and as a society choose not to participate in genocide, torture, inhuman working conditions, or other destructive patterns of behavior and when we resist genocide, human trafficking, torture, and so forth—we work toward a more just society

---

a spousal unit or extended family unit to do? What is God asking a religious community to do? Anne Patrick explores this question in her book on women religious communities. See Anne E. Patrick, *Conscience and Calling: Ethical Reflections on Catholic Women's Church Vocations* (New York and London: Bloomsbury, 2013).

premised on human respect, dignity, and love of neighbor. In other words, all of humanity is our neighbor, and loving our neighbor by following the voice of conscience means serving life, wholeness, and laboring toward a just society rooted in the dignity of each person and acknowledging the breaking in of the Reign of God. The list and tasks can be overwhelming, yet we are called to participate in some fashion as an embodied manifestation of our love for God. I would argue that participation requires an interior changing of attitude that necessitates encountering our own biases regarding others. Stated differently, what cultural and religious assumptions regarding purity, righteousness, and moral behavior connected to a person's dignity have we correctly absorbed and which ones are faulty, requiring conversions?

Per the wisdom of *GS*, both individuals and groups need to turn away from sin and toward grace. This interior movement and conversion manifests itself outwardly in our actions and approaches to others. Thus, *GS* 16 states that the more individuals or communities follow "right conscience" the more they turn from blindness toward truth (defined as objective norms of moral conduct). "Right conscience" matters because conscience can be wrong; it can err. Yet, if conscience errs because of "invincible ignorance" (unavoidable ignorance), conscience retains its dignity.

Nevertheless, we can become undignified and subsequently risk creating an undignified conscience. *GS* 16 conveys the reality of both the undignified human being and the undignified conscience in this manner: "This cannot be said of the person who takes little trouble to find out what is true and good, or when conscience is gradually almost blinded through the habit of committing sin." In other words, humans undermine and betray their inherent dignity when they ignore truth and goodness because they seek and live from other values, such as thirst for power, control, and personal gain. Repetitious sinful behavior distorts one's perception, leading to unclear vision or the inability to notice the good, true, and beautiful. Like an unexercised muscle or an overgrown garden due to neglect, our conscience can be rendered less effective at perceiving grace, goodness, truth, and beauty and cherishing the obligation to love both God and our neighbor (in all the messiness of the human condition). This "practically sightless" conscience often results from habitual sin that is unexamined or deemed unimportant.[34] "Practically sightless" indicates

---

[34] The Vatican translation of *GS* 16 uses the phrase "practically sightless" instead of "almost blinded." "Almost blinded" calls to mind the various biblical passages where Jesus

that sight still exists; therefore, we can still respond to the glimmers of light, goodness, and grace present in our lives through our encounters with God, our neighbors (all of humanity), and the rest of the created world. But we see much less, and what we do see is distorted by our near blindness. In another paragraph, we are cautioned not to be like the rich man who disregarded Lazarus but to remember that in caring for those around us we care for Christ (*GS* 27).[35]

Given our limitations, finitude, and blindness, the search for truth must take place together, as one human community across belief systems. As stated in *GS* 16, "Through loyalty to conscience, Christians are joined to others in the search for truth and for the right solution to so many moral problems which arise both in the life of individuals and from social relationships." In other words, while Christians have a perspective on truth grounded in belief and relationship with the living God, others too are searching for the truth. Therefore, searching for the truth, the good to be done, and solutions to humanity's suffering and problems requires cooperation among Christians, other theists, agnostics, and atheists.

Thus, the first ten instances of the term "conscience" in *GS* occur in the preface, the introduction, and paragraph 16. Conscience was alternatively defined as a dimension of the human being and as a voice speaking to our hearts. Conscience directs us toward truth and the good to be done. Following one's conscience is manifested in love of God and neighbor. Conscience can err. It can be disfigured and become undignified if error is avoidable. Conscience maintains its dignity, however, when its error is unavoidable. Finally, seeking truth, goodness, and solutions to the problems of the human condition are communal virtues grounded in relationships.

After paragraph 16, the term conscience can be found scattered fifteen more times throughout *GS*. Conscience is mentioned in discussions on atheism (19), the dynamism between the individual's rights and the common good (26), duties of conscience (27, 31), and the role of the church and its members (41, 43). These instances continue to develop the idea that conscience is a part of the human being and crucial to human dignity, contextualized and understood in a relationship with the Divine, a

---

heals those who are blind. Thus, "blinded" reminds us of the need for God's grace. While if we are "sightless," it could be due to our own actions, or the participation in structures of sin that we do or do not recognize as sinful.

[35] References are made to Luke 16:19-31 and Matthew 25:40. For a connection to the broader tradition of Catholic Social Teaching, see Bernard Evans, *Lazarus at the Table: Catholics and Social Justice* (Collegeville, MN: Liturgical Press, 2006).

relationship mediated in and through the church.[36] Part 2 of *GS* concerns certain urgent problems, so conscience is discussed in relationship to marriage (47, 50, and 52), cultural education (61), political life (74, 76), war (79), and economic life (87). In the contexts just mentioned, conscience functions in the practical, social, relational aspects of daily life. In other words, conscience aids in making practical judgments.

Taken together, the brief remarks on conscience in the context of other concerns illuminate other aspects of conscience's form and function. Conscience's dignity and humanity's dignity when we follow our conscience is reiterated and reaffirmed. Attention to those who awaken conscience highlights that morality has a deeply social dimension that requires an outward response to social ills. In associating conscience with the laity's work, marriage, economic life, and war, what emerges is the connection between social structures, communal values, and personal decisions for action. Furthermore, there is both a corporate and an individual responsibility to form and inform conscience as well as follow it. Forming, informing, and following conscience fosters human dignity and common, communal undertakings, service to God in freedom by love of neighbor, and activity in the world.

Additionally, it is clear by references to scientific advances and references to other humanities that *GS* recognizes that informing consciences requires engagement with fields besides theology. Engagement with culture and other disciplines remains a both/and endeavor. On the one hand, it requires learning about and incorporating knowledge from other fields into various theological areas. On the other hand, it requires analyzing and offering a specific life-giving stance rooted in the scriptural message, and person of Christ, mediated through the church to the rest of the world. In this vein, following one's conscience requires attention to not only formation, information, and conscience's dignity; it also necessitates recognizing one's position and role within the church. In what capacity is the individual or communal body acting, as a citizen, in the name of the church, as members of the church but acting in their own name? The implications and complications surrounding these distinctions are referenced later in the book in the chapters on formation and dissent. Finally, *GS* also mentions the dignity of conscience connected to religious liberty, which Vatican II's decree on religious liberty, *Dignitatis Humanae* (*DH*) more fully elaborates.

---

[36] Church should be understood within the context of how the council defined church in *Lumen Gentium*, the Dogmatic Constitution on the Church.

Dignitatis Humanae (DH) [37]

The experience of the Catholic Church in the United States and certain European and some Asian countries influenced the drafting and promulgation of *Dignitatis Humanae*. Catholics who immigrated to the United States from the 1700s through the early 1900s came as outsiders to the predominately Protestant cultural ethos. Catholics founded their own educational system, hospitals, and other institutions to aid their fellow Catholics. Their capacity to be civic-minded citizens was often called into question because of misunderstandings regarding the relationship of Catholics to the papacy in Rome. This began changing with the election of the first and only Catholic US president, John F. Kennedy, in 1960. Meanwhile, across the Atlantic and Pacific Oceans in Europe and Asia, Catholics in many countries were not permitted to freely practice their faith. In some instances, the church was underground, or Christians' ability to practice was severely curtailed by governmental mandates and controls. These general experiences affected the conciliar approach and debates regarding *Dignitatis Humanae*. [38]

Bishops and cardinals from these various regions advocated for a document on religious freedom and liberty. Other bishops and cardinals wanted a document more tightly aligning church and state. [39] Despite the debates and disagreements, *Dignitatis Humanae* was promulgated on December 7, 1965, on the eve of the council's conclusion. While falling into the third category of a declaration and thus technically carrying less weight than a constitution or decree, *Dignitatis Humanae* was still important at the time of the council. Furthermore, its influence has grown because of its use and

---

[37] Like any conciliar document, a variety of writings concerning *Dignitatis Humanae* exists. See, for example, Ladislas Orsy, "The Divine Dignity of Human Persons in *Dignitatis Humanae*," *Theological Studies* 75, no. 1 (March 2014): 8–22; Catherine E. Clifford, "The Ecumenical Context of *Dignitatis humanae*: Forty Years after Vatican II," *Science Et Esprit* 59, nos. 2–3 (May 1, 2007): 387–403; Mary Doak, "Resisting the Eclipse of *Dignitatis humanae*," *Horizons* 33, no. 1 (March 1, 2006): 33–53; Leslie Griffin, "Commentary on *Dignitatis humanae*," in *Modern Catholic Social Teaching*, 244–65; John Courtney Murray, "The Declaration on Religious Freedom," in *Change in Official Catholic Moral Teachings*, ed. Charles E. Curran (New York/Mahwah, NJ: Paulist Press, 2003); F. Russell Hittinger, "The Declaration on Religious Freedom, *Dignitatis Humanae*," in Lamb and Levering *Vatican II*; David L Schindler, "Freedom, Truth, and Human Dignity: An Interpretation of *Dignitatis Humanae* on the Right to Religious Liberty," *Communio* 40, nos. 2–3 (2013): 208–316.

[38] O'Malley, *What Happened at Vatican II*, 211–18, 254–58. O'Malley gives an overview as well as additional references in his footnotes.

[39] Ibid., 211–18.

practical employment since its promulgation.[40] John O'Malley points out that, over forty years after the council, "the distinction between decrees and declarations, no matter what it originally meant, has become meaningless." This is because some decrees have fallen by the wayside, "virtually forgotten," while declarations like *Dignitatis Humanae* and *Nostra Aetate* (On Non-Christian Religions) have maintained their importance.[41] In other words, the effective history of interpretation and application has in part determined *Dignitatis Humanae*'s value in the tradition.[42]

DH recognizes that the world's nations are implementing and people are demanding limits to the "powers of government" regarding "rightful freedom of persons and associations" (*DH* 1). Therefore, the document includes religion and its free practice as part of the trend toward limited powers of government over persons' and associations' freedom to act.[43] In the contemporary context of the Affordable Health Care Act in the United States, questions, debates, and arguments have ensued about how to interpret the free practice of religion as it pertains to living from conscientious positions possibly at odds with secular mandates. I turn now to what *DH* says about conscience.[44]

---

[40] The most recent example is in the United States where the United States Conference of Catholic Bishops and various Catholic institutions are using the language from *Dignitatis Humanae* on conscience and religious liberty to fight aspects of the Affordable Health Care Act. These groups are specifically challenging provisions in the act regarding the contraception coverage in the AHCA by claiming they are following their consciences.

[41] O'Malley, *What Happened at Vatican II*, 3.

[42] Structurally, *DH* has an introduction and two chapters. It is a relatively short document encompassing only fifteen paragraphs. *DH*'s introduction is paragraph 1. Following a brief description of various obligations and duties, chapter 1 discusses "the general principle of religious freedom" in paragraphs 2–8. Chapter 2 explores "religious freedom in the light of revelation" in paragraphs 9–15.

[43] The United Nations Declaration of Human Rights was promulgated in 1948. While *DH* does not explicitly refer to this document, it is possible that the UN's declaration forms part of the background here.

[44] The Vatican's Latin and English translations can be found at http://w2.vatican.va /content/vatican/en.html. The Latin uses *conscientia* in paragraphs 1–3, 11, 13–15. Paragraphs 1–2 and 11 have two usages; paragraph 3 has four, and the others one. The Latin version of *DH* uses *conscientia* or a declension of this term thirteen times. The Vatican's English translation uses conscience ten times: once as a clarifying term in paragraph 3, and nine times consistent with the Latin. The four additional times the Latin uses a form of *conscientia* the Vatican's English version translates it as consciousness, awareness, or convictions. The commonly used translation edited by Austin Flannery matches or closely matches the alternative usage in the Vatican's English translation. Thus, the English translations agree on the use of *conscientia* or its declensions.

The ten times *conscientia* is translated as "conscience" occur in five of the fifteen paragraphs of *DH* (1, 3, 11, 13, and 14). Half of its occurrences are in paragraph 3, making this paragraph key when exploring the church's teaching on conscience and religious freedom. Conscience is first mentioned, though, in the introduction (1).

Conscience appears in the introduction after the conciliar fathers set the stage for understanding conscience in the context of this document on religious freedom. They connect freedom and the practice of religion to people's spiritual aspirations, whereby the church aids in the determination of how the spiritual aspirations cohere with truth and justice, aided by tradition and church teaching. The council professes several beliefs. First, God has revealed to humanity how to serve God, have salvation, and "reach happiness in Christ." Second, while open to others, the council believes "that this one true religion exists in the Catholic and Apostolic church." Third, humans are required to seek the truth, "especially in what concerns God and the church." This truth is to be embraced and held onto as it is learned and found. Following this three-point list is the statement: "The sacred council likewise proclaims that these obligations bind people's consciences. Truth can impose itself on the human mind by the force of its own truth, which wins over the mind with both gentleness and power" (*DH* 1). In other words, revelation binds conscience; belief about the status of the Catholic Church binds conscience; the quest for truth binds conscience. Truth is not coercive but persuasive because of its merits. Stated differently, conscience is shaped by revelation in the context of the Catholic and Apostolic Church, requiring the ongoing pursuit of or quest for truth. The realization by the council fathers that the fullness of truth continues unfolding can be found in their own words: "Furthermore, in dealing with the question of liberty the sacred council intends to develop the teaching of recent popes on the inviolable rights of the human person and on the constitutional order of society" (*DH* 1).

The conciliar fathers go onto argue that religious freedom is a right because of human dignity. This right cannot be taken away even if people do not live up to it and the right cannot be interfered with "as long as the just requirements of public order are observed" (*DH* 2). Since we have the capability of participating in divine law, guided by God, we all have an obligation and "the right to seek the truth in religious matters so that, through the use of appropriate means," we may "form prudent judgments of conscience which are sincere and true" (*DH* 3). Not only do we have the right to form judgments of conscience, we are required to do so. While not directly stated, the need for discernment regarding what constitutes prudential judgments of conscience is implied. Two criteria are given for this discernment. Prudent judgments must be sincere and they must be true. Teaching, communication, and dialogue are the ways in which humans "share with each other the truth they have discovered, or think they have discovered, in such a way that they help one another in the search for truth" (*DH* 3). Thus, both judgments and the search for truth have a communal dimension that should remain noncoercive and nonoppressive. Furthermore, the council acknowledges that humans can both discover truth and be mistaken in thinking we have discovered truth. Hence, the need exists for ongoing discernment, dialogue, and engagement with each other, testing insights for their validity and truthfulness.

As noted above, *DH*'s largest discussion of conscience in occurs in 3. The full passage reads:

> The human person sees and recognizes the demands of the divine law through conscience. All are bound to follow their conscience faithfully in every sphere of activity so that they may come to God, who is their last end. Therefore, the individual must not be forced to act against conscience, especially in religious matters. The reason is because the practice of religion of its very nature consists primarily of those voluntary and free internal acts by which human beings direct themselves to God. Acts of this kind cannot be commanded or forbidden by any merely human authority. But the social nature of the human person requires that individuals give external expression to these internal acts of religion, that they communicate with others on religious matters, and profess religion in community. Consequently, to deny the free exercise of religion in society, when the just requirements of public order are observed, is to do an injustice to the human person and to the very order established by God for human beings.[45]

The verb choices indicate a dynamic movement toward God that conscience mediates, whereby conscience functions as a conduit to God. This mediation, movement, and following of conscience does not conform us to the world but aids Christians in knowing and coming to God. Therefore, our consciences are the final guide on the path to knowing and being in relationship with God. The individual cannot be coerced into acknowledging or

---

[45] This paragraph cites two recent popes. See John XXIII, *Pacem in Terris*, encyclical, April 11, 1963: AAS 55 (1963), 270; Paul VI, radio message, December 22, 1964: AAS 57 (1965), 181–82.

coming to God. Rather, the individual must respond in freedom and of his or her own accord. However, the conciliar fathers do move the following of conscience into a communal context when they speak of religion. Religion by its composition, by its structure, is communal. By invoking conscience in matters religious, they place the following of individual conscience and the coming to God within the matrix of religious institutions. In this context, what we also see is the religious community being asked to follow its conscience when religious sensibilities regarding proper courses of action might differ from the broader societal notions of correct action. What is unclear is whether practices include more than how one worships. If so, and practices include patterns of actions and behaviors in society, then practical differences may arise not only within the Christian community but also between the Christian community and the broader society.

Conscience is next mentioned in chapter 2, paragraph 11 as part of the discussion on religious freedom and revelation. Reiterating it in various ways, the council claims that the human response to God must be free. God calls us to God and does not coerce us; rather, God invites us into a relationship and into service. Conscience joins, connects, and binds us to God (*DH* 11). Furthermore, recognizing that the demands of faith are often different from societal demands, citing Romans 4:12 the council argues that Christians ultimately must give an accounting to God for their lives and thus "we are all bound to obey our conscience" (*DH* 11).

Conscience, then, is about more than right judgment, or doing the good. In the context of faith and religion, conscience draws our attention and focus back to humanity's relationship and covenant with God. We are ultimately responsible to God, even as we have duties and responsibilities to the governments under which we live. This dual responsibility entails service, preaching the Gospel, being Gospel leaven, supporting faith in a noncoercive manner, and maintaining faithfulness to God's ways and God's truth.

In a discourse related to the church's function within civil society, *DH* rearticulates the belief that not only Christians but also all people have the right to live freely according to their consciences. Institutionally, the church must have religious freedom to do its work of promoting the Gospel and to live according to the requirements of Christian faith. Yet Christians and all people "have the civil right of freedom from interference, the right to lead their lives according to their conscience" (DH 13). Yet there is a tensile relationship between civil society, religious institutions, and the individual when it comes to religious liberty and the following of conscience. This tension manifests itself within the document, for example, when the right to religious freedom is qualified by the requirement that a just social order be maintained. There needs to be consensus about what is a just social order that has space for people to practice their faith.[46] Additionally, this means that any claim to following "conscience" cannot be a trump card overriding any other argument or rationale for action. The validity of conscience claims can be subject to an appraisal by one's community or society. Therefore, freedom from coercion does not mean freedom from ongoing assessment of one's claims or actions originating in conscience. The tension in these different areas might be undergirding various challenges within the United States to components of the Affordable Care Act by religious communities and private organizations like Hobby Lobby using the argument of religious liberty. We see the difficulty in adjudicating and prioritizing various rights to live from conscience in these instances. People have arrived at different judgments about specific issues and courses of actions stemming from varying interpretations of what religious freedom means within society.

Finally, *DH* 14 cites a radio address by Paul VI in a brief mention of conscience formation. The purpose of forming consciences is not to be judgmental but to form the faithful so they may spread charity, the life-giving Gospel message, and engage those in error or ignorance with charity and patience. This formation of conscience requires that the "faithful must pay careful attention to the holy and certain teaching of the church" because "the Catholic Church is by the will of Christ the teacher of truth" (*DH* 14). This paragraph talks about the holy and certain teachings of the church. The use of the term "certain teaching" implies that some teachings are not certain. No mention is given, however, for determining certain from uncertain teachings. Furthermore, the document uses the term "church," not "magisterium," in reference to teaching and teacher of the truth. Given the various models of church that are articulated at the Second Vatican Council and present in Scripture—how we understand and define "church" matters—it seems to me that this means we come to truth about Christ and Christ's will together, all of us. This has implications for understanding how conscience is formed and who is involved in that formation.

---

[46] While beyond the scope of this chapter and book, there is a need to consider how the chapters in *Gaudium et Spes* on the development of culture, economic and social life, along with the political community shed light on resolving these tensions within *Dignitatis Humanae*.

What can be seen with this overview of a few key passages from *Gaudium et Spes* and *Dignitatis Humanae* is that the conciliar documents use the term "conscience" in various ways with different emphases. These different emphases sometimes occur in the same paragraph of a given document, for example, *GS* 16. What has begun emerging is a multifaceted perspective of conscience. Conscience metaphorically is described as a place, a sanctuary, highlighting that it is a safe refuge where one meets God. Conscience is a mediator, a conduit between individuals, institutions, and God's revelation. Conscience functions as a signpost pointing toward good and away from evil. Conscience is rooted in the dignity of the human person and therefore has an inviolable dignity itself—although this dignity can be harmed or betrayed. Following conscience can lead to errors in judgment and action, but not the loss of conscience's dignity. Habitual sin can render conscience and its judgments ineffectual. Therefore, the shaping and forming of conscience must occur so that conscience can more fully illuminate and permit proper perception of the good. According to *DH*, religion and communities have a central role in forming consciences as they sincerely seek the truth. Given the importance of the church as a teacher of the truth, we turn to the reception of Vatican II's teaching on conscience in two postconciliar magisterial sources, the *Catechism of the Catholic Church* and *Veritatis Splendor*.

Catechism of the Catholic Church (CCC) [47]

The *CCC* is included in this chapter because it contains outlines of Catholic teaching, and it is where many Catholics would turn for information on conscience. The *Catechism* developed as an outgrowth of the 1985 extraordinary assembly of the Synod of Bishops convened by John Paul II on the twentieth anniversary of Vatican II. John Paul II approved it in 1992.[48] Therefore, what the *CCC* says regarding conscience becomes part of Vatican II's effective history and a factor in ongoing debates,

---

[47] *The Catechism of the Catholic Church*, 2nd ed., can be found on either the Vatican's or United States Conference of Catholic Bishop's websites. See http://www.vatican.va /archive/ENG0015/_INDEX.HTM or http://www.usccb.org/beliefs-and-teachings/what -we-believe/catechism/catechism-of-the-catholic-church/epub/. All of my references to the *Catechism* are from the English print version: *The Catechism of the Catholic Church*, rev. 2nd ed. (Vatican City, Rome: Libreria Editrice Vaticana, 1994, 1997).

[48] John Paul II, *Fidei Depositum*, apostolic constitution (On the publication of *The Catechism of the Catholic Church*), in *CCC* 1–3.

conversations, and dialogues concerning Vatican II's implementation, interpretation, and purpose.

Speaking both to pastors and to the faithful, John Paul II wrote, "This catechism is given to them that it may be a sure and authentic reference text for teaching catholic doctrine and particularly for preparing local catechisms."[49] This short sentence touches on many issues; however, it is the term "reference text" that raises some intriguing questions for utilizing the *Catechism* when considering church teaching on conscience or any other issue.

A reference text is usually a dictionary, encyclopedia, thesaurus, or another book of general knowledge or informational websites that did not exist when the *Catechism* was written. A reference text often does not provide in-depth knowledge or information on a given topic; it supplies a general, foundational, topical overview. What does it mean, then, to say that the *Catechism* is a reference text and to use it as such? As a reference text, the *Catechism* is the first stop for deepening knowledge. It is a resource, a starting point, for teaching about the faith, for considering how the faith is lived out and how to engage more contemporary moral questions. A brief story illustrates these realities.

In the undergraduate healthcare ethics course I teach, even though I assign readings from a variety of sources, students sometimes use the *Catechism* as their main source of knowledge on a topic. One day a student came in mad, dropped the *Catechism* on a desk, and voiced frustration that the *Catechism* had no answers regarding the day's topic. Thus, this student demonstrates the point above that the *Catechism* is a starting point for moral consideration, since the moral questions we encounter and try to answer often outpace church teaching or guidance. Therefore, given the *CCC*'s status as a reference text for church teaching, any analysis of conscience in the *CCC* needs to keep in mind that, as a reference text, its consideration of conscience remains a summary of centuries of teaching and tradition on conscience.

The *CCC*'s primary consideration of the term "conscience" appears within the chapter titled "The Dignity of the Human Person."[50] This par-

---

[49] "Apostolic Constitution," in *CCC*, pg. 5.

[50] A word search in the online version of the *Catechism* shows that it uses the term "conscience" 101 times, with approximately 80 percent of these occurrences appearing in part 3. This makes sense, given that in part 3 a description of conscience, its function, obligations, and formation are discussed. Conscience appears after discussions on humans

ticular chapter is itself a subsection of the *Catechism* dealing with the Christian's "Life in Christ."[51] The dignity of the human person and, subsequently, conscience are reflected on as part of the discussion surrounding our human vocation and life in the Spirt. The structure and organization of the *Catechism*, indicates that conscience contributes to the dignity of the human person while being constitutive of our life in both Christ and the Spirit.

The introduction to "The Dignity of the Human Person" summarizes the upcoming discussion and says this related to conscience: "By his deliberate actions (*article* 4), the human person does, or does not, conform to the good promised by God and attested by moral conscience (*article* 5). Human beings make their own contribution to their interior growth; they make their whole sentient and spiritual lives into means of this growth (*article* 6)" (*CCC* 1700).[52] Thus, with these two sentences the *Catechism* connects deliberate actions, passions (emotions), our sentient lives (perceptions and feelings), and spirituality to conscience. Additionally, we contribute to our own growth in conforming to what is good as promised by God.

The *Catechism* addresses the topic of conscience primarily in paragraphs 1776–1802.[53] Paragraph 1776 partially cites *GS* 16 and introduces the *CCC*'s topical treatment of conscience.[54] The topics covered within the *CCC* concern the following: conscience's judgment (1777–82), conscience's formation (1783–85), choosing with conscience (1786–89), and mistaken or flawed judgment (1790–94) followed by a bullet-point summary (1795–1802).

The reader of the *Catechism* would learn that conscience is where we are alone with God, where God speaks to us; it is our core and sanctuary.

---

as the image of God, vocation to beatitude, human freedom, the morality of human acts, and the morality of the passions and before the discussion of the virtues and sin.

[51] The *Catechism* has a four-part structure. Part 1 lays forth the profession of faith. Part 2 explains the celebration of the Christian mystery, focusing on the sacramental life of the church, starting with the liturgy while looking at both sacraments and sacramentals. Part 3 looks at the Christian's life in Christ. It is in this section that the largest discussion of conscience takes place. In its entirety, the section concerned with "Life in Christ" considers what it means to live a "life worthy of the gospel of Christ" through a description of "Man's Vocation: Life in the Spirit" and "The Ten Commandments." Part 4 focuses on Christian prayer.

[52] *CCC*, pg. 424.

[53] Ibid., pgs. 438–42.

[54] Ibid., pg. 438.

Conscience points us toward God's law. Conscience appeals to us to do the good and avoid evil. It helps us judge right and wrong; its judgment is a feature of reason. Conscience can judge before, during, or after acting and helps us be responsible and accountable for our actions. We have a responsibility to both inform and form our conscience. Formation is an ongoing task, done not in isolation but in and through relationships, guided by Scripture (the Word of God) and the Roman Catholic Church's authoritative teaching. Certain judgments of conscience must be followed. While conscience can be wrong, distinctions are made between holding the moral agent more or less responsible for errors, even while acknowledging that actions resulting from error are still evil (wrong). On the other hand, continually following a right and true conscience leads to conversion.

In laying out and explaining these points, the *Catechism's* authors utilize scriptural references; Vatican II documents, specifically *GS* and *DH*; and particular theologians from the tradition.[55] While an assessment of each category could be undertaken, I will focus on the use of the Vatican II document, *GS*, to show the reception of this document.

Despite starting with *GS*, the *CCC* is selective in its use of *GS*, referencing only *GS* 16. Furthermore, the citation of *GS* 16 is partial, subtly shifting how conscience's relationship to laws and various types of authority are conceived. The *CCC* in paragraph 1776, with its partial recitation of *GS* 16, emphasizes law, a law from God. This in itself is not problematic. The only reference to specific scriptural laws, however, is to the ten commandments in 1778, although divine law is mentioned in several places (1778, 1786, and 1787). Are these the only laws the *CCC* considers or should the reader also reflect on additional ritual laws governing communal relationships laid out in Scripture? Does the *CCC* mean to include the fulfillment of the law by loving God and one's neighbor as explained in *GS* 16 in reference to the Gospel? It is hard to say since they do not cite the portion of *GS* that says conscience recognizes the fulfillment of the law when one loves God and neighbor. Nor does the *CCC* cite *GS* 16 that Christians work together with others in seeking truth and answers to the moral concerns of individuals and society. Instead, the *CCC*, with

---

[55] The two theologians cited in the footnotes are Augustine and Cardinal John Henry Newman. Although, if one has familiarity with Thomas Aquinas's thought, the influence of Aquinas can be seen in many statements on conscience. Most of the scriptural references are from the New Testament, with one Old Testament reference to Ps 119.

its citations, subtly implies that guidance comes only from God, fellow Christians, and the teaching of the church. To support this idea the *CCC* cites *DH* 14, which looks primarily at the responsibility of the Christian to Christ and, unlike the openness to the world and to others found in *GS*, advises caution when encountering and engaging those who do not share the faith. Although, in 1788 the *CCC* does say humans are assisted by the advice of competent people, the virtue of prudence, and the Holy Spirit.[56]

Regarding the capacity of our consciences to make mistakes in judgments there is also a subtle difference between *GS* and *CCC*. Both documents acknowledge that mistaken judgments will occur. Both documents make distinctions between avoidable and unavoidable ignorance that leads to mistaken judgments of conscience. *GS* can, however, give the reader the sense that striving together to discover truth, goodness, and solutions to moral concerns is a noble endeavor. Individuals and groups become more attuned to appropriate moral behavior as our consciences make accurate and truthful judgments. *GS* 16 is clear that mistaken judgments will happen due to ignorance, and yet conscience retains its dignity in these instances. We retain our dignity and the dignity of our conscientious judgments if ignorance happens simply because we cannot know everything, new information becomes known after we have made a judgment, or we did not accurately predict possible outcomes resulting from our actions. Only after articulating the positive aspects of conscience and softening the reality of mistaken judgments do we find *GS* mentioning culpable judgments of conscience. *GS* is clear that if we are lazy and do not seek the information we need to make a sound judgment we are culpable for erroneous judgments. Likewise, we are culpable if we make erroneous judgments of conscience due to habitual sin.

While *GS* discusses errors arising from undesired mistakes first, followed by the statement regarding culpability for erroneous judgments, the *CCC* inverts the order. The *CCC* begins its discussion of erroneous judgments in paragraphs 1790 and 1791, utilizing some language from *GS* 16, stating that ignorance is no excuse for an erroneous conscience if the ignorance could have been avoided or if ignorance results from habitual sin.[57] The next paragraph (1792) provides a list of potential reasons for

---

[56] See *CCC*, par. 1785n55.

[57] This leads Brian Johnstone to conclude that, while the *CCC* might not have included certain sections of paragraph 16 from *GS* for reasons of length, the result is a "submissive mode of conscience." See Brian Johnstone, "Erroneous Conscience in *Veritatis Splendor* and

errors in judgment before engaging the possibility that a person's ignorance could be invincible. This ordering implies more deliberate errors by
the person regarding their judgments of conscience than not. In contrast
to *GS*, which upholds the dignity of the moral agent's conscience when
invincibly ignorant, the *CCC* makes a slightly different move. Even though
the *CCC* does acknowledge the possibility of invincible ignorance, the
CCC does not mention the dignity of conscience in instances of invincible ignorance and choses to focus on the resulting evil action and the
need to correct errors. This is a valid point, the need to correct errors
of judgment; however, taken together, the whole article on conscience
in the *CCC* implies that our judgments of conscience will be either correct or incorrect (see 1786). This does not seem to reflect accurately the
experiential reality that our judgments often are partially correct. *GS*'s
description of conscience in the context of a changing world permits a
space to grapple with judgments of conscience that yield both positive
and negative effects, granting a space for ongoing growth and conversion.

From this brief overview, it can be argued that the *CCC* does function
as a starting point for understanding conscience, since it articulates some
areas of Vatican II's teaching on conscience and neglects others. The *CCC*,
if read on its own, represents a narrowing of the tradition and magisterial
teaching on conscience. As a result, the *CCC* remains a starting point for
understanding conscience, and interested persons should read the conciliar documents and other sources informing the *CCC* in their entirety.

There is one other magisterial source frequently referenced or read by
those wanting to understand Catholic teaching on conscience: John Paul
II's encyclical *Veritatis Splendor*.

Veritatis Splendor

If people consulted the *CCC* first, they might then want to know
what the pope says about conscience, or they might even go to papal
documents first. John Paul II's fundamental moral theology encyclical,
Veritatis Splendor, was promulgated on August 6, 1993.[58] John Paul II

---

the Theological Tradition," in *The Splendor of Accuracy: An Examination of the Assertions
Made by* Veritatis Splendor, ed. Joseph A. Selling and Jan Jans (Grand Rapids, MI: William
B. Eerdmans Publishing Co, 1995), 114–35, at 116–17.

[58] John Paul II, *Veritatis Splendor* (1993), http://w2.vatican.va/content/john-paul-ii/en
/encyclicals/documents/hf_jp-ii_enc_06081993_veritatis-splendor.html.

indicated his intention to write the encyclical, however, on August 1, 1987 (the second centenary of the death of Alphonsus Liguori, patron saint of moral theologians and confessors). *Veritatis Splendor* is concerned with addressing developments in moral theology since the conclusion of Vatican II. During the time between Vatican II and the writing of John Paul II's encyclical, moral theology had undergone many methodological changes. These changes occurred for several reasons. Moral theologians had to deal with a changing moral theological landscape and the need to address contemporary issues not in the typical textbooks (manuals of moral theology). Vatican II had called for moral theology's renewal, specifically in the decree *Optatum Totius* and with its approval of *Gaudium et Spes*. Methodologically, questions arose, for example, over how to utilize and incorporate adequately the tools of analysis from different sciences (human, social, empirical, psychology, sociology, anthropology, philosophy, and so forth). There have been efforts to reintroduce Scripture into moral methodology and reflection, which meant a philosophical deductive approach to moral reasoning was no longer sufficient. In this context, John Paul II wrote his encyclical in response to moral theological writings and method after the council.

The response to the encyclical by the theological community was mixed. Some appreciated its tone and saw it as settling the disputes and debates within moral theology. Others responded by stating that *Veritatis Splendor* should be carefully interpreted, "not as the last word in a controversy put to rest, but rather as a call to participate further in the process of discernment, clarifying the issues at hand and making suggestions for the way forward."[59] While it would be interesting to explore the full reception of *Veritatis Splendor* by the theological community, even as the encyclical is addressed to John Paul II's brother bishops, the focus here concerns what John Paul II says about conscience.

Veritatis Splendor starts with Scripture, which in itself is a contrast to the manuals and the centuries-old tradition of relying on natural law

---

[59] Selling and Jans, eds., *The Splendor of Accuracy*, 10. For other analyses of *Veritatis Splendor*, see the following collection of essays: Michael E. Allsopp and John J. O'Keefe, eds., Veritatis Splendor: *American Responses* (Kansas City, MO: Sheed & Ward, 1995); and J. A. DiNoia and Romanus Cessario, eds., Veritatis Splendor *and the Renewal of Moral Theology* (New Rochelle, NY: Scepter Publishing, 1999).

for moral theology.[60] Nevertheless, John Paul II's approach to conscience is framed less by Scripture and more by the moral theological debates after the council and his concern over dissent from church teaching. He mentions conscience in the encyclical's introduction and we see here that John Paul II has problems with how conscience is understood in contemporary moral theology. For him, conscience does point to truth and goodness, yet individuals can easily be lead astray. The majority of John Paul II's discussion of conscience takes place in chapter 2, paragraphs 54–64.[61] He starts his discourse on conscience with these words: "The relationship between man's freedom and God's law is most deeply lived out in the 'heart' of the person, in his moral conscience" (*VS* 54). He then quotes from *GS* 16, but not the full paragraph, emphasizing the portion that talks about law (*VS* 54). He then draws on Paul in Romans 2:14-15 to identify conscience as a witness, which confronts us with what we have done and whether we have been "faithful or unfaithful" to the law. Conscience as witness applies both to ourselves as witness and, more important, to God as witness (*VS* 57–58).

Furthermore, conscience also functions as an inner dialogue with God. John Paul II, citing Bonaventure as support, says that conscience binds because what is demanded of us by conscience comes from God, calling us to obedience.[62] He then returns to the idea of conscience as judgment regarding what to do or not do, as well as judgment regarding what has already been done (*VS* 58–59). In this consideration of conscience's judgment on actions, John Paul II distinguishes the general, universal norm to "do good and avoid evil" from the practical application of the norm in specific situations. Conscience judges our ability to apply the universal norm (*VS* 59).

---

[60] The encyclical has three chapters. Chapter 1 has been described as an extended homily as it features a meditation on the gospel story of the rich young man. Chapter 2 comprises the technical discussion and engagement with moral theology and method by theologians over the prior twenty years. Chapter 3 discusses authority and discipline in the church.

[61] Chapter 2 as a whole discusses and engages the following methodological debates in moral theology: the role of Scripture; whether faith is autonomous, theonomous, or heteronomous; questions surrounding human freedom, will, sin, and grace; absolute norms; natural law; moral action; moral truth; fundamental option; and, of course, conscience. He mentions conscience in paragraphs 30–32, 34, 36, and 52, prior to his more focused discussion. In these other paragraphs, John Paul II misses the opportunity to address the positive understandings and workings of conscience in the tradition by emphasizing what he sees as the distortions in theological descriptions of conscience.

[62] An assessment of how Bonaventure understands conscience and John Paul II's use of him is beyond the scope of this work.

While this vision of conscience resonates, John Paul II's certainty that all situations fall into the binary framework of judging actions as all good or all evil poses some difficulties. He does not acknowledge or provide guidance for how conscience should judge the application of the universal norm to do good and avoid evil in situations that are morally ambiguous because actions or responses will have both moral goods and moral evils in them. How do we account for these types of situations and judgments of conscience where one needs to act and the actions are not pure?[63]

John Paul II does, however, make the case for the requirement to follow conscience. We must follow conscience because while conscience's judgment "does not establish the law" it does testify to the objective universal truth given by natural law, which participates in God's divine law (*VS* 60–61). This obligation to follow conscience's judgment requires us to take responsibility for our actions, as well as serving as a reminder of our need for God, God's grace, and to ask for forgiveness.

Given that we need to follow conscience's judgment, John Paul II considers how conscience can error. We make errors in practical judgments, in perceiving the good, and about the goodness of our actions. We do not always recognize how we are blind in these areas. John Paul II references *GS* 16 and argues that the erroneous conscience due to nonculpable ignorance retains its dignity. He stresses the distinction between the objective truth that remains and the subjective perception of the truth made by the person. It is at the level of subjective perception where mistakes or errors are made. In other words, we can be wrong about our perceptions of the truth. This distinction preserves objective truth while implicitly acknowledging that humans' subjective perceptions can be skewed.

Furthermore, while we might not be culpable for our errors, the resulting action is still evil, which John Paul II defines as "a disorder in relation to the truth about the good" (*VS* 63). In other instances, we are culpable for our sinful action. John Paul II succinctly describes how we are culpable for our erroneous judgments by citing this passage from *GS* 16: "when man shows little concern for seeking what is true and good, and

---

[63] The moral theological tradition has often dealt with situations that are ambiguous by utilizing the principle of double effect or the principle of cooperation. It seems to me, however, that both of these principles focus, as does John Paul II, on our human capacity for sinfulness and the negative effects of actions. How do we more adequately focus on our capacity for graced responses and the positive effects of actions so that we see how we are helping foster God's reign? This is an area for ongoing study and reflection.

conscience gradually becomes almost blind from being accustomed to sin" (see *VS* 63). He buttresses his argument with an appeal to Scripture (Matt 6:22-23) and Jesus' warning that the eye needs to be sound so that the body is sound. In other words, our perceptions (sight) influence our actions and behaviors.

Finally, John Paul II considers the formation of conscience and the need for its ongoing "conversion to what is true and to what is good." In this conversion, however, knowledge of the good is not enough. The heart must be "converted to the Lord and to love of what is good," for this is "really the source of *true* judgments of conscience." This conversion is grounded in and supported by the various virtues, more particularly, the theological and cardinal virtues. He specifically mentions prudence, the virtue that supports and enables practical judgments. This would lead one to think John Paul II was going to uphold insights of practical judgments from the community writ large, yet he concludes this section on conscience by stating that he sees the formation of conscience aided by the Magisterium and teaching authority of the church with no mention of other sources (*VS* 64). This move, particularly in light of *VS*'s chapter 3, which explores the relationship between theologians and the teaching authority of the bishops, can make one wonder if there is a role for the *sensus fidelium*, the whole body of the church, when rightly perceiving objective truth and their exercising of prudence. Alternatively, is prudence a virtue solely for the Magisterium? This question is especially pertinent when one considers that *GS* can be read as saying we discover the truth through conversation and encounters with God, our neighbor, and the world. Given that *VS* cites *GS* and responds to other interpreters of Vatican II, how does John Paul II reinterpret *GS* on conscience?

Mary Elsbernd examines how *VS* reinterprets *GS* in several key ways.[64] Regarding conscience, she believes that *VS* recontextualizes *GS* 16 "into a framework of law." She draws on the hermeneutic of silence and looks at the portions of *GS* 16 not cited by *VS*. The omissions are striking. *VS* ignores the *GS* 16 statement that the law "is fulfilled by love of God and neighbor" and that Christians join in with other humans in search for both truth and solutions to the world's problems. Thus, Elsbernd concludes

[64] Mary Elsbernd, "The Reinterpretation of *Gaudium et Spes* in *Veritatis Splendor*," *Horizons* 29, no. 2 (2002): 225–39. She analyzes conscience on pages 233 and 234. See also Brian Johnstone, "Erroneous Conscience in *Veritatis Splendor* and the Theological Tradition," in *The Splendor of Accuracy*, 114–35.

that "obedience of conscience to the law of love and the engagement of Christians with others in the quest for truth and solutions to contemporary problems are de-emphasized in *Veritatis splendor* by this omission."[65] In other words, our capacity and the requirement to embody love, the phenomenon that good people with good intentions miss the mark, the reality that new situations require an uncovering of the truth and possible actions are all truncated. In this area, we can see that the *CCC* and *VS* both refocus conscience on following the law: a law that already sets out a predetermined, stipulated, proper course of practical action. It is actually surprising, however, that John Paul II does not attend to the love of God and neighbor when he quotes *GS* since he starts *VS* with a meditation on the story of the rich young man. This parable, while not directly quoting Jesus requiring the love of God and neighbor, discusses what must be done in addition to keeping the commandments (law). Sell all, give to the poor, and follow Jesus (Mark 10:17-31; Matt 19:16-30). The story points to the need to attend to the poor (neighbor) among us. This is the fulfillment of the law, the following of our conscience according to *GS*.

Yet, in one area, regarding conscience's dignity, *VS* more adequately follows *GS* than does the *CCC*. Brian Johnstone notes that *VS* reintroduces into the discussion of conscience sections of *GS* relating to conscience's dignity and the distinction between a culpable and nonculpable erroneous conscience.[66] The description of conscience's dignity, and the difference between culpable and nonculpable erroneous conscience requires attention to the moral agent, the subjective element of morality. Thus, *VS* attends at least in part to the person who acts in conscience even as its predominant framework is law, understood primarily as specific, practical applications of universal truth claims.

Conclusion

This chapter began with a brief description of hermeneutics. It then examined the development of conscience as a theoretical category for moral theology during Vatican II and in the half century since the council. Priests, bishops, theologians, and the faithful need time to incorporate

---

[65] Elsbernd, "*Gaudium et Spes* in *Veritatis Splendor*," 233. She references Johnstone's article and his point that this passage of *GS* 16 was an addition to the final text. See Johnstone, "Erroneous Conscience in *Veritatis Splendor* and the Theological Tradition," 116n10.

[66] Johnstone, "Erroneous Conscience in *Veritatis Splendor* and the Theological Tradition," 115–18.

a new worldview or conceptual framework into their thinking patterns and behaviors. Thus, while Vatican II revived ancient teaching and held together various understandings about conscience, changes in moral theology or understandings of moral agency did not immediately happen. Following the council, debates, disagreements, and even confusion as to conscience's role in moral agency occurred, including when to follow it and what constitutes its proper formation. This resulted in part from the various descriptions of conscience embedded in the Vatican II documents themselves. *Gaudium et Spes* alternatively discusses conscience as the voice of God, a sanctuary where the voice is heard, as needing to be informed as well as formed. A person with a well-formed conscience will act from love of God and neighbor, seeking justice in all manners of life. *Dignitatis Humanae* highlighted the more communal dimension of conscience by highlighting the social nature of the individual who participates in religion.

John Paul II sought through his teaching office, as pope, to clarify and reiterate the teaching on conscience. The *CCC* and his encyclical *Veritatis Splendor* at times reaffirm *GS*'s teaching and at other times recast the teaching. Most specifically, the *CCC* and *VS* ignored the more relational aspects of conscience articulated by Vatican II regarding loving God and neighbor as manifested in responses to the world's problems, as considered in part 2 of *GS*.

The method of examining magisterial documents in chronological order indicated that the use of Vatican II to describe and define conscience in later magisterial documents was itself an exercise in hermeneutics. The reception and interpretation of Vatican II on conscience in the *Catechism* and John Paul II's encyclical in some instances subtly changed Vatican II's approach to conscience. This subtle shift could be partially responsible for the false perception that a well-formed conscience means waiting for a magisterial pronouncement on new issues or questions. Likewise, John Paul II's emphasis on certain aspects of Vatican II's approach to conscience shifts emphasis away from the gospel demands in particular ways. Law, for many, has become the law of the Roman Catholic Church rather than the covenantal law detailed in Sacred Scripture. This is in spite of John Paul II's use of Scripture in his writings.

Thus, questions still linger regarding conscience. Questions such as these: Have we understood what the council said about conscience? Given John Paul II's suspicion of theological interpretations of GS on conscience, what exactly have theologians said about conscience? Is the proper formation of conscience predominately a matter of obedience to the teachings in ecclesial documents? Therefore, the hermeneutical task continues in chapter 2, which takes a much longer view of the intellectual tradition on conscience. It briefly explores the biblical roots of conscience, Thomas Aquinas in the medieval period, and Cardinal John Henry Newman in the nineteenth century. This work indicates that the tensions and debates about conscience are not new. The second half of the chapter examines how theologians Bernhard Häring and Anne Patrick, writing after Vatican II, have understood and interpreted conscience. Their work recaptures and refocuses our attention on the Vatican II insight that the formation of our consciences (our moral formation) is grounded in relationship to God and manifest in both love of God and love of neighbor. We embody this love of God and neighbor in our actions for justice and rightly ordered living.

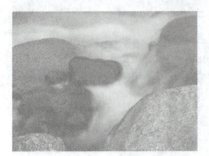

Chapter 2

Conscience through the Ages:
An Overview of Its Intellectual History

Introduction

The last chapter examined late twentieth-century magisterial teaching about conscience. Were these twentieth-century statements on conscience new developments or retrievals of a broader theological tradition on conscience? If one starts with Pope Gregory XVI's (1831–1846) statement and teaching in his encyclical *Mirari Vos* (1832) that to hold freedom of conscience for everyone is an erroneous position, then yes, Vatican II's teaching could be deemed original.[1] When taking into account Scripture, theological commentary, discussion, and reflection about conscience throughout the centuries, however, Vatican II's teaching retrieves and brings forth insights about conscience from a rich theological tradition. In other words, Vatican II's teaching on conscience did not arise *ex nihlio*.[2] It was rooted, nourished, and informed by the broader theological tradition.

In fact, the broader theological tradition on conscience has often contained a variety of approaches to and explanations of conscience. In this chapter, I do not attempt to resolve any tensions inherent in different approaches to conscience. The objective is neither to provide an exhaus-

---

[1] See the discussion of Gregory XVI and *Mirari Vos* in O'Malley's *What Happened at Vatican II* (Cambridge, MA, and London: The Belknap Press of Harvard University Press, 2008), 58–60. O'Malley contends that while this encyclical was less known than the *Syllabus of Errors* by Pius IX, nonetheless, *Mirari Vos* influenced attitudes and positions for at least half a century. Darlene Fozard Weaver also discusses Gregory XVI's encyclical in her article "Vatican II and Moral Theology," in *After Vatican II: Trajectories and Hermeneutics*, ed. James L. Heft and John O'Malley (Grand Rapids, MI: Wm. B. Eerdmans, 2012), 23–42.

[2] In her book *Confronting the Truth: Conscience in the Catholic Tradition* (New York/Mahwah, NJ: Paulist Press, 2000), Linda Hogan provides a wonderful overview of the treatment of conscience from scripture through the immediate aftermath of Vatican II.

tive examination of conscience throughout the centuries nor to cover all theological developments since Vatican II; either task would require several books. Rather, the goal remains providing one overview of the Catholic tradition, showing that conscience has been an important theme when considering the moral life long before Vatican II. Since Vatican II's description of conscience held together approaches, theologians writing after Vatican II remain rooted in and contribute to that tradition with their writings on conscience.

Therefore, my methodological approach consists of lifting up and explicating a variety of theological approaches to conscience in order to spotlight specific eras and thinkers contributing often overlooked or forgotten insights regarding conscience both pre– and post–Vatican II. The reasons for this methodological approach are to show that conscience as a theological category has a broad and deep history, thus helping demonstrate that the teaching on conscience emanating from Vatican II was neither innovative nor unique. An exposition of how several post–Vatican II theologians have reflected on and explained the term "conscience" serves as an example of how the hermeneutical task is endemic to theological work.

Section 1 begins with a brief examination of biblical understandings of conscience. This overview shows that the concept of conscience in Scripture, while concerned with judgments, places those judgments within the context of intimately knowing God and following the covenant. Sections 2 and 3 provide a brief explication of how medieval theologian Thomas Aquinas and nineteenth-century theologian Cardinal John Henry Newman define and discuss conscience. Their thought provides one sweeping historical arch for understanding twenty-first-century debates on the primacy and formation of conscience. Section 4 considers writings by several moral theologians on conscience after Vatican II. Bernard Häring was committed to the renewal of moral theology before the council[3] and was an influential presence at the council itself.[4] After the council, he wrote a three-volume manual continuing his pursuit to renew moral theology,

---

[3] Bernard Häring writes in his autobiography about his interest in renewing moral theology. His first manual was a three-volume work focusing on Christ and Scripture, a renewal approach. See Bernard Häring, *Das Gesetz Chrisit* (Freiburg: Verlag Wewel, 1954), translated as *The Law of Christ* (Paramus, NJ: Newman Press, 1961). Bernard Häring, *Free and Faithful: An Autobiography* (Liguori, MO: Liguori Publications, 1998).

[4] See James Keenan, *A History of Catholic Moral Theology in the Twentieth Century: From Confessing Sins to Liberating Consciences* (New York: Continuum, 2010), 95–98; Häring, *Free and Faithful*, 69–106, 147–76.

including how we conceive conscience.[5] Anne Patrick has written three monographs in which she explores the interplay of conscience, conscience formation, and decisions within and by women's religious communities as they engage the world: an engagement advocated by *Gaudium et Spes* and framed by their religious vocation.[6]

Bernard Häring's and Anne Patrick's interpretations and applications of Vatican II's teaching on conscience deepen, enrich, and contribute to moral theology's renewal. While other theologians do so as well, Häring and Patrick highlight that conscience and its judgments are at their core profoundly about our relationships in all their forms—to God, neighbor (both human and other creatures), self, and the rest of the created universe. Furthermore, conscience aids us in living from our core values, fostering the formation of the moral agent who grows in love of God and neighbor through lived experience, as witnessed in their lives. Finally, they offer us guidance for holding together individual responses that are attentive and responsive to various communities.

Taken together, the four sections serve to highlight the relational component of conscience. This does not negate the need for conscience to identify, recognize, and know the difference between good and evil. Rather, the relational dimension of conscience reminds us that, while objective order can be known, the moral agent acts within and is shaped by a variety of relationships.

Section 1: Scripture

Retrieving insights into conscience from Scripture requires several caveats. First, as James Bretzke points out, "conscience is not primarily a scriptural term."[7] The term "conscience" does not exist in the Hebrew Bible even as the Hebrew Bible captures the realities described by that term. While the Hebrew does not use the term "conscience," English translations of the Hebrew Bible (Old Testament) occasionally use "conscience." This occurs because versions of the Scriptures translated from the Greek or

---

[5] Bernard Häring, *Free and Faithful in Christ* (New York: Crossroad, 1978–1981).

[6] Anne E. Patrick, *Liberating Conscience: Feminist Explorations in Catholic Moral Theology* (New York: Continuum, 1996); *Women, Conscience, and the Creative Process* (New York and Mahwah, NJ: Paulist Press, 2011); *Conscience and Calling: Ethical Reflections on Catholic Women's Church Vocations* (London and New York: Bloomsbury, 2013).

[7] James T. Bretzke, *A Morally Complex World: Engaging Contemporary Moral Theology* (Collegeville, MN: Liturgical Press, 2004), 116.

Latin have sometimes translated the Hebrew term for "heart" into the English "conscience."[8] Other times a reference to conscience in the Old Testament resulted from translation choices by St. Jerome, translator of the Vulgate (Latin version of the Bible), or later transcription errors by scribes who copied the Vulgate.[9] However, the term "conscience" periodically appears in the Greek New Testament as *"synderesis* and/or *syneidesis"* and from the Greek into the "Latin as *conscientia."*[10]

Second, Linda Hogan argues that early Christians did not always use either the Latin *conscientia* or the Greek *syneidesis*, equivalents of the English "conscience," exclusively in a moral sense. There were many non-moral meanings of the term.[11] For example, *conscientia* can mean knowing with or knowing together, and *syneidesis* can mean awareness of or con-sciousness.[12] Given the reality regarding conscience's more philosophical rather than scriptural basis, Hogan turns to the scriptural and early Christian terms "heart," "wisdom," and "prudence" as corresponding to conscience. She states that these three terms "carry many of the meanings of *conscience* without the explicit terminology and are particularly important in the early history of the concept."[13] Given the importance of conscience within moral theological reflection, and the limited appearance of the term within Scripture, what can be learned from Scripture?[14]

---

[8] Linda Hogan provides examples of this move in *Confronting the Truth*, 46–47.

[9] Charles E. Curran, "Conscience in the Light of the Catholic Moral Tradition," in *Catholic Moral Tradition Today: A Synthesis* (Washington, DC: Georgetown University Press, 1999), 172–96; Linda Hogan, *Confronting the Truth*, 59–61; Robert A. Greene, "Synderesis, the Spark of Conscience, in the English Renaissance," *Journal of the History of Ideas* 52, no. 2 (April–June 1991): 195–219; Dennis J. Billy and James F. Keating, *Conscience and Prayer: The Spirit of Catholic Moral Theology* (Collegeville, MN: Liturgical Press, 2001), 4–6; John Mahoney, *The Making of Moral Theology: A Study of the Roman Catholic Tradition* (Oxford: Clarendon Press, 1987), 184–93.

[10] Bretzke, *A Morally Complex World*, 116.

[11] Hogan, *Confronting the Truth*, 36–38.

[12] Joyce Shin, "Accommodating the Other's Conscience: Saint Paul's Approach to Religious Tolerance," *Journal of the Society of Christian Ethics* 28, no. 1 (2008): 1–23, at 6.

[13] Hogan, *Confronting the Truth*, 38. For her brief overview of the use of conscience in Greek and Roman philosophical traditions, see pages 36–46. She also discusses the use of the term in the patristic period on pages 55–61. Joyce Shin argues on page 6 in her article, "Accommodating the Other's Conscience," that the closest term to "conscience" is the Hebrew word for "heart."

[14] I agree with Hogan and others that while the term "conscience" does not appear frequently in Scripture, the ideas related to conscience as it developed in the tradition are captured in other ways.

As already noted, the Hebrew Scriptures do not contain the word "conscience." Rather, the concept of morality in the Hebrew Bible requires the believer to act in line with the law and covenant. This does not mean that the moral agent follows an externally imposed system of laws and norms assented to through an overly rational exercise aimed at determining the system of laws and the norms validity. Instead, obedience to the law and covenant requires attention to the relationships that the law and covenant govern. The primal relationship binding moral agents' obedience is the Divine-human one. Obedience to the law and covenant requires attending first to God and then to others with one's complete self, acting from God's concept of justice, mercy, and wholeness. Obedience of this kind is not rote acquiescence but should ultimately increase awareness of and engagement with others, behaviors that promote life for all God's creation, self-knowledge, self-understanding, and an overall moral life.

The heart metaphor in Scripture captures these ideas along with the reality that we often fail to conform to God's law and worldview. Therefore, in Scripture, we read of hearts that need reproach and that are hard, contrite, or stubborn. We pray with the Psalmist for clean hearts.[15] As Hogan writes, the heart "became an important metaphor for describing certain features of the person's moral faculty."[16] Additionally, the heart metaphor alongside the concept of obedience to the law and covenant suggests the necessity to attend to both internal (feelings, proper dispositions) and external (actions, behaviors) features when assessing either a moral life or individual decisions. Thus, "heart" language indicates that the moral agent must not only act well externally; internally, they must also have certain dispositions and affections connected to proper action and properly formed relationships.

Turning to the New Testament, "conscience" or its Greek equivalent *syneidesis* appears a handful of times, mostly in the Pauline corpus and only once in the gospels. Scripture scholar Joyce Shin writes that the "term 'conscience,' or 'syneidesis,' appears in the New Testament thirty-one times," mostly in Paul's writings.[17] Therefore, it can be argued that the Pauline corpus is primarily responsible for conceptions of conscience

---

[15] Hogan, *Confronting the Truth*, 46–49.

[16] Ibid., 48.

[17] Shin, "Accommodating the Other's Conscience," 20n6. The thirty-one times she identifies are "once in John 8:9; fourteen times in Pauline letters; and sixteen times in post–Pauline letters."

deriving from the New Testament. Paul uses the term "conscience" while neither defining nor explaining the term.[18] Shin, however, sees Paul's use of the term reflecting "the forensic role of conscience as witness (Rom. 2:15, 9:1; 2 Cor. 1:12), the notion of a painful awareness of transgression (1 Cor. 10:25, 27, 28; Rom. 13:5), as well as a gnostic definition of conscience as the agent of knowledge (1 Cor. 8:7, 10, 12)."[19] Shin is using the term "gnostic" here to mean "the primacy of knowledge for one's salvation."[20] In other words, conscience helps us identify what we need for salvation.

Hogan, on the other hand, focuses on how Paul's use of conscience in several contexts influences how we see conscience and its function in moral decision making. Hogan identifies that conscience is present, albeit in different ways, in the Gentiles and Jews (Rom 2:14-15).[21] Paul perceives conscience as having both objective and subjective dimensions (Rom 9:1). The objective dimension of conscience refers to both "its divine character" and "the requirements of faith." Romans 14 also discusses the objective dimensions of conscience, which shapes the subjective dimension ("personal response to our circumstances"), whereas 2 Timothy 1:3 and 2 Corinthians 1:12 reference conscience's subjective dimensions.[22] In these examples we see that each community was living their faith in Christ.[23] Hogan also identifies the notions of a weak, correct, and erroneous conscience that later receive more development in Christian theology in Paul's letters, specifically in 1 Corinthians 8:7-13 and 10:27-29. Additionally, the Corinthians passage also indicates that conscience has a deliberative function, a function prior to acting. As a result, Paul paved

---

[18] Shin, "Accommodating the Other's Conscience," 7. Shin discusses the various ways conscience was used in the Hellenistic literature of Paul's time that could have influenced his understanding and use of the term.

[19] Ibid., 8.

[20] Ibid., 21, n. 25.

[21] A review of the literature surrounding Paul's use of conscience is beyond the scope of this section. For a discussion of Paul's use of the term "conscience," including a brief overview of the biblical scholarship and some of the debates, see S. J. Gathercole, "A Law unto Themselves: The Gentiles in Romans 2.14-15 Revisited," *Journal for the Study of the New Testament* 85 (2002): 27–49; and Joyce Shin, "Accommodating the Other's Conscience," 3–23. Shin's footnotes are particularly helpful.

[22] Hogan, *Confronting the Truth*, 51–52.

[23] As each early faith community lived out their faith in Jesus Christ (objective dimension) in various ways due to different contexts and concerns (subjective dimension), contemporary Christians might also incarnate the demands of Christian discipleship in various ways.

the way for further explanation and understanding of conscience's role in the individual's moral life.[24] Conscience participates in our forethought, and we must recognize that it can be correct, weak, or wrong.

Shin, on the other hand, takes issue with much of the scholarship on the 1 Corinthians passages around eating meat. She argues that Paul was advocating for "accommodating the other person's conscience, rather than stressing the autonomy of conscience," and she sees this as a significant contribution by Paul.[25] Rather than focusing solely on the personal autonomy of conscience, Shin highlights that other people's judgment of conscience makes a claim on us. In other words, we not only have to consider our own conscience before acting; we must also be in conversation with others regarding the judgments of their consciences. Shin's insights here have implications for how we understand scandal and the obligation to follow our consciences if we must pastorally consider the other as making a claim on us. In other words, prior to acting we must factor the consequences of acting on other people, especially in matters of faith. The individual must remain aware of his or her interconnectedness with others. We are responsible for ourselves, but we are also our siblings' keepers.

This very brief foray for understanding conscience in Scripture indicates several things that are important when thinking about conscience. Connecting conscience to the heart highlights the transformative, internal and relational aspects of moral agency. The moral agent must not be concerned only with the moral law, or objective order of things. The moral agent must also be engaged in the lifelong task of conversion and transformation of their hearts (understood in the Hebraic sense as referencing their whole being).

Likewise, though not discussed here, the terms "wisdom" and "prudence" implicitly indicate that knowledge and appropriate applications of conscience develop through lived experience. As indicated in chapter 1, however, experience does not automatically equate to insight. Experience must be subject to reflection, analysis, and interpretation. The Pauline corpus contains these insights as the letters respond to various activities and experiences within specific communities where judgments are made regarding communal practices and norms.

---

[24] Hogan, *Confronting the Truth*, 50–55.
[25] Shin, "Accommodating the Other's Conscience," 9–12, at 12.

Finally, the New Testament provides the seeds for describing conscience as a judge, its deliberative function, its objective and subjective dimensions, its individual and communal considerations, and further classification regarding different types of consciences. These seeds for describing conscience in this way also point to the relational character of conscience. The next section examines some of the ideas briefly presented here as they were developed in the theological tradition, starting with the medieval period. The medieval period was chosen because it is the era of Thomas Aquinas, an influential thinker on the development of conscience.

Section 2: The Medieval Period and Thomas Aquinas

No century, monastery, or theological center of study has a monolithic approach to theology and its various loci. The medieval period is no exception.[26] Medieval theologians such as Bonaventure, Peter Abelard, Peter Lombard, and Thomas Aquinas contributed by their writings, debates, and clarifications to the development of a "theory of conscience." This included various understandings of conscience over time.[27]

For theologians in the early Middle Ages, St. Jerome's use of both *synderesis* and *conscientia* in the Vulgate posed difficulties and confusion. The two terms that seemed to describe a similar reality necessitated clarification. Did the two terms refer to the same reality? Did the human reality named by the two terms reside in the same faculty? While individual theologians answered these questions differently, they frequently had areas of agreement. For example, some theologians located the working of *synderesis* in the human will, and other theologians located its workings

---

[26] See, for example, Peter Godman, *Paradoxes of Conscience in the High Middle Ages: Abelard, Heloise, and the Archpoet* (Cambridge: Cambridge University Press, 2009); Dirk Volkertszoon Coornhert and Gerrit Voogt, *Synod on the Freedom of Conscience: A Thorough Examination during the Gathering Held in the Year 1582 in the City of Freetown* (Amsterdam: Amsterdam University Press, 2008); M. V. Dougherty, *Moral Dilemmas in Medieval Thought: From Gratian to Aquinas* (Cambridge: Cambridge University Press, 2011); Linda Hogan, "Discerning Moral Principles: Conscience from the Medivalists to the Manualists," in *Confronting the Truth*, 64–99; Eric D'Arcy, *Conscience and Its Right to Freedom* (London: Sheed & Ward, 1961); Timothy Potts, *Conscience in Medieval Philosophy* (New York: Cambridge University Press, 1980); and "conscience" in *Cambridge History of Later Medieval Philosophy: From the Recovery of Aristotle to the Disintegration of Scholasticism, 1100–1600*, ed. Norman Kretzmann, Anthony Kenny, and Jan Pinborg (New York: Cambridge University Press, 1982) 687–704.

[27] Hogan, *Confronting the Truth*, 65.

in the human intellect. Linda Hogan argues that the various schools of thought and the resulting debates solidified the distinction between *synderesis* and *conscientia*.

Thus, the differentiation was made "between the general orientation toward the good" held by all (*synderesis*) "and the concretization of this orientation in particular decisions (*conscientia*)."[28] This innovative differentiation "enabled theologians to deal more precisely with the complex matter of the interior dimensions of moral judgment. It allowed them to draw a distinction between the person's moral sense and his/her actions." Hogan carefully notes that the distinction was not rigid, because the medieval theologians kept a connection "between *synderesis* and *conscientia*" or, in other words, a connection between "moral orientation and action."[29]

Even though medieval theologians held a dynamic connection between moral orientation and action, a narrow focus on either moral orientation or action can sever this connection. Separating moral orientation from action poses problems for human beings seeking to live a moral life, since this separation leads to a truncated description of moral action, a reductionist view of the moral agent's capacity for growth, and an underestimation of the importance of narrative for living a moral life. *Gaudium et Spes* strives to hold the connection between *synderesis* and *conscientia*. *GS* 16 states that "men and women discover a law which they have not laid upon themselves and which they must obey. Its voice, ever calling them to love and to do what is good and to avoid evil, tells them inwardly at the right moment: do this, shun that." This is the general orientation to the good. Connecting moral orientation to action, *GS* 16 says, "By conscience, in a wonderful way, that law is made known which is fulfilled in the love of God and of one's neighbor." In other words, orientation toward the good and away from evil is not sufficient; a proper moral orientation is embodied in actions that make manifest one's love of God and neighbor, the criteria for which is spelled out in various places within the Torah, the Prophets, and the New Testament. Therefore, *Gaudium et Spes*'s description of conscience, which includes both moral orientation and action, propels moral agents and moral communities to consider, reflect upon, and grapple with the distinct yet deeply entwined interior and exterior dimensions of moral judgment and action.

Moving back to the medieval period, I turn to the work of Thomas Aquinas. While exploring the theological diversity among medieval theo-

---

[28] Ibid., 67.
[29] Ibid., 66–72, quotes on pages 71–72.

logians is a worthwhile endeavor, several reasons provide the impetus to focus on Thomas Aquinas. Many people are aware of Thomas Aquinas's work on conscience, if not by name at least by experience. Furthermore, Pope Leo XIII in *Aeterni Patris* advocated the restoration of Christian philosophy, commending those who had returned to Thomas Aquinas's work and encouraged others to do the same.[30] As a result, various schools of Thomistic thought arose in the latter half of the nineteenth century and into the twentieth that influenced the theology of priests, bishops, and theologians.[31] Aquinas's thought can be seen in various Vatican II statements on conscience, and his thought forms one background refrain for contemporary debates on conscience.

Whereas his predecessors clarified the distinctions regarding *synderesis* and *conscientia*, Aquinas explored the nature and workings of conscience and its authority for the moral agent.[32] For Aquinas, *synderesis* refers to the ability of the human being to recognize foundational principles for moral behavior. It is a "habit of practical reason" or that which moves us toward the good and away from evil. Notice that there are two movements here: recognition and habit. Habits, for Aquinas, result from practices aimed to foster certain virtues or attributes. So already embedded in Aquinas's description of *synderesis* is the dynamic interplay between practices/habits that foster virtues and our capacity to acknowledge or perceive foundational principles for moral behavior. We develop the ability to recognize foundational principles for acting through practice. While *synderesis* is the ability to recognize foundational principles, *conscientia* is the means for applying the foundational principles in concrete situations. Stated differently, it can be said that *synderesis* deals with recognition and *conscientia* deals with application.[33]

It is helpful knowing that conscience has two necessary tasks: the recognition of foundational principles and the application of those principles.

---

[30] Pope Leo XIII, *Aeterni Patris* (On the Restoration of Christian Philosophy), 1879, paragraphs 25–33, http://w2.vatican.va/content/leo-xiii/en/encyclicals/documents/hf_l-xiii_enc_04081879_aeterni-patris.html.

[31] Gerald A. McCool, *Nineteenth-Century Scholasticism: The Search for a Unitary Method* (New York: Fordham University Press, 1989); idem, *From Unity to Pluralism: The Internal Evolution of Thomism* (New York: Fordham University Press, 1989).

[32] Hogan, *Confronting the Truth*, 75–87; Mahoney, *The Making of Moral Theology*, 187–93, 207, 290.

[33] Hogan, *Confronting the Truth*, 76–79; Mahoney, *The Making of Moral Theology*, 187–89; see Thomas Aquinas, *Summa Theologiae* (ST), 1a, q. 79, a. 12; ST, 1a2ae q. 94, a.1 and 1a, q. 79, a. 13.

Keeping these two tasks in mind can foster appreciation for the differing emphases within contemporary debates about conscience. Foundational principles (or objective moral standards) are crucial; yet, by virtue of their universality, general norms usually require more specificity for application in different contexts. Thus, for Aquinas, the application of first principles is not a simple matter of straightforward deduction. In other words, employing foundational principles is not a mechanized application of rules or laws. The moral agent must first identify which foundational principle is pertinent; accurately understand the problem, and assess all the morally relevant features of the issue. As a result, the application task can be and often is difficult.[34]

While we often recognize and apply principles appropriately, we must be equally mindful that our reasoning can be flawed, that we sometimes misunderstand problems, that we are frequently blinded to morally relevant features, and that a course of action might not be clear. These realities require modesty and highlight the provisional nature of conscience's determination and application of foundational principles, subsequently raising questions and doubts concerning our ability to have "certain" judgments of conscience and to act from doubtful judgments. These contemporary concerns are not new. They existed in the medieval period as well and were often debated under the question of whether a conscience rarely, sometimes, or never binds the moral agent to act.[35]

Aquinas weighed in on the debate about whether conscience rarely binds, sometimes binds, or always binds by concluding that conscience always binds. This binding of conscience necessitates that the moral agent follow their conscience and its judgment even if it is erroneous. Hogan argues that "Aquinas's argument revolves around the claim that the conscience seeks to identify the good in each situation."[36] Thus, conscience "must follow the good as it perceives it."[37] Aquinas's conclusion about following an erroneous conscience is more nuanced than it appears on the surface. Since our perceptions can be wrong and there are consequences

---

[34] Hogan, *Confronting the Truth*, 75–78.

[35] The question here eventually leads to debates over probabilism. See Hogan, *Confronting the Truth*, 94–96; Mahoney, *The Making of Moral Theology*, 135–43; Bernard Hoose, *Proportionalism: The American Debate and Its European Roots* (Washington, DC: Georgetown University Press, 1987).

[36] Hogan, *Confronting the Truth*, 81; see also Mahoney, *The Making of Moral Theology*, 191–92.

[37] Hogan, *Confronting the Truth*, 82; Mahoney, *The Making of Moral Theology*, 192–93.

and effects stemming from any action, following an erroneous conscience is not a free pass regarding actions. We can be culpable or held responsible for following an erroneous conscience. If we are mistaken about what is good due to voluntary, neglectful, or careless ignorance, then Aquinas argues we assume culpability and responsibility for following an erroneous conscience.[38]

Conversely, if due to invincible ignorance (or ignorance due to no fault of the person) we follow an erroneous conscience, then we are blameless.[39] To be clear, Aquinas does not call the actions arising from either a culpable or a nonculpable erroneous conscience good. The actions stemming from an erroneous conscience can be sinful. The conclusion regarding an erroneous conscience, however, concerns the subject, the moral agent, and the moral agent's accountability for his or her actions. On the one hand, when we act from a vincible conscience, whether voluntarily or through neglect or carelessness, the community can reprimand and hold us responsible for our actions and their effects. On the other hand, when we act from an invincible conscience, since we are blameless even if the actions are sinful or have bad effects, a different response is required. Appropriate responses to actions from an invincible conscience are compassionate ones that seek to explain, teach, and instruct the person in order to form a conscience more properly.

Several of the themes Aquinas considered in his work on conscience appear in *Gaudium et Spes* 16, even without direct reference to Aquinas. The recognition of first principles can be found in the statement regarding doing good and avoiding evil. *GS* affirms the dignity of an erroneous conscience along with the distinction between the vincible and invincible erroneous conscience. Part 2 of *Gaudium et Spes*, which looks at various issues confronting the modern world, is a testament to the idea that practical application of norms is difficult. Seeing some resonances between Aquinas's thought and the thought on conscience in *GS* demonstrates that intellectual ideas have an effective history; ideas can influence future thoughts and projects.

Nevertheless, even after Vatican II questions remain about conscience. For example, how does one determine the culpability from ignorance? Does

---

[38] Hogan, *Confronting the Truth*, 82–83; Aquinas, ST, 1a2ae, q. 19, a. 6.

[39] Hogan, *Confronting the Truth*, 83–85; Mahoney, *The Making of Moral Theology*, 192–93; Aquinas, ST, 1a2ae, q. 19, a. 6.

conscience help mediate between the objective and subjective elements of morality, and, if so, can we define this relationship more specifically? Under what circumstances can there be divergent applications in good conscience of first principles for morality in practical circumstances? When individual or communal consciences diverge from magisterial teaching, should we consider the conclusions and subsequent actions of individuals and communities automatically as dissent? How do we navigate the possibility that magisterial teaching is sometimes wrong without disparaging the Magisterium's teaching authority? What role does the authority of a well-formed individual or communal conscience have in the broader ecclesial community in their discernment regarding proper courses of action in living out the Gospel message?[40] These questions frequently appear in various forms whenever I teach or present on conscience.

Cardinal and convert John Henry Newman's lifetime spanned the nineteenth century. Given the nineteenth century's influence on twentieth-century theology, and the fact that Newman considers several of these questions in his writings on conscience, he is a good figure from which to seek guidance for possibly answering these recurring questions.[41]

Section 3: Cardinal John Henry Newman

While references to conscience can be found throughout Newman's works, two specific writings, a sermon and a treatise written shortly after Vatican I, will be the focus here.[42] These readings were chosen because they address our relationship with God, to whom the moral agent owes obedience, and the relationship of the individual conscience to papal authority and teaching. Together these readings show how Newman helps

---

[40] Linda Hogan discusses the status of the contemporary debates around conscience in chapter 1 of her book, *Confronting the Truth*. James Keenan looks at developments regarding conscience in his historical book on moral theology, *A History of Catholic Moral Theology in the Twentieth Century*.

[41] For autobiographical information on Cardinal John Henry Newman, see Ian Ker and Terrence Merrigan, eds., *The Cambridge Companion to John Henry Newman* (Cambridge: Cambridge University Press, 2009) 1–28; information can be found online at the National Institute for Newman Studies at www.newmanreader.org.

[42] For studies that explore the various ways conscience appears in Newman's thought, see Gerard J. Hughes, "Conscience," in Ker and Merrigan, *The Cambridge Companion to John Henry Newman*, 189–220; Walter E. Conn, *Conscience and Conversion in Newman: A Developmental Study of Self in John Henry Newman* (Milwaukee, WI: Marquette University Press, 2010).

illuminate how we might understand conscience's relationship to papal and magisterial authority, contextualized by obedience to God.

Newman, while still an Anglican, preaches about conscience in his 1840 sermon, "The Testimony of Conscience."[43] Newman starts the sermon with Paul's brief line on conscience in 2 Corinthians 1:12.[44] Newman does not directly connect conscience to judgments of external actions; conscience does not judge or point us toward good or evil. Rather, Newman preaches that conscience passes judgment on our "heart" and how we are serving God: whether singlemindedly, deceptively, conflicted, or imperfectly.[45]

According to Newman, since humans are "very sinful and corrupt" we often ignore our conscience as it ascertains how we are serving God.[46] Newman preaches that if we are falling short in our service, we are often unwilling to change and serve more readily since change requires something of us. Furthermore, Newman believes that we dull our conscience by ignoring it. He also argues that we can pretend to follow our consciences by outward actions and words, while at the same time we deny and ignore what God desires of us—a full surrender to God. Yet despite our sinfulness, God can facilitate and affect in us "the desires, affections, principles, views, and tastes which a change implies." While God facilitates change, any change also requires our willingness to "surrender" to God and let go of our old selves.[47]

Our willingness to follow God manifests itself in our following Christ. Newman preaches that over time we grow and are more completely able to follow Christ. As an example, he contrasts Peter's two confessions of Jesus as Christ. Newman sees in the first "a reserved devotion," a willingness to follow Christ only so far; a part of Peter's heart was not given to Christ. On the other hand, Newman sees Peter's second confession after the resurrection as a fuller surrender of his self (and heart) to Christ.[48]

---

[43] John Henry Newman, "The Testimony of Conscience," in *Parochial and Plain Sermons*, vol. 5 (Waterloo, London: Rivingtons, 1882), 237–53; a digitized copy of the text was accessed online at http://babel.hathitrust.org/cgi/pt?id=nyp.33433068279722;view=1up;seq=11.

[44] 2 Corinthians 1:12 says, "Indeed, this is our boast, the testimony of our conscience; we have behaved in the world with frankness and godly sincerity, not by earthly wisdom but by the grace of God—and all the more toward you" (NRSV).

[45] Newman, "The Testimony of Conscience," 236–40, 242–44.

[46] Ibid., 240.

[47] Ibid., 241.

[48] Ibid., 245–46.

In other words, Peter's capacity to committed discipleship matures and deepens, becoming less flawed and more integrated.

In this sermon, Newman considers conscience within the context of faith and as a verdict concerning our commitment to following Christ. In this way, conscience's findings concern our relationship with God, our discipleship and "heart." Yet, this is not the only way Newman ponders conscience. Fast forward to 1875, thirty-five years after this sermon and thirty years after becoming Catholic, and Newman again tackles the concept of conscience.[49] In the aftermath of Vatican I's definition of papal infallibility, there are concerns about Catholics' ability to be good citizens in England. Newman indirectly responds to William Gladstone, one of those concerned, in a letter to the Duke of Norfolk, a Catholic, while devoting a full section to conscience.[50]

Newman defends the concept of papal infallibility, albeit in a limited way, while also arguing for the primacy of conscience. Unlike Gladstone, Newman does not see a collision between papal authority and the authority of the private conscience. Newman's capacity to embrace both papal infallibility and the primacy of conscience can be seen in his four-point argument in the letter's section 5 on conscience.[51]

In the first point, Newman provides what he calls "the first principle," which is his understanding of conscience "as a dutiful obedience to what claims to be a divine voice, speaking within us."[52] Earlier he argued that God implanted God's law, "which is Himself in the intelligence of all [God's] rational creatures." Citing Aquinas's definition of natural law, as human participation in eternal law (which is God's law), Newman says the natural law, "as apprehended in the minds of individual men, is called 'conscience.'"[53] In a move that he does not develop explicitly, Newman says that the law (here natural), while "it may suffer refraction," because

---

[49] John Henry Newman, *A Letter Addressed to His Grace the Duke of Norfolk on the Occasion of Mr. Gladstone's Recent Expostulation*, 4th ed. (London: B. M. Pickering, 1875). A digitized copy was used and can be accessed at https://archive.org/details /a13300673500newmuoft.

[50] Sheridan Gilley, "Life and Writings," in *The Cambridge Companion to John Henry Newman*, ed. Ian Kerr and Terrence Merrigan, 1–28 (Cambridge: Cambridge University Press, 2009), 22; Newman, "Letter to the Duke of Norfolk," 5. I am not delving into the historical debate regarding papal infallibility. My concern remains Newman's explication of conscience.

[51] Newman, "Letter to the Duke of Norfolk," 61–74.

[52] Ibid., 69.

[53] Ibid., 61.

it is mediated, still has efficacy and demands obedience.[54] In other words, because God communicates with limited, finite creatures, God's communication is received in a fractal, partial, mediated manner. Consider by way of analogy that we perceive light normally as white, yet when diffused or refracted into its various wavelengths, light appears to us as a rainbow. This event gives us a new perspective on both light and color. If God's law suffers refraction because of the recipients' capacity to receive God's communication, then we, the recipients, must be mindful that our comprehension and perception of God's law is limited and partial. We can perceive truth, God's laws and grace, yet incompletely. We are still obliged to follow this incompletely understood law; however, this means we can both err and increase in our knowledge of what the law obliges.

In his second point, Newman articulates the theological domain where conscience functions. Conscience's domain is not "speculative truth" or "any abstract doctrine." Rather, conscience's domain is "conduct, on something to be done or not done."[55] Using Aquinas, Newman argues that conscience is the practical judgment of actions focused on doing good and avoiding evil. Given the distinctions between speculative truth, abstract doctrine, and practical judgment, Newman concludes that "conscience cannot come into direct collision with the Church's or the Pope's infallibility; which is engaged in general propositions, and in the condemnation of particular and given errors."[56] In other words, papal infallibility and conscience have distinctive purviews. Papal infallibility concerns areas of speculative truth and general propositions (abstract doctrine). Conscience's arena is practical judgments involving actions.

In his third point, Newman acknowledges that conflict can and does occur between conscience and papal statements in the domain of practical judgments. He writes that since conscience is a "practical dictate," then yes, a "collision is possible between it and the Pope's authority only when the Pope legislates, or gives particular orders, and the like. But a Pope is not infallible in his laws, nor in his commands, nor in his acts of state, nor in his administration, nor in his public policy."[57] Neither papal infallibility nor papal authority is negated here, just qualified. Rather, Newman argues that papal error might occur in matters of practical

---

[54] Ibid., 61–62.
[55] Ibid., 69.
[56] Ibid.
[57] Ibid., 69–70.

judgment or in particular areas like administrative duties. Papal practical judgments are not infallible; they are fallible.[58] Since Newman argues that papal infallibility does not extend to these types of practical judgments, he detects "no deadlock" as occurring "between conscience and the Pope" in matters of practical judgment.[59]

In his fourth point, Newman reiterates that in this work he is referring to conscience, properly understood, not contemporary misappropriations of conscience. He clarifies that only conscience properly understood can oppose the non-infallible papal authority. Any opposition by conscience to something emanating from the papacy should be taken seriously and only with several caveats. The caveats require the moral agent who disagrees with the papacy to engage in serious thought and prayer and to recognize that the burden of proof rests on them to show that their conscience is correct. Additionally, one must use "all available means of arriving at a right judgment on the matter in question." When considering a question of conscience that opposes a papal injunction, one must interrogate and examine one's own motivations, concerns, and vices before following the voice of conscience.[60] Newman contends that following these steps means that "collisions between the Pope's authority and the authority of conscience would be very rare."[61]

In considering these points, we glean several insights from Newman regarding conscience that are important for us today. Conscience only makes sense in the matrix of a relationship with God (prayer). Reflection (serious thought) is important. Papal judgments about practical matters are to be followed unless the moral agent supplies persuasive arguments that his or her conscience is correct (burden of proof). Finally, when disagreeing with papal judgments, conscience can be followed if the moral agent considers the purification and proper attribution of their motives, concerns, vices, and, I would add, gifts. Stated differently, Newman rejects the idea or definition of conscience that reduces it to mere opinion, feeling, or an individualized personal approach to morality. Conscience is relational. The moral agent has to consider his or her relationship to God, self, and the communities within which he or she is embedded. As such,

---

[58] Ibid., 69–71.

[59] Ibid., 70–71.

[60] Ibid., 71.

[61] Ibid., 70–71. Finally, to buttress his argument about conscience and show that it is traditional, on pages 72–74 he cites historical figures, and contemporary theologians on conscience.

obligations or duties that result from God's call and law are set within an ecclesial context, providing boundaries for conscience's deliberations regarding practical judgments.

Newman's focus on relationality and the ecclesial context for practical judgments of conscience mitigates one contemporary temptation to reduce conscience to unreflective opinion. Likewise, his emphasis on God as the ultimate adjudicator of objective truth and the narrow constraints on infallibility should moderate the movement toward increasing the scope of magisterial infallibility. Only when one realizes that Newman prioritizes conscience's obligation to God and does not mean the individual person's opinion, as well as the narrow scope he ascribes to infallibility, can someone avoid misappropriating his statement where he notes that he toasts conscience first and the pope second.[62]

Given that Newman believes that "collisions" between the pope's authority (meaning judgment in practical matters) and the faithful's consciences are rare, however, does he offer anything for the twenty-first century regarding debate within the community? This is important because of the seemingly increasing disagreements around judgments in practical matters.

Insights occur if we turn to the human person, the one who acts. Terrence Merrigan makes the case that Newman saw the human being as one who comes to know him- or herself "through conscientious moral action within the framework of a history that is inevitably—even necessarily— ambiguous."[63] According to Merrigan, Newman wrote in a time, similar to our own, when religion's influence in "shaping thought and public life" was decreasing. Aware of this reality, "Newman's apologetic takes as its starting point the individual's encounter with God in conscience."[64] Newman takes this starting point of the individual's encounter with God and connects it with a profound respect for, engagement with, defense of, and recognition that an individual functions within a tradition. In other words, the option is never between an individual conscience and tradition. Rather, the belief that both individual conscience and a shared tradition

---

[62] Ibid., 74.

[63] Terrence Merrigan, "Conscience and Selfhood: Thomas More, John Henry Newman, and the Crisis of the Postmodern Subject," *Theological Studies* 73, no. 4 (December 1, 2012): 841–69, at 841–42. While Merrigan also examines the thought of Thomas More, I am only looking at what he says regarding Newman, the human person, and conscience.

[64] Ibid., 843.

are crucial creates a necessary tension "basic to the Catholic mind."[65] Merrigan sees Newman holding these two ideas together, thereby modeling "the quest to hold in tensile unity the responsibility for one's self and the responsibility toward the community of faith."[66] Both the individual and community are important in the quest for truth and right action.

Merrigan highlights that Newman attends to the way conscience "has an intimate bearing on our affections and emotions."[67] The feelings of conscience often follow actions. In other words, conscience's judgment and workings are made present when we use practical reason and acknowledge and attend to our emotions, feelings, and affections. Our emotions and affections can tell us conscience is operating—which has theological significance since Newman believes emotions, affections, and conscience help direct us toward God.[68] Hence, through conscience we get to know the self and the self-in-relation to God. God revealed in conscience is "the 'echo' of God's voice in us" even as God's "presence is always mediated."[69] The reality that God's presence and voice as "echo" are mediated requires that we interpret, consider, look at, and discern whether our perceptions and articulation of actions are accurate. This interpretation, consideration, and discernment always occur within the context of an ecclesial community. We need the community since "conscience alone cannot sustain the moral and religious commitment it urges upon us."[70] In an age that calls

[65] Ibid., 843. Tension is not always a negative thing. It can hold things together; it can be a sign that there is disagreement and that consensus is still not reached. For example, the tension in the springs of a garage door makes the garage door work. When the tension is too much or too little the springs do not work and neither does the garage door.

[66] Ibid. I would contend that certain impasses in contemporary Catholicism exist because we no longer hold this unity-in-tension. Imbalance exists, on the one hand, because of an incorrect understanding of conscience as opinion rather than an informed judgment of practical reason. On the other hand, imbalance occurs when a person incorrectly believes that a formed correct conscience means assenting to everything coming from the pope or Magisterium. Therefore, it remains crucial to remember that unity is different from uniformity. We can have unity and still differ in our perspectives leading to life-giving responses to the world's questions about meaning and purpose. What might temper the temptation to focus only on the individual or the pope would be to expand our communities of consultation beyond the Vatican to include local bishops' synods, the lives of the saints, local parishes, various religious orders and their charisms within Catholicism, in other words, the whole people of God.

[67] Ibid., 849.

[68] Ibid., 849–50.

[69] Ibid., 866.

[70] Ibid., 855.

God's existence into question, the church should support the individual or community in their belief and relationship with God.

Humans, however, err: we often do not support each other; we can overemphasize and miscomprehend both obedience to authority and individual freedom of conscience; as many twentieth-century events made abundantly clear to contemporary peoples, human sinfulness can and does become embedded in social structures, institutions, and governments. This social sin in its various forms requires critique, challenge, and resistance by individuals and communities. In so doing, we respond to conscience and discover our very selves. Merrigan, drawing on Newman, states it this way: "The self is always being constituted by the 'other'—the other *for* whom one is responsible, and the Other *before* whom one is responsible. The being of the self is, therefore, essentially gift (or grace) and task (or call), something to be actualized in every authentic response to the voice of conscience."[71]

Once again, our attention is drawn to and focused on the relational character of human existence. This relational aspect forms the context within which we act. We have obligations to our fellow human beings, and God is the one to whom we ultimately answer. Thus, the exercise of individual freedom in acting conscientiously is always constrained by our relationships. Yet, it is in acting and responding to our conscience that we find ourselves. Connecting conscience to self-actualization or, in theological terms, becoming a new being in Christ requires attention to external actions as well as internal motivations, dispositions, affections, and loves. It requires multilayered, complex considerations regarding the moral formation of moral agents and confronting the hard truth that discipleship, while not easy, requires ongoing conversions and sacrifices to live justice and love as mandated by God. Bernard Häring and Anne Patrick are two post–Vatican II theologians who consider conscience, moral formation, responsibility to the other, and the relationship of the individual and community within the context of the human response to God's call.

---

[71] Ibid., 868. While valid, this claim raises further questions. What does it mean to be responsible to the other? How do we navigate competing claims from others? How does one discern and verify an authentic call and response to conscience?

Section 4: Post–Vatican II Select Theologians, Bernard Häring and Anne Patrick

Bernard Häring

Bernard Häring's theological career spanned Vatican II, much as Newman's spanned Vatican I.[72] Häring's experiences with war, his desire to renew moral theology, his travels, and being a Redemptorist priest all influenced and shaped his work.[73] While Newman considered conscience in relation to papal infallibility after Vatican I, Häring, both before and after Vatican II, remained focused on conscience's connection to the moral agent's responsibility to live authentically.[74] James Keenan writes that Härings' pre–Vatican II writings on conscience "anticipated, inspired, and informed some of the most important words from the Council, the now famous definition of conscience [in *GS* 16]."[75]

After Vatican II Häring also writes about conscience in volume 1 of his three-volume work, *Free and Faithful in Christ*. Häring did not see this work as a rejection of his prior work, *The Law of Christ*. For him, *Free and Faithful in Christ* continues the Christocentric approach of *The Law of Christ* with the purpose of presenting "responsibility and co-responsibility as key concepts in a Christian ethics for people of today." This responsibility remains grounded in a commitment to Jesus Christ while addressing concerns regarding themes of "liberty, liberation, and fidelity" as signs of the times.[76] Häring's approach to these themes should be read against the backdrop of influences that he describes; most crucial, it seems, is the following statement:

> But what most influenced my thinking about moral theology was the
> mindless and criminal obedience of Christians to Hitler, a madman

---

[72] For a sense of Häring's overall approach and his voluminous output, see Kathleen A. Cahalan, *Formed in the Image of Christ: The Sacramental-Moral Theology of Bernard Häring* (Collegeville, MN: Liturgical Press, 2004); James F. Keenan, "Synthesis: Bernhard Häring," in *A History of Catholic Moral Theology in the Twentieth Century*, 83–98.

[73] Keenan, *A History of Catholic Moral Theology in the Twentieth Century*, 89; Häring, *Free and Faithful: An Autobiography* and *Embattled Witness: Memories of a Time of War* (New York: Seabury Press, 1976).

[74] Häring not only wrote on conscience before the council; he also served as secretary for the committee on *Gaudium et Spes* and has been called its "quasi-father" by Charles Curran. See Keenan, *A History of Catholic Moral Theology in the Twentieth Century*, 96.

[75] Ibid.

[76] Häring, *Free and Faithful in Christ*, 1:1–2.

and tyrant. This led me to the conviction that the character of a Christian must not be formed one-sidedly by a leitmotif of obedience but rather by a discerning responsibility, a capacity to respond courageously to new value insights and new needs, and a readiness to take the risk.[77]

Keenan writes that Häring saw "the need to develop not a conforming, obediential moral theology, but rather one that summoned Christians to a responsive and responsible life of discipleship."[78] Häring's emphasis on Christian responsibility in his discussion of conscience makes sense considering his concern stemming from World War II that unquestioning obedience can lead to criminality and evil. He does not negate communal concerns, norms, or standards. Rather, he focuses attention on the reality that humans cannot go blindly or unreflectively through life giving obedience to any authority. Our foundational authority is Christ. How we act and live reveals and witnesses to our commitments. Therefore, we must take responsibility for our lives; we are accountable for what we do and do not do. Obedience to earthly authority does not relinquish us from this responsibility and accountability.

Häring does not unmoor the individual from a communal context broadly understood or from a religious context. On the contrary, theologically he sees the church as the place where God calls us and we enact our faithfulness to that call. We have a responsibility to those who went before us, to those who journey with us now, and to future generations. The importance of the community for the responsible, responsive, and faithful moral agent to God's call is coupled with a realism that acknowledges that the church has "dead traditions in contradiction with our faith in a living God who works with his people at all times."[79] Furthermore, liberty (authentic freedom) and fidelity are not mutually exclusive. Häring is clear: we are faithful to Christ first. Living from the liberty that Christ provides becomes the backdrop for considering the formation of moral agents who take responsibility for their lives "as discerning people and with the creativity and fidelity that characterizes those who believe in

---

[77] Ibid., 1:2. He points the reader to a further explanation of how war affected his thinking in his book *Embattled Witness*, esp. pgs. 67–72.

[78] Keenan, *A History of Catholic Moral Theology in the Twentieth Century*, 90.

[79] Häring, *Free and Faithful in Christ*, 1:2.

the living God."[80] The themes of obedience, fidelity, responsibility, and freedom (liberty) repeat in his discussion about conscience.[81]

Häring begins his discussion on conscience in *Free and Faithful in Christ* by quoting *Gaudium et Spes* 16, followed by an extremely short section where he makes five succinct points pertaining to conscience, which he later develops. His points and explanations provide a brief interpretation of *GS* on conscience.

First, Häring uses *GS*'s language describing conscience as an "inner-core and sanctuary." *GS* says this inner core and sanctuary is where we encounter God. Häring expands upon *GS*, explaining that in the sanctuary of conscience we encounter ourselves through our engagement with God. Furthermore, we also encounter our fellow human beings in this sanctuary. We only know ourselves insofar as we "genuinely encounter" God and others. Thus, for Häring, conscience described as a sanctuary does not concern judgments regarding exterior actions but concerns our ability to know ourselves because of our authentic engagement with God and others.[82]

Second, Häring talks about the "re-echo" within our conscience. Häring quotes *GS* 16 as saying that "conscience is the most secret core and sanctuary of a person. There he is alone with God, Whose voice echoes in his depths." In reading this quote, Christians ideally would consider the triune God when seeing the term "God." It is possible, however, that when hearing or reading "God," most people think of one person of the Trinity, often God the Father.[83] Therefore, it is particularly interesting that Häring connects the "re-echo" to the Word that creates us and the Master's call (invitation) "to be with him." The Word stirs our conscience and calls us to discipleship. This shift in language from God to the Word accentuates more clearly that the re-echoing of the law points us toward relationships: our relationship with God as creator, the one who spoke and breathed creation into being; with Christ, the Word made Flesh, who continually calls us to discipleship, to action in the world; and finally with the Holy Spirit, the giver of life who supplies the power to make discipleship possible.

While *GS* 16 uses the term "God," and does not mention the Word or the Holy Spirit, Häring specifically references the Holy Spirit and implic-

[80] Ibid., 1:4.

[81] Häring discusses conscience in chapter 6 of *Free and Faithful in Christ*, 1:223–301.

[82] Häring, *Free and Faithful in Christ*, 1:224.

[83] Karl Rahner discusses what he calls almost "mere monotheism" in Karl Rahner, *The Trinity*, trans. Joseph Donceel (New York: Crossroad Herder, 1998, original English 1970).

itly Christ with his language of the Word. Therefore, it can be argued that Häring implies that the moral agent's responsibility is to the demands of discipleship. The Holy Spirit assists disciples in applying the law and living discipleship in new contexts and circumstances.[84] This is an important move because the Spirit is given to all, not just a select few. Therefore, all have a stake in defining the contours of Christian discipleship.

Third, Häring writes: "In the depth of our being, conscience makes us aware that our true self is linked with Christ, and that we can find our unique name only by listening and responding to the One who calls us by this name."[85] Häring draws attention to the reality that discipleship begins with a call and response and that our identity depends on our relationship with Christ. Our conscience's attunement to goodness requires a relationship with Christ. Our conscience grows in "sensitivity and truthfulness" both externally by the teachings of Christ, or, as Häring says, "the divine Master," and internally because Christ sends "us the Spirit of Truth."[86] *GS* 16 states that in our depths is a law written on our hearts that we must obey as it points us toward good and away from evil.

This move by Häring to discuss Christ and the Spirit in his analysis of *GS* 16 draws attention to the reality, affirmed time and again in Scripture, that the triune God provides us with our identity first by calling us and then by accepting our response in the form of relationships lived by loving God and neighbor. More specifically, our Christian identity and very self is contingent not on a yes to propositional statements but on a yes to Jesus Christ's call to live a life of Christian discipleship and the ongoing response to the Spirit who renews, vivifies, and points the way forward. Once again, moral agents are challenged to place their actions and conscientious judgments into the context of discipleship.

Fourth, Häring articulates his understanding that conscience has a voice. He distinguishes between voice and the Word. Each conscience has a voice but not an individual word. Rather, each conscience (voice) mediates the word that comes from the Word who became incarnate.[87] The voice should not pronounce individual opinions but should speak of salvation history promoting the vision of the triune God, manifested in the truth spoken, lived, and illuminated by Christ. Of course, this means

[84] Häring, *Free and Faithful in Christ*, 1:224.
[85] Ibid.
[86] Ibid.
[87] Ibid.

we have the capacity to hear and listen to the Word, even if this listening and hearing does not always occur.

Finally, Häring claims that "in the search for truth, man's conscience is the focal point for sharing experience and reflection in a reciprocity of consciences."[88] This assertion agrees with *GS* 16 that together humans search for, seek, and find truth. Because of *GS*'s language that we search together in conscience to solve the world's problems, and the discussion of a correct conscience holding sway to follow "objective norms of morality," however, someone could interpret *GS* as focusing conscience's judgments primarily in the area of external action. Häring does not dismiss objective norms of morality, the results of a common search for truth. He focuses on the shared search for truth, which occurs through the "encounter of consciences." In other words, the process for arriving at truth is important too. So he argues that the encounter of consciences requires a sharing, giving, and reception of knowledge, experience, and our very selves.

Häring's depiction of the need to share, give, and receive the self is of our authentic self, not the self that hides behind various masks. Häring also says this sharing, giving, and receiving must occur freely; all must be willing to give of themselves in the search for truth. This process of truth seeking requires honesty and trust that we will be received, as well as our willingness to receive others without their masks. This means a commitment not to manipulate, coerce, or harm the other. The encounter requires an embodied response that manifests concretely how we respond in love to God, neighbor, and self.[89] One result of Häring's attention to process is that we see that seeking the truth is about the disposition and attitude with which we seek the truth, along with the more traditional concerns about actions and common objective norms.

Häring argues that conscience functions as the integrative working together of the emotional, intellectual, and volitional aspects of the human being so that we can respond to and be touched by the "creative Spirit."[90] Karl Rahner sees conscience in a similar manner. Conscience has an "existential-function" whereby in the application of universal norms in the particular situation, conscience "grasps" "what has to be done by me individually" within the context of the love of God and the search

[88] Ibid.

[89] Ibid. See also pages 265–70, where he discusses the reciprocity of consciences in more detail.

[90] Ibid., 1:234–36

for truth.[91] Conscience's accomplishments require the integration and working together of the will, intellect, and emotions. Conscience, then, as a concept, describes the integration of different features of the human being so that decision making and practical, prudential judgments account for the cognitive, intellectual, affective, interpersonal, and situational considerations for action. We must bear in mind that this human movement toward integration and deepening integrity remains within the matrix of loving God and searching for the truth.

Since humans make mistakes in the search for truth, Häring holds that consciences can err without losing their dignity. Drawing on the work of Thomas Aquinas, Häring sees this as particularly true if a person (or, I would add, community) is willing to "expunge" sources of error to correct one's conscience.[92] Häring concludes that conscience's dignity remains intact despite erroneous decisions, particularly if the person in light of new information or consideration remains open to revisiting the decision.[93] He also, however, develops *GS*'s teaching that a human's dignity is harmed when conscience errs because of blindness and sin.[94]

Sin, especially repetitive unrepented sin, blinds, distorts, and corrupts conscience. We become distant from our self; we can lose sight of our identity and foster unhealthy relationships rather than healthy ones. "Alienation, falsehood, and abuse" result.[95] For Häring, the severely corrupted conscience leads to a disintegration of human integrity, the potential destruction of one's very self-identity.[96] Eventually, according to Häring, a person, who for whatever reason does not heed the call of conscience to conversion and repentance with remorse, can "integrate," but in a manner where their "enormous energies will reach out only for their own dark goals."[97] In this way, one's human dignity is harmed, distorted, and betrayed.

---

[91] Karl Rahner, "On the Question of a Formal Existential Ethics" in *Theological Investigations*, vol. 2, trans. Karl-H. Kruger (Baltimore, MD: Helicon Press, 1963), 217–34 at 229.

[92] Häring, *Free and Faithful in Christ*, 1:242, n. 40. He references Thomas Aquinas, ST I, II q. 19, a. 6, ad. 3.

[93] Häring, *Free and Faithful in Christ*, 1:242.

[94] *Gaudium et Spes* 16 states, "This cannot be said of the person who takes little trouble to find out what is true and good, or when conscience is gradually almost blinded through the habit of committing sin."

[95] Häring, *Free and Faithful in Christ*, 1:260.

[96] Ibid., 1:239, 259–63.

[97] Ibid., 1:268. Häring specifically references Hitler and Stalin here. Thus, he implies that Hitler and Stalin became who they were through the choices they made over time. As a result, Hitler and Stalin are not a foreign species, unhuman; rather, they could be us.

Despite this dark potential, Häring nevertheless maintains that conscience's "strong tendency" is "towards living in the truth and acting on it" and that God can always return us to this tendency through grace.[98] This tendency toward living in and acting on truth requires five foundations: (1) the God-imbued desire for wholeness and openness; (2) the clarity and strength of a person's decision to live under the covenant in solidarity with others and in affirming the desire for wholeness and openness; (3) development and fortification of the virtues of vigilance and prudence, among others, which embody the desire for wholeness, integration, and living the communal covenantal relationship oriented toward God; (4) active engagement with other consciences that must be coupled with gratitude and respect for the other's contributions; and (5) the search for truth, which includes a readiness to "act on the word."[99] In other words, conscience properly conceived and cultivated does not foster stasis or a minimalist morality. Rather, conscience properly cultivated fosters growth, maturation, and increasing responsibility in one's moral life. Proper formation also results in a deepening self-realization of one's identity, character, and relationship with the triune God, other human beings,[100] and the rest of creation.

Häring's work highlights several things about conscience, many of which emphasize the relational character of conscience identified earlier. His focus, however, is more specifically Christocentric with pneumatological impulses. Conscience's foundation lies in faith, marked by the encounter with Christ and the moral agent becoming a new being in Christ. As a result, merely following doctrines or a normative ethic would not properly form a conscience. The cultivation of Christ-like attitudes and dispositions fostered by the sacraments and the Word are key to conscience formation. In this way, the person focusing on God's boundless love shifts from simply avoiding sin to identifying and utilizing one's gifts and talents as a response to the call to discipleship. Thus, conscience's judgment takes on a more personal tone connected to discipleship—have I used my gifts and talents, has the community used their gifts and talents, to build up and support God's kingdom?[101]

---

[98] Ibid., 1:239 and 264–65, respectively.
[99] Ibid., 1:238. All five points can be found here.
[100] Ibid., 1:239.
[101] Ibid., 1:250–52.

The idea of gifts, how we engage the world, not as minimalists attending only to behavior to avoid, but rather focusing on what we are called to do, is what *GS* and other Vatican II documents require of us. Anne Patrick, in her writings on conscience, contemplates what this call and invitation looks like, while developing the idea that conscience formation is about the formation of the moral agent holistically considered. To her work, I now turn.

Anne E. Patrick

Theologian Anne Patrick is a Sister of the Holy Names of Jesus and Mary (SNJM) and professor emerita at Carleton College, Minnesota.[102] Several reasons exist for choosing her work from among the theologians who have written on conscience. First, her three books focus on conscience.[103] Second, her books all appear after the publication of *Veritatis Splendor*, even as her theological career began in the decades before its promulgation. Thus, while steeped in the theological tradition on conscience that proceeds *Veritatis Splendor*, including Vatican II, her work provides a window into how one theologian conceives and understands conscience in a post–*Veritatis Splendor* ecclesial world. Third, her methodological approach overlaps and differs from the other theologians referenced up to this point, including an intentional consideration of women's voices, experience, and theological research. Most important for me is that Patrick's work alters the conceptual map for considering conscience. The span of her writing demonstrates this conceptual remapping. In addition to established tradition and church teaching, her work highlights the necessity that theologians who follow her example consider spirituality, narrative, prayer, and communal formation when discussing conscience.[104]

---

[102] For a brief introduction to her accomplishments, see Anne E. Patrick, *Women, Conscience, and the Creative Process*, v–vi.

[103] They are as noted earlier (1) *Liberating Conscience*; (2) *Women, Conscience, and the Creative Process*; and (3) *Conscience and Calling*. The second monograph is the printed and expanded version of her 2009 Madeleva Lecture given at St. Mary's College in South Bend, Indiana.

[104] Patrick sees her scholarship as beginning this task, while hoping others will engage and carry the work further. See *Liberating Conscience*, 5, 13–14. She continues developing her thoughts on conscience in her two books *Women, Conscience, and the Creative Process* and *Conscience and Calling*. Both books were written after *Liberating Conscience*.

The need to reenvision the theological discussion about conscience is captured in her definition of conscience. She writes:

> I define conscience as personal moral awareness, experienced in the course of anticipating future situations and making moral decisions, as well as in the process of reflecting on one's past decisions and the quality of one's character. This leads me to affirm the value of the church's teaching authority, the legitimacy of dissent in certain circumstances, the importance of personal responsibility, and the urgent need for persons in locations of social privilege to attend to voices from the margins. More recently, . . . I suggest that we can avoid the tendency to reify and depersonalize conscience by thinking of it as "the creatively responsible self."[105]

Her definition of conscience focuses on the human person who comes to "personal moral awareness" through his or her experiences, moral decisions, reflections on past decisions, and a consideration of character. While it is the human person who reflects and comes to moral awareness, this personal moral awareness cannot be separated from relationships, whether ecclesial or societal. By defining conscience in this way, Patrick's concern that we do not reify conscience by conceiving of it as an object or as residing in one human faculty is evident and seen most clearly in her suggestion that we think of conscience as the "creatively responsible self."

Patrick believes the term "conscience" should be employed with great care. In order to avoid giving the impression that the reality to which it refers is either separate from the moral agent or some sort of thing within the agent, it may be helpful for a while to substitute for the phrase "formation of conscience" something like "formation of the creatively responsible moral agent."[106] Patrick's suggestion of a change in language regarding conscience formation means conscience functions as shorthand for the larger reality of the human person's awareness of moral realities and their subsequent moral agency. Just as the term "heart" functions in the Hebraic Scriptures as a metaphor for the whole person, the term "conscience" acts as a metaphor describing the awareness of the whole person. Considering conscience in this way prevents us from reifying

---

[105] Patrick, *Conscience and Calling*, 18. She references her own work in this definition. See *Liberating Conscience*, 35–39, 198–99; and *Women, Conscience, and the Creative Process*, 52–54.

[106] Patrick, *Women, Conscience, and the Creative Process*, 52–53.

conscience, and we might avoid the temptation to treat conscience as a thing separate from the moral agent.[107]

Patrick's own commitment to personalize conscience and consider the "creatively responsible self" is evidenced in the way she writes about conscience. Her methodological approach provides a theoretical construct for discussing conscience while her use of other sources demonstrates how conscience (the creatively responsible person) functions in practice. She uses literature to provide examples of theory in action while also attending to the concrete narratives of people's lives. The narratives of historical events and decisions that she chooses are both individual and communal. This calls to mind the scriptural metaphor of the communion of saints and the belief that those who have gone before us offer models and encouragement as we also run the race.

Patrick's narrative analysis does not yield to a hagiographic temptation, even as her choice of narratives deliberately portrays primarily women's stories of living from conscientious decisions.[108] Moreover, the tensile relationship between individual agency, external and internal communal factors, and political and ecclesial institutional circumstances informs her analysis. In other words, both individual and communal narratives are studied within their social contexts. She lifts up the communal nature of conscience by her willingness to enter the existential space where judgments, decision, and actions are sometimes clear, sometimes mixed, and always fraught with costs for being committed to God's justice, compassion, mercy, and salvific vision. As a result, Patrick highlights that the struggle to reach responsible moral judgments and decisions for action occurs within the concreteness of daily life, can be at odds with received teaching, and has implications for people's self-identity and character development.

These ideas of struggle, concrete daily living, responsibility, self-identity, and character development are also found in other theological work. When seen through the lens of conscience as the "creatively responsible self,"

---

[107] I would like to thank Anne Patrick for a phone conversation about her work in general and specifically the ideas in this paragraph. Any errors remain mine.

[108] She characterizes her methodological approach as a feminist liberationist one, which seeks equality for all women and a correction of injustice through a reformed society and its social structures. See Patrick, *Liberating Conscience*, 5–7, where she provides details regarding her placement among the many types of feminist liberationist theologies. Some of this information can also be found in the footnotes for the text cited.

however, Patrick's attention to context and narratives in her analysis provides an especially rich, textured accounting of conscience's workings. This includes seeing discussions about conscience's judgment about any moral issue in both the individual and social contexts. Her approach also moves beyond an emphasis on sexual concerns to consideration of other areas included in *Gaudium et Spes*: questions of economic justice, war, human dignity, racism, gender inequality, and any other issue that would come under the theme "reading the signs of the times." These issues should trouble a moral agent as they try to live the Gospel message.[109]

Patrick highlights the reality that our experiences are both individual and profoundly social, with a deep connection between conscience, justice, discernment, and discipleship.[110] Drawing on Vatican II themes, Patrick describes what she does in this way:

> I attempt to illustrate what "liberating conscience" can mean: freeing persons from whatever inhibits a full response to the divine invitation to love God, neighbor, and self in ways that are recognizably good. The goal of moral discernment, after all, should be deeds that "bring forth fruit in charity for the life of the world." Our consciences will be functioning, as they should, it seems to me, when those who suffer most from oppression and injustice experience our lives and deeds as expressions of God's liberating love for us all.[111]

While Patrick uses the term "conscience" in this statement, she articulates what a morally aware person who acts freely and lives a life of discipleship looks like. The human person responds to God, others, and the self. This requires the need to pay attention, be self-aware, and acknowledge, listen to, and learn from the other. Liberation means being unbound from that which prohibits a full, loving response to God, self, and others in good, healthy ways. The goal is life-giving engagement with the world that brings forth new nourishing structures and responses (fruit) in charity (*caritas*, a fully committed love).

---

[109] She examines justice concerns throughout her books. See, for example, chapter 3, "A Ministry of Justice: The 25-Year pilgrimage of the National Assembly of Religious Women (NAWR/NARW)," in *Conscience and Calling* for her description of women religious' work embodying the search for justice.

[110] Patrick, *Liberating Conscience*, 8–16.

[111] Patrick, *Liberating Conscience*, 16. The idea of bringing "forth fruit in charity for the life of the world" comes from the call to renew moral theology in Vatican II's Decree on Priestly Formation. The idea of loving God and neighbor can be found in *GS* and of course Scripture.

Therefore, conscience needs to do more than assent to norms and avoid certain behaviors. The human person properly engaged confronts and works to resist and, when possible, change structures of oppression and injustice. The criteria for success come not merely from our own analysis but also from the assessment of those most affected by structural sin. For example, those most affected by racism or police brutality would be the primary assessors of whether structural changes are working. Whites or the police, on the other hand, would need to listen deeply to those affected by white privilege or police brutality about what is needed to root out racism and change a culture of police brutality.

Those most affected by structural sin become one of our communities of accountability. According to Patrick, a community of accountability challenges us to live our values, ideals, and professions of faith while also providing models of "liberated consciences" and responsible moral agents in the individuals who make up the community.[112] The community of accountability holds together two realities: we have an individual obligation before God for our lives and a responsibility to those with whom we interact here on earth.

Another community of accountability is the church. Patrick writes:

> The church does not supply the perfect answer to all our moral questions, but it gives us a community where faithful moral reasoning can go on, always with attention to the values Jesus cherished and with confidence in his continued presence in our midst. In addition, the church gives us saints to inspire us, friends to support us, spiritual guides to assist us, and teachers to challenge and instruct us. Properly understood and exercised the church's teaching authority is a marvelous gift for our moral and spiritual development, for it offers the wisdom gained from centuries of experience with the human heart to individuals who might otherwise have to reinvent the ethical wheel for themselves.[113]

This brief explanation of how the church functions as a community of accountability and inspiration draws on *GS* and the idea that the church does not supply all answers; rather, the church aids the moral agent in his or her search for truth and a proper perception of goodness. Patrick

---

[112] Patrick, *Liberating Conscience*, 34–39.
[113] Ibid., 38–39.

provides examples of what the church offers individuals as we seek to live moral lives of responsibility and responsiveness to the signs of the times. Whereas Häring consistently references Christ, Patrick, with her reference to Jesus, recalls the fact that the divine Christ is also the human Jesus, thus connecting our relationship with the transcendent God to our relationships with others here on earth. In other words, we also need to learn from the earthly ministry of Jesus. Finally, she provides a positive framework for understanding the exercise of the church's teaching authority. The teaching authority is not about requiring blind obedience and acquiescence. Rather, teaching authority provides wisdom and a foundation for ethical reflection so no one starts from scratch.[114]

While Patrick does advocate for a positive role for the community of accountability and how the community helps form moral agents, she does not foster an uncritical acceptance of the community's standards. Given her goal of liberating conscience for the task of justice, she describes and analyzes instances where communities and individuals face conflicts with church authorities over teachings or potential courses of action.[115] In reading Patrick's narratives of conflict, disagreement, dissent, oppression, and injustice along with the creative responses of the individuals and communities, and considered within the context of her overarching work on conscience, several ideas emerge for considering the moral agent's formation within communities of accountability.

The first idea concerns knowledge. Patrick writes that knowledge "is inherently hermeneutical, social, and historical, is never perfect but always in process."[116] In other words, knowledge has several features. "Historical" means there is a given event, some facts that can be identified. "Social" indicates the relational component, and "hermeneutical" touches on the interpretive element when considering any type of knowledge. Given that when human beings act they are responding from values, any values at stake must be properly articulated when considering a course of action. Discourse, conversation, debate, and disagreement help us clarify our

---

[114] Patrick more fully develops her argument for the proper use of magisterial authority attending to concerns for mutuality, attention to power dynamics, and an egalitarian not a patriarchal structure, among other things, in her books. See especially her chapter "Contested Authority" in *Liberating Conscience*, 102–33.

[115] These narratives are interspersed throughout all three of her books. See, for example, chapter 1, "'His Dogs More Than Us': Virtue in Situations of Conflict between Women Religious and Their Ecclesiastical Employers," in *Conscience and Calling*, 27–49.

[116] Patrick, *Liberating Conscience*, 61.

values, what is happening, and what needs to be done, as well as the language we might want to use.

Given that acquiring knowledge is never complete, or, as Patrick says, "never perfect but always in process," we ultimately still need to make judgments and act. Therefore, any ambiguity in decision making and judgments need not lead to stasis. She argues that our conscience can rely on God's mercy in the event of error because "all human moral striving is relative in the light of divine goodness and mercy, and changing times require changing emphases and interpretations of what human goodness entails."[117] While she wrote these words in 1996, resonances exist with elements of Pope Francis's thought and his ongoing challenge to engage the world, knowing we will make mistakes, while trusting in God's mercy and compassion.

When engaging the world by working to resist oppression and injustice, when thinking about change, power must be considered and taken into account. Who holds power, who wields it, and whether power is appropriately applied are all considerations when discerning actions to oppose injustice and oppression. Creativity is required to foster changes and resist improper uses of power. Creativity becomes one of many virtues that enable us to respond profoundly to contemporary challenges in a manner like Jesus. This does not mean acting exactly as Jesus did with particular, specific responses. Rather, our actions and responses should reflect the emotions, motivations, and imagination Jesus portrayed in living out the commands of God.[118]

Knowledge gathering, clarification, and creativity do not end with action. Questioning and assessing our actions is an ongoing event with insight unfolding even after we act. This resonates with Klaus Demmer's contention that experience does not equate to insight; rather, a hermeneutical process exists for arriving at insight. Action, insight, and creative responses to the world might require dissent. Patrick sees dissent not necessarily as a problem but as a reality that requires respect because it contributes to the search for truth and faithful living of the Gospel. In other words, dissent can help us clarify what is happening, what values are at stake when acting, and can be a creative response to contemporary challenges.

---

[117] Ibid., 100.

[118] Patrick, *Women, Conscience, and the Creative Process*, 24–31. She relies on William C. Spohn's work and his description of analogical imagination in her approach to creativity. See Spohn, *Go and Do Likewise: Jesus and Ethics* (New York: Continuum, 1999).

Forming oneself, or a community, in this manner as a moral agent requires prayer, time, self-knowledge, consultation, and proceeding with trust and confidence in God's mercy and in our capacity to make provisional judgments.[119] It could, however, lead to communities prophetically living vocations that manifest group judgments about what God is calling them to in conscience.[120] Vocations can then be focused on seeking justice and alleviating all forms of oppression; these types of vocations can be individual and also communal. Other times, the religious community of formation and discernment might be called to support specific individuals in prophetic work and ministry.[121]

Taken together, these considerations support Patrick's critique of certain understandings of "conscience" and "conscience formation." They support the recommendation, at least for a time, to talk less about conscience formation and more about the "formation of the moral agent," or, even better, the formation of the "creatively responsible moral agent."

Almost fifty years after Vatican II, Anne Patrick provides Catholics with a definition of conscience that honors the value of the Magisterium's teaching authority while not making all magisterial teaching infallible. While John Paul II in *Veritatis Splendor* and the *Catechism* risks reifying conscience and limiting conscience to agreement with the Magisterium, Patrick seeks to "liberate conscience" from these stultifying constraints. On the one hand, she agrees with the Magisterium that the moral autonomy of conscience unmoored from a community is problematic. On the other hand, an unreflectively obedient conscience adhering unquestioningly to communal standards is problematic as well. She avoids a creeping infallibility and thus preserves the ability of all Catholics to participate in the church's growth in moral knowledge and virtue.

She also connects action and being, while moving the emphasis of moral awareness from solely individual concerns to the arena of social justice, communal concerns. The personal is public, and the public is personal. Our moral awareness and subsequent action must attend to

---

[119] Patrick, *Liberating Conscience*, 200–212; *Women, Conscience, and the Creative Process*, 33–54.

[120] An example of a community working together is the French village of Le Chambon-sur-Lignon during World War II. The village sheltered, fed, and helped many Jews escape into other countries during the war.

[121] Patrick, *Conscience and Calling*. This book explores this point in detail, focusing on the vocations of Catholic women.

the concerns of the least among us, drawing us out of our own social location and perspective. We are accountable to each other. Patrick's understanding of conscience informed by the theological tradition, history, and the narratives of people's lives supplies necessary tools for fostering judgments and decision making for action in a world that needs creatively responsible moral agents who seek to "bring forth fruit in charity for the life of the world." In so doing, she challenges us to reconsider how we define and discuss conscience and its formation.

Conclusion

The purpose of this chapter was to provide one perspective on conscience's intellectual history. This overview focuses on several pre–Vatican II theologians who help situate Vatican II and other magisterial statements on conscience in a centuries-long intellectual tradition. The post–Vatican II theologians were chosen because their lives spanned Vatican II and their work demonstrates the ongoing hermeneutical exercise that occurs with the reception of any magisterial document.

It was seen that while the Hebrew Scriptures do not directly use the term "conscience," the term captures the idea of heart and wisdom in the Hebraic text. The term "heart" functioned in the ancient world not simply as a reference to a specific organ but as a metaphor for the whole person. Resonances exist between a scriptural heart and Anne Patrick's claim that conscience functions metaphorically for the moral agent holistically understood. It is in the New Testament where Paul begins describing and using conscience in various ways that reappear in multiple forms throughout the tradition. Conscience is seen as a judge, witness, and agent of knowledge. It has both objective and subjective dimensions. It can be weak, correct, or strong.

Briefly revisiting the portrayals of the main theological figures in this chapter we see that Aquinas's and Newman's work provide some context for understanding conscience's intellectual history. They yield insights into some statements about conscience in the council's documents. Even as these two theologians were innovative in their approaches and insights, a more scholastic, debate model still shaped their methodology. A brief explication of some medievalist work, including Aquinas, supports the claim that Vatican II's teaching on conscience was not new. Rather, it shows that *Gaudium et Spes*'s definition of conscience has echoes of medieval thinking on conscience. The medievalists' attention to the internal aspects of moral judgments (general orientation to the good) is seen in *GS*'s statement that we do good and avoid evil. The medieval recognition that conscience also deals with external moral action is seen in *GS*'s emphasis on loving God and neighbor with insight into specific ways this love manifests itself. Aquinas's discussion of how the conscience binds resonates with twentieth-century teaching that conscience has dignity and can be followed even if in error. There are caveats to this claim, though, that include the action could still be objectively wrong (sinful) and the moral agent must be seeking and pursuing the good (even if they are wrong about what the good entails).

Newman in the nineteenth century provides some clarity for considering the relationship between papal infallibility and following one's conscience. Newman was clear that conscience is responsible to God first. We can cultivate or dull our consciences through a relationship or lack thereof with God. The church helps foster that relationship and what the relationship demands of us. Conflicts within the area of practical judgments can, however, occur because the church and pope are fallible in this arena.

Subsequent to Vatican II, Häring's work offers perspectives for understanding the emphasis on the moral agent's responsibility in following conscience's judgments and prioritizing obedience to Christ. While he helped usher in the renewal of moral theology, he frequently worked within the constraints of renewing the moral manual. Nonetheless, Häring draws attention to the moral agent's relationship with the triune God. He clearly articulates that individuals must become moral agents responsible for their decisions and actions. Yet the search for truth and our conscience formation occurs in relationships through dialogue, honest communication with a willingness to be wrong and possible subsequent change. Here Häring expands on *GS*'s teaching that we seek the truth with others.

Patrick also describes and emphasizes the communal relational feature of the individual conscience. Like Häring, she explicates the need for conscience formation to include all dimensions of our humanity. This leads her to see the term conscience functioning as a metaphor for the moral agent (human being). She sees value in focusing on the formation of the moral agent, rather than on the shaping of a "conscience" abstracted from the person. Additionally, Patrick engages the broader theological tradition and magisterial teaching on conscience. Her approach embodies Vatican II's call to engage other disciplines and the conditions of the world (the signs of the times). In so doing, she moves the conversation from individual moral piety to social engagement whereby individuals and communities are accountable to others as constitutive of morality.

Several ideas emerge from this chapter regarding conscience. They include deliberation; discernment; desire for the good; forming relationships with God, the self, and the community; the relationship between judgments of conscience and magisterial teaching; dissent; responsibility; and discipleship. While questions involving the ability of individuals or communities to disagree with authoritative teaching remain perennial, this issue will be saved for chapter 4, which explores the question of dissent. Discipleship will be considered in chapter 5. The next chapter delves into the moral agent's formation (formation of conscience) by discussing several influences that form, tutor, and mold the moral agent, factoring in the importance of communities in this regard.

Chapter 3

Conscience Formation
(Formation of the Moral Agent)

Introduction

One theme that has emerged in various ways throughout the last two chapters is the need for conscience formation. The formation of conscience is ongoing, continuing its schooling in virtues—practices that aid in the seeking, knowing, judging, and developing of healthy, authentic relationships with God and others. Ongoing formation includes examining and learning from past decisions, behaviors, and attitudes. A properly formed conscience seeks and utilizes well relevant data and advice; considers, examines, and explores various arguments and insights from other disciplines; and researches church teaching and the tradition in order to make good judgments about living the Gospel message.

Chapter 3 describes various streams influencing and contributing to conscience formation. Methodologically, I have chosen to highlight thinkers and concepts that indicate the complexity and plurality of influences going into conscience formation. The language of conscience and conscience formation will be used in this chapter. Nevertheless, the reader is encouraged to remember the insight from Anne Patrick's work that conscience formation language functions metaphorically for the whole person. Therefore, the following discussion about conscience and its formation refers to the person's whole being: mind, body, spirit, interior lives, external relationships, and the dynamic interconnected nexus of influence and effects between them.

This perspective on conscience and its workings is summed up beautifully in psychologist Sidney Callahan's description of how conscience works. She sees the work of conscience as a more winding, cyclical, and retracing process encompassing all our human dimensions. Her description sets the stage for exploring, in section 1, the reality that conscience's work functions differently from a Euclidean geometry proof.

Revisiting how conscience has been described theologically occurs in section 2. Richard Gula's discussion of conscience contributes to the project of de-objectifying and personalizing conscience. He does so by articulating how conscience actually describes dimensions of the human person. Section 3 once again uses Richard Gula's work to consider how conscience formation requires forming the various aspects of the human person. His work demonstrates that conscience formation is an ongoing, complex endeavor influenced by a multiplicity of personal and communal contexts, factors, and events. The communal component includes the church community. This section also considers how the church forms believers in three ways: as a shaper of moral character, as a bearer of moral tradition, and as a community of moral deliberation. Exploring these themes highlights the complexities of and myriad influences by the church (broadly understood) on the formation of conscience.

The chapter concludes by arguing that conscience formation is ongoing. Formation must account not only for magisterial teaching, but also for people's habits, virtues, spirituality, and prayer lives to name a few other areas.[1]

Section 1: Sidney Callahan on Conscience as Dynamic Engagement

Psychologist Sidney Callahan's book *In Good Conscience: The Role of Reason and Emotion in Moral Decision Making*[2] frequently appears in the footnotes of theologians navigating the relationship between reason and emotion. Her work demonstrates that theological dialogue with psychology can be a resource for considering and thinking about the human person's many interconnected dimensions as well as formation. Callahan illuminates the danger of fixing unblinkingly on reason for moral theology by discussing psychological disorders rooted in a lack of emotional capacity. She draws attention to the importance of emotions, feelings, and all forms of affectivity in moral development. Callahan proposes a vision

---

[1] Kenneth R. Himes, "The Formation of Conscience," in *Ethics and Spirituality*, ed. Charles E. Curran and Lisa A. Fullam, Readings in Moral Theology Series, no. 17 (New York: Paulist Press, 2014).

[2] Sidney Callahan, *In Good Conscience: Reason and Emotion in Moral Decision Making* (San Francisco: HarperCollins, 1991).

of the moral agent wherein neither affections nor reason are ignored and where the moral agent works to integrate these aspects of him- or herself.[3] Furthermore, she remains highly aware of and accounts for our human relationality. Thus, Callahan describes a more integrated vision of the human being who decides and acts conscientiously.

Her description of conscience's working also draws on her commitment to integration and helps us consider further how conscience is not a place where one goes to "find" objective truth about an action or decision. Rather, conscientious decisions result from a process whereby one seeks truth and a good decision for acting well. She writes, "I think we best make decisions of conscience through an integrated, recursive process in which we direct and focus attention back and forth, within and without, activating, mutually testing, and monitoring all our human capacities of thinking, feeling, and self-consciousness."[4] A striking thing about this description of conscience's work is her selection of verbs. They are not linked with an arrival at a place or the finding of an object. Instead, the verbs are concerned with behaviors and dispositions more readily associated with the moral agent's internal life, discernment, and ongoing formation. The verbs help us see that conscience is not an identifiable object or space; nor is it limited to one human faculty. In a different way than Anne Patrick, Callahan articulates that conscience language metaphorically signifies the whole human being. Conscience—we could say "the human person"—engages in a process when making decisions and judgments, a movement requiring several virtues: attention, thoughtfulness, self-awareness, and a willingness to test both feelings and rationality.

Callahan's descriptive words "integrated, recursive process" indicate that this process needs to be holistic, accounting for all aspects of the moral agent. For example, if we rely on reason and ignore feelings, or rely on feelings and ignore rationality, then any judgment of conscience is incomplete and fragmented. "Recursive" highlights the revisiting phase of conscientious decisions; we must circle back after activating, testing, and monitoring all of our capacities. We question and test whether our initial reasons and feelings for a decision retain validity. Have we come to a new understanding of ourselves that sheds light on the judgment we made or need to make? Is change required?

---

[3] Ibid., 134–38; see also Sidney Callahan, "The Role of Emotion in Ethical Decision Making," *Hastings Center Report* (June/July 1988), 9–14, at 9.

[4] Callahan, *In Good Conscience*, 115.

The "integrated, recursive" process includes a movement that is both internal and external, or individual and communal. Furthermore, Callahan's statement about the "back and forth, within and without" alludes to the consultative dimension of conscience formation. We attend to and consult with other people accounting for their wisdom, views, reasons, feelings, values, and perceptions in our moral lives. Accounting for others' insights does not always mean adaptation in our own lives; it does mean taking seriously that others might have insights and wisdom that we do not and, thus, learning from them.

Meanwhile, "attention within" requires us to do a self-examination of our motivations, rationales for action, and feelings. We need to name and acknowledge our motives for considering certain courses of action. Likewise, part of the process necessitates identifying our rationale for acting and our judgments. Naming and recognizing feelings is also part of the internal attention.[5] Are we in a desired emotional space or do adjustments need to be made? Do we ask God for God's grace to change? Often before we can answer these question, we must acknowledge our motivations and emotions.

As a result, Callahan's use of the term "activating" indicates that our conscience's capabilities, including our rationality, feelings, and self-awareness, need to be engaged since they can be dormant or ignored. We need to awaken the process for conscientious judgment. Knowing our strengths, weaknesses, preferred modes of decision making, and so forth is important. Thus, activating means we must deliberately not always rely on our preferred mode of operation, for example, our rationality or our affectivity. Instead, we must intentionally attend to all dimensions that permit conscience (ourselves) to function holistically and effectively as moral agents.

Callahan claims that this "activating" requires "mutual testing and monitoring" of our thinking, feeling, and self-awareness. Both our reasoning processes and our emotional responses can be either inaccurate or accurate. We realize that our reasoning can be flawed and illogical, or it can be accurate and logical.[6] Thus, we are often willing to entertain arguments that help us see the strength or weakness in our cognitive

---

[5] The Spiritual Exercises of Ignatius of Loyola requires the practitioner of the exercises to pay attention to patterns and movements of the Spirit. Ignatius names two major movements: consolation and desolation. Attending to these movements requires facility in naming, recognizing, and living with various emotions and their connection to human behaviors and capacity to respond to God.

[6] Callahan, *In Good Conscience*, 10, 66–70, 74.

conclusions. The same needs to hold true for our feelings, since they are also a source of knowledge. Feelings or emotions, like our reasoned positions, can be well tuned, perceptive, and accurate. Feelings or emotions can also, however, be flawed, misplaced, or inaccurate.[7] Thus, both reason and feeling or emotion provide information about a situation and need to be tested, examined, and monitored for accuracy and reasonableness.

This means checking whether our thoughts and feelings are accurate, logical, and reasonable. Alternatively, are distortions present in our thinking? Are we attending to the wrong feelings, emotions, and affections? Do we have something to learn from others, therefore needing to change our perspective and chosen course of action? As a result, a conscientious decision requires not only putting in motion a particular process for organizing or causing change; it also means being aware of the moral agent in his or her totality.

One important aspect of Callahan's definition is the recognition that the human person remains in relationship, connected to and affected by others. The phrase "mutually testing" seems to reference only our human capacities. Yet, mutually testing can also reference our willingness to subject our process and provisional and actual decisions to others, whether individuals, communities, or God. We must honor our relationship with God while at the same time remaining in conversation with and accounting for the insights of our communities of accountability.[8]

While stated slightly differently from the descriptions of conscience given in chapter 2, Callahan's summary description of conscience's work overlaps with them. She highlights the need for integration, verifying the judgments of conscience both internally (subject) and externally (communities or other individuals). As moral agents, we must not abdicate our moral responsibility for our own actions and judgments; nor should we forget *Gaudium et Spes*'s statement that conscience's judgments should foster love of God and neighbor. Responsibility requires staying in the conversation around issues, recognizing that one is not a rule unto oneself,

---

[7] Ibid., 101–3.

[8] Callahan does not use Anne Patrick's language of the community of accountability. In a recent book, however, Callahan considers how faith and psychology help people find happiness. In the course of the book Callahan examines and explicates how specific communities function to structure people's lives, providing insight into meaning and leading to happiness. One case study is Alcoholics Anonymous. See Sidney Callahan, *Called to Happiness: Where Faith and Psychology Meet* (Maryknoll, NY: Orbis Books, 2011).

owning one's decisions and actions, fostering virtues, correcting vices, and standing firm when conviction in conscience requires it. In short, Callahan's description helps us resist the temptation to reify conscience. She avoids making conscience an object or a place and provides further ground for arguing that the language of conscience formation functions as shorthand for considering the moral agent's holistic formation.

Section 2: Richard Gula on Conscience as Capacity, Process, and Judgment

The intellectual history of the term "conscience" is varied and long, lending to changes in the term's meaning. As Richard Gula writes: "Whereas in the past we tried to restrict conscience to a function of the will or of the intellect, today we understand conscience as an expression of the whole person. Simply put, conscience is 'me coming to a decision.' It includes not only cognitive and volitional aspects, but also affective, intuitive, attitudinal, and somatic aspects as well."[9] In other words, we see the term "conscience" functioning here as shorthand for the human being holistically considered: intellect, will, spirit, instinct, attitude, affection, and body.

Gula argues that his description of conscience, in the holistic manner just cited, is what helps make sense of the Roman Catholic tradition's three dimensions of conscience. These traditional three dimensions for describing conscience are a capacity (*synderesis*), a "process of discovering" specific goods and naming actions right or wrong (moral science), and a judgment (conscience) for action in particular situations.[10] All human beings make use of these three dimensions of conscience, and the dimensions are interconnected in any consideration of action, behavior, or character development.

---

[9] Richard Gula, *Reason Informed by Faith: Foundations of Catholic Morality* (New York: Paulist Press, 1989), 131.

[10] Ibid., 131. See also Richard Gula, *Moral Discernment* (New York: Paulist Press, 1997), 18. In *Reason Informed by Faith*, Gula references Timothy O'Connell's work on conscience and O'Connell's language of conscience 1, 2, and 3 as a way of simplifying nomenclature. Gula simultaneously uses the language of capacity, process, and judgment, O'Connell's nomenclature, as well as the traditional language of *synderesis*, moral science, and conscience in a narrow sense. In his book *Moral Discernment*, however, Gula uses the language of capacity, process, and judgment.

Capacity

Conscience as a capacity is something we all have. The capacity is our ability to know the good, the ability to do the good, the ability to see and recognize values, and to engage in conversation and discussion to determine a specific good. Conversely, this capacity also helps us identify the evil we need to avoid.[11] Different people, however, have different levels of this inherent capacity for various reasons. Yet, this capacity can be developed through our own experiences or by learning from the experiences of others. We then have a history of knowing, perceiving, and doing the good as well as recognizing and avoiding evil. This general orientation and recognition of right and wrong, good and evil, does not give specific instructions for every situation or decision we encounter, especially in the more quotidian areas of our lives. This is the reason we need a discussion of process (moral science) as a dimension of conscience.[12]

Process (Moral Science)

The dimension of conscience named "process" or "moral science" is where we seek the right thing to do grounded in "objective moral values," and the values we profess to live by.[13] In other words, can we recognize whether we are becoming good persons through living well? Can we identify what makes an action right or wrong? The process of determining right from wrong requires both right perceptions and good moral reasoning. Therefore, we must ask, are we seeing correctly? Do we correctly perceive the pertinent information or contours of a situation? Is our reflection and analysis accurate, in-depth enough?[14] Our ability to reflect on experiences, data, and insights to determine the good or what makes a good person develops through our experiences and those of others. Experiences in turn sharpen our sensitivity to good, evil, and the recognition of operative moral values. Experiences on their own do not yield insight; rather, as argued in chapter 1, insight arises from analysis and interpretation of experiences.

---

[11] *Gaudium et Spes*, in its definition of conscience in paragraph 16, says we are called to do good and avoid evil. Gula recognizes that the ability to do good and avoid evil must be developed.

[12] Gula, *Reason Informed by Faith*, 131–32.

[13] Ibid., 131; Gula, *Moral Discernment*, 18.

[14] Gula, *Reason Informed by Faith*, 131–32.

This second dimension (process) is also important when, as Ignatius of Loyola realizes, decisions need to be made about the best course of action when deciding between multiple goods. Or, as Margaret Farley points out, when our commitments or values compete with each other.[15] Competing values or goods exist as part of our finitude in the search for moral truth as we often wrestle with prioritizing values and goods. Eventually, each person or community must decide upon a course of action, truth claim, or moral value to be lived leading to the third dimension of conscience: judgment.

Judgment

While judgment precedes action, it follows and is dependent on conscience's capacity (*synderesis*) and process (moral science). Judgment is the determination of what we think a given situation calls for, what an individual or community must do.[16] Stated differently, we make practical judgments regarding specific actions in a given context. In a communal context, the judgment dimension might mean recognizing that individuals might need to act differently than others depending on their role, their function, or their identity within the community. A person's position can and must inform what one can and must do in light of all known relevant circumstances and information. Judgment also functions after the fact, after an action has taken place, as part of the ongoing reflection, consideration, and analysis about any decision and action.

According to Gula, following one's judgment does several things. We become owners of our actions grounded in our grasp of the values at stake. In so doing, we become morally responsible agents and shape our character by our actions.[17] Following one's conscience should move humans

---

[15] Margaret A. Farley, *Personal Commitments: Beginning, Keeping, Changing* (San Francisco: Harper & Row, 1986). Farley also discusses the reality that we make decisions for future actions and then act differently when the time comes. This is because of competing values that we are deciding between when making decisions. See Margaret Farley, "Freedom and Desire," in *The Papers of the Henry Luce III Fellows in Theology*, ed. Matthew Zyniewicz (Atlanta, GA: Scholars Press, 1999), 57–73. Farley's claim is that as humans we experience conflicts and tension between our values, virtues, and commitments. This means that different situations can lead us to reorder or reprioritize our commitments, or to act from different values.

[16] Gula, *Reason Informed by Faith*, 133; Gula, *Moral Discernment*, 18.

[17] Gula, *Reason Informed by Faith*, 132–33; Gula, *Moral Discernment*, 19.

toward a deepened relationship with the triune God, both manifested in personal relationships and embodied in our lived responses to people and all God's creation. Judgments should also take into consideration whether or not a decision helps us live more deeply our relationship with this triune God and, in doing so, live more deeply and authentically the relationships with our fellow human beings and the rest of God's creation, becoming more fully ourselves. This consideration serves as a reminder that we come from God and ultimately return to God; thus, the living triune God remains at the center of our reflections, the pivot point, the Being around which all decisions rest. Given that we often fail to respond to God well, the need for transformation and conversion is always in the background of conscientious decisions and formation.[18]

While Gula separately considers conscience as a capacity (*synderesis*), a process (moral science), and a judgment (conscience), these areas comprise a single reality termed "conscience." While Gula and others discuss each dimension separately, their interrelatedness must always be kept in mind. Each area needs ongoing formation. Well before we as individuals make any conscientious judgments, however, we are born into communities and families with worldviews, values, and beliefs already defined that influence our formation. Familial or cultural worldviews can affect our capacity to see the good and avoid evil. We learn certain methods for problem solving or decision making. Our familial and cultural formation can affect our judgments.

Section 3: Spheres of Influence on Conscience Formation

Richard Gula examines the relational aspects of the moral agent's formation and, likewise, the social nature of our consciences. He writes, "convictions of conscience are shaped, and moral obligations are learned, within the communities that influence us."[19] Looking at conscience formation in the context of the process of moral discernment that yields a judgment about what to do (practical judgment of conscience) means we must account for the various spheres of influence in our lives. Gula

---

[18] Many Scripture passages allude to the reality that the human–divine relationship shapes the human in particular ways. One image that comes to mind is God as the potter and humans as the clay (Isa 64:8; Jer 18:1–10), drawing attention to the reality that as humans we are always in the state of formation and needing conversion.

[19] Gula, *Moral Discernment*, 21.

argues that these spheres of influence fall into three general categories: the personal sphere, the social sphere, and the situational sphere.[20]

Briefly, the personal sphere is defined as the self or community as moral agent. The social sphere encompasses the various communities where the moral agent participates. Overlap can exist between some of these communities. For example, when I attend communal prayer where I work, two spheres overlap: a faith sphere and a work sphere, since I enter into worship with fellow believers, some of whom are also professional colleagues. The situational sphere is where the moral agent meets his or her values, beliefs, and the question regarding what is happening here and now.[21] Together these arenas demonstrate the richness and multivalent ongoing nature of conscience formation (formation of the moral agent).

Personal Sphere

The personal sphere, as noted, comprises the self. As beings and as moral agents we are complex and created by God with a mind, will, body, and soul. Moral agents have emotions, intuitions, beliefs, values, ideals, virtues, vices, and imagination. We think and feel in both body and spirit. These areas, along with capabilities for logical thought, shape and affect the moral agent's perception regarding possible responses to events, situations, or experiences.[22]

Our emotions and intuitions can point to values being threatened or values that need protecting by a given decision or experience. Thus, naming our emotions becomes important since they point to values, influence what and how we see, and indicate possible courses of action to consider. As a result, can we name when we act or are thinking about action from fear, love, mercy, retribution, mutual correction, kindness, or vengeance? Naming and recognizing the difference between various emotions becomes an important kind of self-knowledge. This type of discernment distinguishing between the sometimes subtle differences

---

[20] Gula talks about contexts of influence. The term "context" could imply that if we change contexts the formation from another area no longer influences us. This is not what Gula is arguing, however. Therefore, I prefer to the language of spheres because spheres can overlap, they can be linked, and, in some instances, they can be broken. Even when relationships or spheres break the shards still exert some formative influence on us; albeit in a different way.

[21] Gula, *Moral Discernment*, 57–101.

[22] Ibid., 85–101.

in emotions requires a richer vocabulary than often attributed to our emotional landscape.

Connected to the discernment of emotions is the reality that our bodies can be a source of knowledge. Do we know our body well enough to identify and consider its wisdom? In other words, do we recognize when we are sick due to illness as opposed to our emotions manifesting themselves in bodily form? The insight that our bodies carry knowledge and speak to us is embedded in our language. Consider these few examples and sayings: He is a pain in the neck. I have butterflies in my stomach. Doing that made me sick to my stomach. She danced for joy. She wept out of gratitude. My hands are shaking. Each of these sayings referencing the body has an attached emotion or emotions by allusion or name. Naming the emotion when accompanied by reflection on the emotion can lead the moral agent to have greater awareness or insight about an event, an experience, or a possible course of action. Together, our emotion, rationality, and body more holistically help us reflect on and consider the values, beliefs, and fundamental convictions that orient our actions.

Our fundamental convictions help orient us toward the good in various circumstances. We need to know what we value and what we find important. What do we most need to pay attention to? What is "noise" or not important? What stories or narratives do we tell each other or about ourselves? Our narratives reveal something about our foundational commitments and values. The narratives might also reveal areas that need changing or transformation. Stories are multifaceted and often have multiple experiences embedded in the narrative.[23] Narratives told and heard from a different perspective can emphasize new and different elements, revealing new possibilities for living well. Envisioning or perceiving new possibilities for living a life of discipleship requires imagination.

Richard Gula argues that most people are not failures in the moral life. Rather, we are poor actors in the moral life because of a failure of imagination. Imagination helps us see, perceive new ways of being and acting, and

---

[23] The recent literature on the Second Vatican Council is a good example of how narrative can showcase new information and new ways of understanding an event. Scripture is also replete with examples of different narratives explaining or interpreting the same event. Therefore, it is extremely important to listen to a variety of voices before making conscientious decisions. As an individual this consultative feature is part of good discernment. For a community, consultation hopefully leads to some consensus, helping ensure that feelings are not hurt and people are not unintentionally oppressed, even if they do not agree with a decision.

envision how the kingdom of God breaks into the world now. First-century Palestine, with its different political and economic situation, required a different embodiment of the Good News than third-century Rome, or twenty-first-century United States. As a result, while core scriptural values remain the same, how they are inculturated in different places and eras requires imagination.[24] For example, I have lived in several Midwest states, several East Coast states, and for a time in southern California. While all are in the United States of America, each place has different sensibilities and cultural nuances. The variability arises because of the geography of the place, the way the state came into the Union, the first settlers' and immigrants' heritage, and a host of other factors. Therefore, while I remain Catholic in each of these settings, how I understand what mercy, compassion, and justice look like depends in part on the needs of the people in each of these places. For example, housing is cheaper in Minnesota than in either New York City or San Diego. Yet Minnesota has a greater need for people to advocate for public transportation than in the East. It does not matter if housing is cheaper if people cannot afford the necessary cars to get them to their jobs because of poor public transportation.

Social Sphere

Contemplating, however briefly, a geographic location's effect on living Gospel values subtly draws attention to the individual's establishment in communities. Presbyterian Beverly Wildung Harrison argues that communities, and more specifically the people in them, shape and form us. She argues that taking seriously the moral life requires that we face "the awe-ful, awe-some truth that we have the power through *acts of love* or lovelessness literally to *create one another*."[25] We have the ability to maim, hurt, help, heal, or encourage growth in each other. In other words, we form each other. Karl Rahner makes a similar claim in his argument that we cannot self-actualize in isolation; we know the self only in deeply

---

[24] Gula, *Moral Discernment*, 94–98. See also William Spohn, *Go and Do Likewise* (New York: Continuum International Publishing Group, 2007), 50–74.

[25] Beverly Wildung Harrison, "The Power of Anger in the Work of Love," *Union Seminary Quarterly Review* 36 (1981): 41–57, at 47. Emphasis is in the original text. Paul Wadell references this same passage from Harrison during his discussion on the role of friendship in the everyday moral life of human beings. See Paul Wadell, *Friendship and the Moral Life* (Notre Dame, IN: University of Notre Dame Press, 1989), 162.

interconnected relationships of response to God and others. Rahner argues that God's revelation (self-gift) is a call to become who we were created to become. The ability of parents to exert influence over and help "form" their children is just one illustration of these ideas.[26]

In addition to families, individuals are formed by a plurality of communities of influence. Communities of influence include family, friends, coworkers, and our ethnic communities. Specific religious influences include Scripture, the triune God, church, and religious communities. Laws, media, role models, expert authorities, and culture are other sources that shape and form moral agents and the communities to which they belong.[27]

Focusing on Christianity, within the larger institutional body of Christianity are smaller communities that form and shape its members. Both influence and shape the moral agent. Local churches must make decisions that affect their local church while keeping the larger ecclesial and human community in view. In other words, communities must keep in mind their larger ecclesial identity while working to address the neuralgic social issues of the day.

The two Benedictine communities connected to my place of work illuminate how this can occur. They are committed to Central Minnesota, the place they were founded. They manifest an approach that accounts for universal concerns while addressing those concerns within the context of the particularity of Central Minnesota and from the framework of the Benedictine charism. The Benedictine women of Saint Benedict's Monastery are involved in a variety of ministries and concerns. These include spiritual direction, retreat work, a common ground garden, health care, immigration reform, working to end sex trafficking in Minnesota, and advocating for and helping build affordable housing by partnering with Habitat for Humanity. Environmental concerns led to a moral decision to eliminate coal as an energy source. For the Benedictine men of Saint John's Abbey, this has meant a commitment to a solar plant for energy. In a different way, the abbey's decision to commission *The Saint John's Bible*, the first hand-illustrated and handwritten Bible in over five hundred years, was rooted in their sense of place, mission, history, charism, and identity. Both communities demonstrate how commitment to a geographic place affects the issues one considers.

---

[26] For an exploration of the implications of this thought for friendship and our interactions with people in general, see Wadell, *Friendship and the Moral Life*, 142–67.

[27] Gula, *Moral Discernment*, 57–74.

Social Sphere: Church and Moral Formation

Sometimes Roman Catholics and/or their bishops associate a well-formed conscience with intellectually assenting to a magisterial or episcopal teaching. Intellectual assent to a teaching typically requires particular behaviors and actions that are sometimes also described by the Magisterium or episcopacy. While this is an important insight that moral agents must account for and assent to magisterial teaching, this vision of a formed conscience is, however, truncated. Intellectual assent to propositions often focuses on doctrine and has orthodoxy as its primary concern, with orthopraxis (right actions) as a secondary concern. Yet even a rightly construed concern with orthodoxy and orthopraxis can be reductionist if it ignores the heart. Ignoring the need for a rightly formed heart (orthocardia) leads to the malformation of moral agents (consciences) and a distorted, if not an ignored, life of discipleship.[28]

Consideration of the rightly formed heart—understood in the Hebraic sense where the heart represents the totality of the human person—recalls scriptural allusions to God as the ultimate formation director of the human being. Considering what constitutes a rightly formed heart draws attention to the need to consider right formation of our emotions (or what Aquinas calls the tutoring of the emotions and inclinations),[29] dispositions, habits, virtues (which shape our character), and even habits of our intellect. Therefore, the formation of conscience speaks less to agreeing with this or that magisterial teaching and more to how this or that magisterial teaching fits into the broader framework of the moral agent's formation as a Christian disciple living the Gospel message. This holds true for communities of believers as well.

As a result, we need to clearly distinguish between ongoing conscience formation that develops virtues, dispositions, and emotions and ongoing conscience formation that develops skills for conscientious decision making. Thus, when we use the term "conscience formation" we implicitly recognize that there are two operative dimensions: character formation (the being) and the formative process for decision making in particular

[28] Edward Vacek, *Love, Human and Divine: The Heart of Christian Ethics* (Washington, DC: Georgetown University Press, 1996). My use of the language of orthocardia is borrowed from Edward Vacek's treatment of our need to rightly form our hearts.

[29] For an examination of Thomas Aquinas on the emotions, see Diana Fritz Cates, *Aquinas on the Emotions: A Religious Ethical Inquiry* (Washington, DC: Georgetown University Press, 2009).

instances.[30] A dialectical interconnection exists between these two features of conscience formation, yet we often tend to focus on the latter when considering conscience formation. When we are overly concentrated on the decision-making process of conscience formation, we risk conflating a formed conscience with an informed conscience. Furthermore, we risk equating conscience formation with intellectual assent to magisterial teaching. In so doing, we reinforce the emphasis on orthodoxy to the detriment of orthocardia and possibly orthopraxis. While orthodoxy is important, single-minded attention on it has the consequence of an overemphasis on dissent while underemphasizing discipleship. Therefore, considering the formation of conscience as character development (or the formation of the moral agent) reilluminates the connection between relationships, discipleship, conversion, spirituality, and morality. Formation as an ongoing event requires honesty, conversion, repentance, and receptivity to the triune God's grace. In turn, it helps us recall the fact that we (our consciences) are always in the process of formation through our relationships, practices, and actions.

Richard Gula argues that when we limit the understanding of the church's role in the moral life to "the relationship between conscience and the official teachings of the magisterium" we are being "overly restrictive."[31] Expanding the role of the church in conscience formation means seeing the church as a "shaper of moral character," a "bearer of moral tradition," and a "community of moral deliberation."[32]

The church can be seen as shaper of moral character in various ways. It shapes us through instruction, rituals, liturgy, art, music, and so forth. Various religious communities and their spiritual charisms within the church—for example, Franciscans, Jesuits, and Benedictines—also shape us. In talking with a colleague who also works at a Benedictine school, we noted that with our greater attention to the Liturgy of the Hours we are being influenced and shaped by Scripture in different ways than we have in the past. Furthermore, the Rule of Benedict contains wisdom that pertains to both small and large communal life. The Rule provides guidance for living together, meals, norms, decision making, truth tell-

---

[30] Gula, *Moral Discernment*, 22.

[31] Gula, *Reason Informed by Faith*, 199.

[32] Ibid., 199–200. Gula is drawing on the theological work of Bruce Birch and Larry Rasmussen with his description of church here.

ing, willingness to listen, learning from each other, and the dangers, for example, of gossip or murmuring.

The church is a bearer of the moral tradition in various ways as well. We bear tradition using the same means by which we shape our moral character. For example, tradition is borne through instruction and rituals, as well as in official moral teaching, school systems, catechetical programs, the family, monastic communities, and the faithful in a variety of church programs. The formation of the next generation occurs only when the prior generation demonstrates the relevance of their faith, if they keep growing in and learning about the faith themselves. In this way they acknowledge and model to the people they are teaching that the faith matters, that spiritual growth or regression is possible, and that God is always faithful. In other words, when we enact what we believe, we teach and hand on the faith, our beliefs system, and practices through the example of our lives.

Avery Dulles, citing *Dei Verbum* 8, writes that tradition "includes everything that contributes to the holiness of life and the increase of faith of the people of God." Therefore, the church bears and hands on moral insight not only in its teaching but also through its life, worship, and the "practice of the believing and praying church."[33] Liturgy, then, is key for the handing on of the faith, since it is an experience of the saving mystery and a reflection on the contents of faith. The scriptural narratives and psalms read and preached are crucial. Scripture, along with its interpretation through preaching or study, instructs, shapes, and influences our moral imagination.[34]

The church functions as a community of moral deliberation in myriad ways. According to Karl Rahner, we need to be a community of moral deliberation because of gnoseological concupiscence. Gnoseological concupiscence captures the reality that in the contemporary world there is too much information and no one person can know everything. We also see things differently from each other. Therefore, on the one hand, we need to live with the reality that our judgments or insights might be

---

[33] Avery Dulles, "Faith and Revelation," in *Systematic Theology: Roman Catholic Perspectives*, ed. Francis Schüssler Fiorenza and John P. Galvin, 2nd ed. (Minneapolis, MN: Augsburg Fortress Press, 2011), at 102.

[34] This is why the dearth of biblical narratives read and preached about the women in Scripture is problematic. It sends the subtle message that males are the actors with God in history.

correct. On the other hand, we might need to revise our judgments and teachings in light of new information, new experiences, and new insights into what has already been revealed.

A community's ability to take responsibility for moral deliberation is important. Our world, society, and culture are changing, as the world, society, and cultures always do. Yet there are constants within that change. I would contend that it is crucial that Catholics are equipped with the foundation to address new questions and topics as they arise and seek solutions together. In the face of new challenges, our initial response might not be the final response. Ongoing deliberation, rooted in our relationship with the triune God, and respect for each other are key components in deepening our understanding of truth, growing in wisdom, and loving God and neighbor.

In light of the reality that we operate fallibly and with limited knowledge, Gula's community of moral deliberation functions in a similar manner to Anne Patrick's community of accountability. Both a community of moral deliberation and a community of accountability place the individual and smaller groups into a web of relationships. Attention to relationships, roles within the community, and accountability to others prevent both relativism and a false universalism that functions to mask the privileging of a particular group. Communities of moral deliberation or accountability are crucial given the human propensity to self-deception and blindness. Standards of "goodness" or norms can function as a means to silence or attempt to silence voices that argue for change in structures that benefit some people while oppressing and discriminating against others. Scholars concerned with gender, race, class, and postcolonial theory consistently analyze how a dominant culture and their agents utilize norms, standards, and laws in order to foster specific ideas of morality while masking blind spots. One example illustrates this point: at one time many Christians supported the enslavement of their fellow human beings. Today, while enslavement of other people is seen as destroying human dignity and sinful, many Christians still have not substantively grappled with the ongoing effects and consequences of slavery. As theologians and other scholars think and write about slavery and its consequences, their scholarship shapes communities and holds us accountable to each other.

Situational Context

The personal and social spheres of influence, including the church, intersect in the situational context. The situational context is where we meet our values, beliefs, and commitments when needing to act. I am not talking about the situational ethics debate in the 1950s and early 1960s, deemed problematic by both Catholic theologians and the Magisterium. Rather, by the situational context I mean the specific event, circumstance, or milieu requiring action (whether in thought, word, or deed). Understanding the framework or situation in which one is acting is important because the situation influences the type of response that might be required. Taking a mundane example, I would not want to wear my gardening clothes to a wedding because of the different norms or standards for clothing.

We make thousands of decisions every day regarding actions and behaviors. Often we do not go through an in-depth reflective, deliberative process where we consider the intellectual, volitional, verbal, attitudinal, affective, or bodily components of our responses or actions. Rather, reflection on our daily actions frequently occurs after we have acted and we determine whether we have lived from our commitments to particular values, virtues, scriptural principles, and so forth. The process of coming to a decision and judgment for acting when we have longer periods for reflection; gathering data; consciously articulating our values, commitments, dispositions, and desires for growth or change does influence us in our day-to-day living. As a result, the character, habits, and dispositions we have and continue to develop influences our actions when we lack time for extended reflection, allowing for a more reflexive response to any particular event. As well as understanding certain norms, as illustrated by the clothing example above.

Questions exist that aid the analysis of a given situation or circumstances requiring future action or even analyzing past actions. Every time we act we cannot ask ourselves these questions since we could become paralyzed. Yet the process of discernment embedded in answering these questions for some decisions instills skills that can be used more reflexively in other instances. In other words, the process of discernment for acting well is formative. The questions focus on answering what, why, how, who, when, where, what if, and what else.[35]

---

[35] Gula, *Moral Discernment*, 76–84.

Asking what is happening requires us to describe the situation. Any description influences analysis since a description focuses us on some details rather than others. For example, while Catholics consider marriage a sacrament, governments do not. The description of marriage as a sacrament shapes discourse about marriage in the church.

Considering why we are going to act requires us to name and attend to our motivations. We also reflect on our purposes for acting. Some motivations and purposes for acting are more appropriate than others. Are we seeking justice, to develop a deeper relationship with the living God, growth in discipleship and charity?

Once we have answered the questions of what is happening and why we are acting, we can deliberate about how we are going to act. The means for acting matter. The Catholic moral tradition has long held that the ends and means of action must align. Furthermore, different modes of acting have different purposes and effects. For example, a person might choose to resolve conflict by either confrontation or consultation, recognizing that each approach would yield possibly different results and interpersonal relationships. We must bear in mind that a person's disposition is important here as well, since we can respond differently to various people. This fact compels us to consider the next set of interrelated questions.

Who is acting and who does the person acting affect? We are connected in a web of relationships where actions have ripple effects. As a result, we need to consider the effects of our actions both on ourselves and on others in our community. At times, this will entail pondering a dyadic relationship. Other times, we are acting as individuals but weighing in on societal matters. In these instances, larger groups would need to be considered. For example, when we vote during elections for candidates or on ballot measures, we act as individuals, but the results are determined by the sum of all votes. As such, we need to consider not just ourselves when voting but also how ballot measures and candidates' positions affect the broader community in which we live.[36]

Answering the question of when we are acting focuses attention on timing. Sometimes, as in the example about voting, the timing for action is

---

[36] The voting example requires examining and considering a host of issues and concerns. Candidates cannot be judged by their stance on one or two issues. The United States Conference of Catholic Bishops had published a voting guide that provides a framework for looking at issues when voting. They consider and list a wide range of societal concerns that have to be weighed, including poverty, economic disparity, and immigration to name a few.

determined for us. In other matters, we need to choose the time for acting or making decisions. Timing for action might require multiple stages or responses, depending on the issue or decision being considered. Timing can determine whether our action leads to the result we desire or seek. The issue of timing relates to where we act. Location can matter since culture influences both the implementation of ideas and the reception of ideas or actions. For example, the New York City tendency to start a meeting without a few moments of chitchat would be considered rude in other parts of the country. Likewise, the practice of chitchat to start a meeting would be considered inefficient by many New Yorkers.

Pondering the "when and where" for actions also leads to a consideration of any foreseeable effects or consequences arising from our actions. Answering the question of if we act or of what will possibly happen helps us consider both negative and positive ramifications. This involves the imagination, the ability to think about the future, and an awareness of the self, and it relies on accurate, honest answers to the other questions. Additionally, answering the "what if" question calls for some comfort level with uncertainty by the moral agent. This is because some effects and consequences are unforeseeable.

Finally, when we contemplate the consequences or possible effects of our acting, we eventually ask the question "what else?" In other words, we ponder other options and possibilities for acting. The "what else" question necessitates the ability to think imaginatively and move beyond the construct of "we have always done it this way" thinking. Moral agents who consider the "what else" question activate their imagination in order to think about alternative solutions to problems and arrive at creative life-giving ways around impasses.

After deliberating and answering these questions, given the element of indeterminacy and the reality of unforeseeable effects, decisions and actions must still be undertaken. Trust and hope become important. Moral agents must trust and hope that the God in whom they live, move, and have their being will work in and through their insights and mistakes. The ability to live in this space that recognizes some ambiguity, while still taking responsibility for acting, requires the moral agent to have reached some level of moral maturity. The ability to hope and trust in the mercy of God, live in spaces of ambiguity, and take responsibility matters, because we will make mistakes in judgments or decisions regarding a course of action that might need reconsideration in light of new information. Therefore, it is important to realize that any decision or judgment might need to be revisited in the future.

Moral Maturity

Moral maturity includes the ability to debate and deliberate. We must know why we believe what we believe: what are the reasons and convictions that cause us to have our moral beliefs and positions? We must take responsibility for our actions and for who we are becoming. In other words, we cannot blame others for our errors, mistakes, and sins. We must also acknowledge and accept our successes, accomplishments, and graced moments. As a result, moral maturity does not always mean just being able to follow orders, laws, and norms. One can follow the law and norms of the faith and not love, not be aware of one's own blindness, and not be self-aware. Of course, we continue to grow in these areas throughout life. Moral maturity requires a sense of self and self-awareness and the capacity to decide how to act for oneself rather than always being told what to do. Additionally, moral agents must be able to be responsive to new situations.

Responsiveness means being able to engage and decide in new situations. It accounts for the individual and the community as well as the proper balance between internal and external authority when we consider our relationship to the church and various communities to which we belong. Magisterial guidance is appropriate. Yet instruction and teaching from the Magisterium (Vatican) often lags behind our need to consider new situations. Therefore, we need to be attentive and respond to new situations since theological and philosophical debates can rage for years before the Vatican weighs in, as happened in the case of bioethics and reproductive technologies. It was nine years after the birth of Louise Brown, the first person born after being conceived through in vitro fertilization, when the Congregation for the Doctrine of the Faith issued *Donum Vitae* in February 1987. Many Catholics suffering from infertility between the years 1978 and 1987 would not have found church teaching on the matter. They would have had to rely on other sources for moral guidance.

Moreover, Pope Francis has also challenged Catholics to get involved in addressing the social issues of the day. He acknowledges that engaging the world is going to be messy, not perfect, and we will make mistakes. Nevertheless, we must live the Gospel and bring the Gospel message to the world.[37] In other words, we must be responsive to the concerns of

---

[37] For more detail, see Pope Francis, *Evangelii Gaudium* (November 24, 2013). This document can be accessed at http://w2.vatican.va/content/francesco/en/apost_exhortations /documents/papa-francesco_esortazione-ap_20131124_evangelii-gaudium.html.

the world and not always wait for guidance from institutional echelons. Responsiveness could entail, as Anne Patrick points out, that we figure out how we can both support and honor the individuals within our communities when needing to make a communal discernment.

The Spiral of Conscience Formation

Formation does not end at action, nor with the recognition that various communities shape our thinking, worldviews, and emotional landscapes. Nor does formation end with the ability to discern courses of actions stemming from critical reflection on the questions described above. Conscience formation is ongoing; the formation of the moral agent is ongoing.[38] As James Bretzke describes it, a spiral of conscience formation exists. This spiral of conscience formation consists of the following components: formation, information gathering, discernment, decision, action, reflection, reconsideration, and potential reform.[39]

Bretzke's spiral of formation and its elements illuminate in a visual manner what Sidney Callahan described in her definition of conscience. Both Bretzke and Callahan contend in different ways that any judgment of conscience does not end with a judgment regarding good or evil, a decision to act, or the action itself. We undergo a process when making conscientious decisions. We do not go to a place where the decision is found. Rather, since decisions about how to respond or act precede action, the decisions themselves are subject to change before action. Additionally, we might make a decision and then need to figure out if it is the right time to act. Also further reflection might mean we reconsider and reevaluate prior decisions, leading to changes or new insights for acting differently in the future.

We do not always go through the steps involved in discernment or in Bretzke's spiral of conscience formation in a deliberate fashion. This is because in our daily lives we form habits of acting; we act from accumulated actions, insights, and dispositions. Since our discernment or judgment

---

[38] Pope Francis, in his addresses, alludes to ongoing formation. While he talks about conversion, the need to consider change, reform, and more authentic responses to living the Gospel, he is also talking about ongoing formation. If the purpose of formation is to shape us into disciples and followers of God, then part of formation is conversion.

[39] James Bretzke, *A Morally Complex World: Engaging Contemporary Moral Theology* (Collegeville, MN: Liturgical Press, 2004). He provides two different diagrams on pages 139 and 144. For a more detailed description of the spiral of formation, see pages 138–44.

from conscience regarding our actions continues after action, however, we need time for reflection, reconsideration, and reformation or conversion. This time for reflection, reconsideration, and identification of areas for conversion occurs in several venues: private prayer, communal prayer, retreats, the sacraments, conversations with others, and assessment by communities of accountability, among others.

Prayer and the Examination of Conscience

Relationship with the triune God appears throughout this chapter. Relationship with God requires, as does any relationship, spending time getting to know the other person. Getting to know the other, in this case the triune God, occurs in conversations, individual and communal prayer, and also through seeing Christ in others. Dennis Billy and James Keating talk about prayer not as a technique but as a "keeping company with God," getting to know God to tune (form) the heart, to listen to the Holy Spirit.[40] For them, prayer fosters the formation of conscience, a formation of conscience that occurs within the practices that attune the disciple to his or her Christian identity. This requires more than using the questions described earlier to facilitate decision making. In highlighting the role of prayer in conscience formation or the formation of the moral agent, the disciple, Billy and Keating focus on the rightly ordered heart. Prayer makes it possible for the person to hear God, to listen, and to recognize God's voice. They contend that "in the formation of conscience the unique characteristic of the prayer-imbued conscience is that the person desires to spend time at the sources of encounter with Christ, be they the Word of God or embedded in the Sacraments."[41] The willingness to spend time in prayer and encounter Christ through Scripture and the sacraments means that the person is willing to subject their own perspectives and judgments to the judgment of God in and through the person of Christ. While Billy and Keating discuss how spending time in prayer forms the conscience, spending time in prayer also shapes our thinking, perceptions, imagination, and emotions. In other words, prayer shapes the person in their totality.

Prayer and the desire to spend time with God is not the only shaper of the conscience: "The conscience is also directly affected by one's service to

---

[40] Dennis J. Billy and James Keating, *Conscience and Prayer: The Spirit of Catholic Moral Theology* (Collegeville, MN: Liturgical Press, 2001), 2–4, 55.

[41] Ibid., 95.

the poor to the extent that the person is open to see Christ in all who are needy."[42] In other words, service is good. Yet, the shaping of conscience also requires seeing Christ in others. In being able to see Christ in those we serve, we remain open to Christ and form ourselves in seeing the world differently. This openness to seeing Christ in others instills in humans a receptivity to recognize our limitations and be open to the workings of the Spirit fostering wisdom.[43]

Billy and Keating's idea that prayer is keeping company with God and listening to the promptings of the Holy Spirit can be seen in the examination of conscience. The examination of conscience is one way of reflecting on whether we have lived our day seeing Christ in others or with the mind of Christ. When used in the context of the sacrament of confession, an examination of conscience helps a person take stock of his or her sins and areas needing conversion. An examination of conscience, however, can be done on a more regular basis at either the end or beginning of a day. If done at the beginning of a day, the reflection refers to the prior day or days. There are various versions that provide questions to help facilitate consideration of both graced and sinful responses to God. For example:

What did I do well? (Where did I respond to Christ?)

What could I have done better? (Where did I fail to respond to Christ?)

Whom did I offend? (To whom did I show hospitality?)

Whom did I help or encourage? (Where did I share the Good News?)

In praying these questions, the person sees not only where conversion is needed but also where virtues are taking hold and where graced responses to God appeared in their day. In learning to recognize graced responses to God in and through daily life, the moral agent instructs themselves in different ways of seeing.

Scripture

Spending time with the Word of God (Scripture) shapes and forms the person. The Word of God when read and preached about during

---

[42] Ibid.
[43] Ibid., 96–98.

liturgy provides one way for understanding how the Scripture informs our worldview and actions. Insights and our formation by Scripture depend in part, however, on what we hear or read from Scripture.[44] The stories shape our imagination, and therefore how one reads the biblical narrative matters. For example, when reading the beginning of Exodus, if the reader focuses on Moses, the story has a particular emphasis. If in reading Exodus the reader focuses on the midwives, then the same biblical narrative reveals other insights.

Similarly, the themes of Scripture matter as well as the narratives. The covenantal theme reminds believers that God calls, we respond, and we are given our identity. Furthermore, both God and the community have responsibilities and obligations. The laws and moral norms provided in Scripture are meant to give structure and help establish boundaries for the moral life. The law or moral norms, however, are not the object in and of themselves. Since the community's relationship with God is central, laws and norms should foster genuine responses to God. In other words, we cannot make an idol out of the law or the moral norm.

Likewise, when we consider the theme of discipleship, which is deeply connected to Christology, the type of Christology matters. Is discipleship premised upon a Christology from above (descending) or below (ascending)? A Christology from above affirms human dignity due to the incarnation. Christologies from above tend to start with Christ, the second person of the Trinity who became human, whereas a Christology from below starts with the human person, Jesus of Nazareth and his life, death, and subsequent resurrection. Christologies from below consider how Jesus "moves toward God." The gospels have both types of Christology operating—descending with John's gospel and ascending with the Synoptic Gospels. There is a value in both, and thus believers need to be mindful not to prioritize one over the other because it fits our own spirituality better or makes us more comfortable. After all, encountering Jesus Christ in the Scriptures should challenge our perspectives, helping us see the world as he did.

As with individual narratives and themes, the books of Scripture we read influence, shape, and form us. The prophets remind us that leader-

---

[44] Biblical scholars and other theologians caution that believers have to be careful not to proof text and use Scripture uncritically. There are four related tasks when using Scripture in a moral endeavor: exegetical, hermeneutical, methodological, and theological. When used together, these four methods for understanding or breaking open Scripture keep the believer from boxing in the biblical text.

ship and the broader community can fail to live out the demands of the covenant. The prophets call us back to right relationship with God, each other, and all of creation. For example, Micah 6:8 reminds us that we are "to do justice, and to love kindness, and to walk humbly with [our] God." The Psalms cover the range of human emotions and experiences, setting them all in the context of praise and worship of God. The Acts of the Apostles details the beginnings of the early church and teaches us about the outpouring of the third person in the Trinity, the Holy Spirit. Like the early church community, we need to ask where the Holy Spirit is moving today and what issues are ours to address. How does the Spirit prompt us to preach the Good News to people today?

While many people hear Scripture once a week during Mass, Benedictine communities communally pray Scripture several times a day. The Benedictine communities in Central Minnesota have morning prayer, midday prayer, Mass, and evening prayer together. There is no choice in the readings when praying the Liturgy of the Hours. One shows up to pray and prays the day's Scripture passages. This means, for example, that in a four-week cycle one will encounter the full range of human emotions in the psalms. Sometimes the psalms resonate, sometimes they do not, and sometimes the psalms illuminate areas that need attention in our individual and communal lives.

Praying the Scriptures multiple times daily together shapes and forms the community and individual in the Word of God. The practice of this type of prayer fosters attention to the Scriptures where the themes, narratives, and insights come through the repetition and silent pauses that foster listening to the Word of God. The Scriptures become the foundation and touchstone for acting, deciding, and being in the world.

In addition to shaping the communal and individual worldview, reading Scripture privately or communally schools people in the virtues. Virtue theory typically focuses on the theological virtues of faith, hope, and love along with the cardinal virtues of temperance, prudence, courage, and justice. Demetrius Dumm, in his book *Cherish Christ above All*,[45] examines how Scripture functions in the Rule of Benedict. In so doing, he actually provides virtues necessary for the formation of the moral agent—virtues such as hospitality, listening, trust, and humility. These virtues are both

---

[45] Demetrius Dumm, *Cherish Christ above All: The Bible in the Rule of Benedict* (Latrobe, PA: Archabbey Publications, 2002, 2008; originally Mahwah, NJ: Paulist Press, 1996).

individual and communal, thus maintaining the symbiotic relationship between the individual and a community of accountability advocated by Anne Patrick. Furthermore, their genesis is scriptural and contributes to the endeavor to connect Scripture to moral theology.

Moreover, in Dumm's work the admonition coming from Benedict to "cherish Christ above all" is not a pie-in-the-sky, overly romanticized account. Cherishing Christ above all relies on the workings of the Holy Spirit and remains rooted firmly in the communal undertaking of living life here on earth. The virtues proposed by Dumm, even though he himself does not refer to them as virtues, help form the moral agent in a manner that fosters liberation from oppression and moves toward greater love of God and neighbor. Reading and praying Scripture schools the moral agent in scriptural virtues necessary to cherish Christ above all and then act accordingly.

Conclusion

In this chapter, I explored further how conscience functions, how formation occurs, and the influences on this formation. Psychologist Sidney Callahan illustrates the nonlinear aspect of formation, reflection, and ultimately decision making. In addition, she describes the value of emotions in our moral formation, judgments, and decision making. The rest of the chapter theologically looked at many of these ideas, including how the church functions as a moral formator, a community of moral deliberation, and how it hands on a moral tradition. It became clear that formation of the moral agent is an ongoing endeavor. Given our human finitude and limitations, part of acting well is reflection on our actions and interactions with others. If change or conversion is necessary, this then becomes part of the formation process.

As in the first two chapters, relationship with God, and others featured as a crucial component for moral formation. While stated slightly differently, Richard Gula's argument that the term "conscience" represents the "expression of the whole person" is similar to Anne Patrick's claim that the term "formation of conscience" operates metaphorically to describe the formation of moral agent. Taken seriously, their claims have the potential to de-reify conscience as a "thing" exterior to the human person and help moral agents recognize their responsibility as practitioners of Christian discipleship. Scripture and the tradition provide models, guidelines, criteria, and virtues for living a life of discipleship.

Prayer as one practice was described as more than a technique; it is time spent with God that develops our perceptive abilities, thus attuning us to the demands and obligations of our Christian discipleship. Thus, a connection exists between the formation of the moral agent, discipleship, discernment, and spirituality regarding right courses of action. Conscience also illuminates the moral agent's character, self-understanding, and central values as well as their response to God's call as a result of formation. While the results of formation can be seen in specific instances, they are also revealed over the arc of one's life history. Consequently, it can be dangerous to judge a person by one observed action or pattern without understanding the fullness of their lives, since we are complex beings interacting with others in a plurality of situations.[46] People can change as well as solidify who they are by their ongoing actions, attitudes, and dispositions. As an ongoing, incomplete process, formation requires its own ongoing analysis. When done well, formation enables us to respond to others and current situations from the wisdom forged in the furnace of life and reflected upon individually and with others (God, friends, neighbors, and the stranger). Likewise, when done poorly, our formation can lead to sinful, evil reactions, vices, and harmful behaviors. Usually our formation is mixed: done well and needing improvement.

Since individuals are formed in communities, dynamism exists between the individual's responsibility to the self as well as to the community. If the community helps shape individuals in its midst, however, the community's health raises questions about the formation of conscience (moral agent) and subsequently following one's conscience. The church as an institution has participated and continues to participate in resisting oppression and spreading the Good News. Nevertheless, the church has participated and continues to participate in and contribute to structural sin. Yet John Paul II, even as he apologized at various points in his pontificate for the past sins of the church, also stressed the conformity of the conscience to the teaching authority of the Magisterium as a means of validating conscience's judgment regarding good and evil. Does the individual have a role in identifying where the institutional church might have a wrong judgment regarding good and evil? The biblical prophets and the stories of

---

[46] The film *St. Vincent* illustrates this reality by exploring the life of a retired Vietnam veteran and his effect on the people in his life. The viewers of the film see how Vincent's brokenness is but one aspect of his being.

various believers throughout history indicate the answer to this question is yes. Pope Francis has begun the hard task of structural reforms within the institutional church, including changes in confronting the sex abuse crisis and scandal. In so doing, he challenges all people to resist, and work to reform, unjust structures.

In considering the formation of the moral agent within the broad context of magisterial teaching, rituals, communal and individual prayer, Scripture, and other influences I did not address what happens if formation leads a moral agent to disagree with established norms or communal insights regarding actions and matters of practical judgments. What does it mean when communities or individuals within a community disagree on the means for following God in the world? Is it simply a matter of conforming to the teaching of the Magisterium? Is disagreement sometimes a sign that correction is needed within the structure itself? Or is it possible that agreement exists around foundational norms or general principles, while a plurality of practices for embodied actions arises from the interpretation and application of the norm? These questions lead to further questions about the role of dissent within the community of moral deliberation, which will be discussed in the next chapter. While dissent has often been associated with sexual matters within the Roman Catholic Church, questions regarding dissent appear in discussions of Catholic Social Teaching as well. This is especially true when considering the economy, workers' rights, immigration policy, and, most recently, the discussion of what Pope Francis's 2015 encyclical on the environment means for Catholic beliefs and future actions.

Chapter 4

Rethinking Dissent

Introduction

The last chapter explored and examined how other people and structures function and participate in the human being's moral formation. This included acknowledging the reality that some people, after forming their consciences, end up disagreeing in some instances with magisterial norms, teachings, or practical judgments regarding how to live a teaching. All too frequently, disagreement is labeled dissent and applied to disagreements with episcopal teaching, as well as practical judgments sometimes perceived as timeless, unchanging, and infallible.

I contend that not all disagreement equals dissent and that both disagreement and dissent have purposes within the church. Historically, when meeting certain criteria, dissent has been permitted and tolerated within the Catholic tradition. Drawing attention to this history is important because dissent, as it is frequently invoked today, functions as a church practice that does not properly form church communities. Frequently, dissent language combined with practices that surround the prohibition and stifling of properly understood dissent deforms and malforms the community of moral deliberation. This malformation contributes to a perception of creeping magisterial infallibility. It functions to silence voices. Furthermore, when malformation occurs we lose the ability to dialogue, to debate, listen to, and see multiple valid responses to questions regarding what constitutes right practices and behaviors stemming from norms, magisterial teaching, and visions of discipleship. Additionally, given that most episcopal teaching is fallible, the concept of dissent needs rehabilitation so that dissent can function as a positive element within the community of moral deliberation.[1]

---

[1] Richard Gula discusses dissent as a feature of the community's moral deliberation. See Gula, *Reason Informed by Faith: Foundations of Catholic Morality* (New York: Paulist Press,

During the twentieth century, theologians engaged the topic of dissent shortly after the Second Vatican Council. An overview of this debate was provided in 1988 by Charles Curran and Richard McCormick, who considered the theological debate around dissent in their edited series Readings in Moral Theology.[2] Each themed volume consists of a collection of influential essays chosen as representing various streams and schools of thought on a given issue. The essays orient the reader to that issue's theological landscape. Volume 6, *Dissent in the Church*, is no exception. The essays indicate a range of theological positions on the type of dissent that is permitted, what constitutes dissent, and how to define it.

The essays and experience point to the reality that dissent exists within the ecclesial community of moral deliberation. Yet, the existence of dissent and a theological consideration of it do not automatically entail an acknowledged or respected practical role for dissent—a practical role that could help in arriving at, clarifying, or correcting moral norms and magisterial teaching. Finding and practicing a more functional role for dissent within the community of moral deliberation that seeks truth is impeded by the current practice of framing "dissent" with the default mode of debate. Debates recognize common problems or questions to be solved and answered. Debaters seek to resolve disagreement through rational argument that one solution is better than another. Debate also implicitly or explicitly recognizes that disagreement exists. Thus, debate can be helpful and constructive when verifiable facts, logical argumentation, and the persuasive use of past precedents are used in arguing the merits of different proposals, ideas, or responses to questions when a

---

1989), 206–7. Despite the US bishops' general norms and teaching in the areas of immigration, housing, and other issues, several topics garner ongoing attention in the United States around the question of dissent. The perennial topics include birth control, abortion, homosexuality, and, more recently, the validity of same-sex marriage. Disagreements regarding responses to or even the need to respond to immigration, affordable housing, the economy, and poverty are frequently seen as differences in practical or prudential judgment rather than dissent within the ecclesial community.

[2] Charles E. Curran and Richard A. McCormick, *Dissent in the Church*, Readings in Moral Theology, vol. 6 (New York and Mahwah, NJ: Paulist Press, 1988). The essays are divided into five parts: theological dissent in general, canonical aspects, academic aspects, moral theology in particular, and the Curran Case and its aftermath. Authors include theologians such as Jon Nilson, Karl Rahner, Daniel Pilarczyk, Roger Mahony, Joseph Ratzinger, Germain Grisez, and Christine Gudorf, among others. The series' first volume, *Moral Norms and the Catholic Tradition*, was published in 1979. After Richard McCormick's death in early 2000, Charles Curran has continued co-editing the series with various other theologians. The series is up to sixteen volumes and Paulist Press continues its publication.

group needs to decide on something. At its best, the medieval practice of exploring disputed questions was a theological, intellectual debate aimed at solving or providing viable solutions to theological questions.

Unfortunately, debate can also be unhelpful and destructive, especially when debate is less about seeking truth and more about winning and losing. This is particularly true when debate tactics include sleights of hand, dismissive comments, and personal attacks on those who present alternative arguments or positions rather than an intellectual engagement with the strengths and weaknesses of various arguments and positions. Debate does not always foster the search for common ground or truth.

Sometimes debate is even lacking. For example, reflect on a time you might have been trying to engage in conversation regarding a matter of church teaching, norms, or practical judgement. You might have been met with an almost immediate response of "You are dissenting" or "That is dissent." Using "dissenting" or "dissent" in this manner can effectively shut down the conversation, dialogue, or potentially healthy debate. This type of response could be heard as saying to the other person, "You have nothing to say to me; nothing you say is valid. Your questions do not change anything. I understand the truth, the whole truth, and the Magisterium has all insight. I do not need to listen to you. I do not need to engage you. Only if you believe as I believe or as the magisterial teaching states without question, then and only then do I need to engage in conversation with you." This is essentially not even a conversation or exploration of truth. It is one-sided, closed, and does not effectively foster communion or shared commitment to the same ideals of the Gospel: love, faith, and hope in the one who creates, sustains, and calls us forth into greater love.

This type of response surfaces differences between people about how they understand and define what constitutes infallible magisterial teaching. Additionally, dissent (disagreement) too often carries a negative connotation theologically, whereby many perceive "the dissenter" as one who dislikes rather than loves his or her church. Therefore, we must avoid the danger of using dissent as an ecclesial trump card or weapon, a bludgeoning tool as a way of stifling authentic and needed discussion, conversation, and even debate. Discussion, conversation, debate, and disagreement can clarify teaching or arrive at new insights for living a life of Christian discipleship.

Set in this context, the intent going forward is not to provide a survey of the current literature on dissent. Rather, I seek a way around the impasse that the word "dissent" currently presents when considering questions that intersect at the nexus of personal judgments of conscience and magisterial authority. Doing so could help clarify whether disagreements are about universal norms, specific norms, or instances of practical judgment regarding the norm's application in very concrete situations. Clarification about what constitutes dissent will help the Body of Christ more fruitfully consider how variances in practical moral judgments may not harm Catholic unity but rather function as an ongoing means of moral deliberation in the pursuit of moral truth. Any approach to disagreements regarding practical judgments must account for the teaching authority of the Magisterium, the moral agent's moral responsibility, the possibility of errors in both teaching and conscience's judgment, as well as the centrality of relationship with the triune God.[3] This multifaceted reality requires moral agents and communities to grapple with questions that stretch beyond the legitimacy of dissent. For example: What are the contours of responsible dissent? When, if ever, should one stay quiet? Does the individual ever have a responsibility to the larger community first, rather than to the self and faithfulness to conscience? Is all disagreement with magisterial pronouncements and teaching dissent or is something else happening? If something else is happening, is it more than "loyalty coexisting with dissent"?[4] My own position is twofold. One, that loyalty to the Magisterium can coexist with dissent properly understood. Two, that not all disagreement with magisterial teaching is dissent from norms or teachings; rather, disagreement can showcase different practices regarding practical judgments about a norm's application.

Section 1: Defining Dissent

This section looks briefly at the term so that the readers and author share a basic understanding outside an ecclesial context. The Oxford English Dictionary (OED) lists dissent as both a noun and verb.[5] As a noun, the dictionary defines dissent as a "difference of opinion or sentiment;

---

[3] Josef Fuchs, "Teaching Morality: The Tension between Bishops and Theologians within the Church," in Curran and McCormick, *Dissent in the Church*, 330–53. The article was originally published in Josef Fuchs, *Christian Ethics in a Secular Arena* (Washington, DC: Georgetown University Press, 1984), 131–53.

[4] Curran and McCormick, *Dissent in the Church*, 1.

[5] Oxford English Dictionary, online version. The dictionary provides quotes illustrating these definitions mostly from the sixteenth and seventeenth centuries. The dictionary was first published in 1896.

disagreement; quarrel, disagreement with a proposal or resolution; the opposite of consent." In a religious context, dissent is defined as a "difference of opinion in regard to religious doctrine or worship."[6] There is a mostly obsolete definition that says dissent is the "want of agreement or harmony; difference of sense, character, nature, meaning, quality, etc."

Etymologically, "dissent" as a verb comes from the Latin *dissentire* with the prefix *dis-*, which signals difference or opposite, and the root *sentire*, to feel or think. In other words, dissent can mean to differ in sentiment, feeling, or thought. The OED defines dissent as a verb in a variety of ways. For example, dissent can mean "to withhold assent or consent from a proposal, etc." or "to think differently, disagree, differ *from*, *in* (an opinion), *from*, *with* (a person)." In a theological and religious vein, dissent is "to differ in religious opinion; to differ from the doctrine or worship of a particular church, esp. from that of the established, national, or orthodox church."

This quick review from the Oxford English Dictionary indicates that the various definitions of the term "dissent" describe points of disagreement, the inability to assent to a proposal, or differences regarding worship and/or doctrine. The definitions, however, do not make distinctions between types of concerns and ideas. Likewise, the centrality of the concerns or ideas for a people's identity or belief system does not factor into the definitions.

A distinction exists between dissent on core matters of the faith and disagreements regarding prudential judgments about different courses of action. On the one hand, disagreements abound as to what constitutes reverent liturgical music that fosters prayer. These disagreements are not core matters of faith but rather prudential judgments concerning practices that nurture prayer. Therefore, varying perspectives on liturgical music typically do not push members outside the boundaries of faith. On the other hand, a core Christian belief remains that Jesus Christ is fully human and fully divine. Dissenting from this belief puts the person outside the boundaries of the faith, in heresy.

Within Catholic circles, however, matters of faith, such as the belief that Jesus is Lord, in the incarnation, and in the resurrection, are not issues discussed when considering dissent. Rather, the category dissent is employed most often in Catholic circles regarding theological ideas

---

[6] More specifically, dissent is described as "the practical expression of disagreement with the form of religious worship which prevails or is authoritatively established in any country; nonconformity." This definition is given with references to England and Scotland.

or writings that question or challenge teaching in the arena of morals. Theological ideas or writings can function positively when they question and challenge teachings that are harmful, sinful or hinder the common pursuit of truth: for example, slavery.

Historically, theologians have been part of this clarification process with their writings and their engagements with each other in conversations, discussions, debates, and critical analysis of each other's work.[7] This is not new; even Aquinas's theological method and insights were subject to critique in his lifetime. The fact that many Catholics do not know the theological and intellectual history of the Catholic Church and the role of theologians has been complicated by contemporary realities. Contemporary technology makes more readily available and accessible material that, prior to the internet, took slightly more time to be disseminated or required physical library research. This dissemination includes theological writings along with the analysis of each other's work or magisterial teaching. Gone are the days when deliberations about theological questions at scholarly conferences were limited to the participants who would have had the benefit of ongoing reflection, refinement of arguments, and less public debate where written material might take up to a year or more to appear. Now information about a scholarly conference can appear almost simultaneously with the event through the use of Twitter, online event postings, blog postings, media stories, and a host of other technological venues that push theological investigations into public scrutiny that, while properly the purview of theologians, have a different effect in an era all too often filled with sound bites. The difficulty of this situation is that the time needed to determine what theological ideas bear fruit in practice is shortened.[8]

Since Vatican II, a conversation reemerged regarding the role of the theologian and whether it is to address new questions, bring the faith into new language (ever ancient, ever new), or simply reiterate what the bishops, cardinals, and pope pronounce as teaching.[9] Problems exist with any

---

[7] Fuchs, "Teaching Morality."

[8] See Anthony J. Godzieba's description of how our current approach to time affects our capacity to understand what we do over time. Anthony J. Godzieba, "'. . . And Followed Him on the Way' (Mk 10:52): Identity, Difference, and the Play of Discipleship," *CTSA Proceedings* 69 (2014): 1–22, at 18–20.

[9] See, for example, John Paul II, *Veritatis Splendor*, paragraphs 109–17; John Paul II, *Ex Corde Ecclesiae* (Apostolic Constitution on Catholic Universities), August 15, 1990, paragraph 29, and article 4.3. Fuchs, "Teaching Morality," 330–32, 336–40.

attempt at narrowing the theologian's role to primarily catechesis. New questions emerge faster than the Vatican can address them, and theological research, scholarship, and debate help inform eventual magisterial teaching. Moreover, bishops themselves are not always educated in every area in which they pronounce teachings. They need consultants.[10] For example, Catholic economists in the United States recognizing the need for consultants have formed an advisory board for bishops and Catholic institutions.[11] Their website notes that bishops or anyone availing themselves of this advisory service should survey several economists since there are areas of disagreement within their field. Therefore, talking with a range of economists would give a more rounded picture of the field, the issues, and possible courses of action.

With this background, current context, and nontheological descriptions of dissent in mind, we now turn to theological descriptions regarding the appropriateness of dissent.

Section 2: Avery Dulles and the 1968 United States Bishops

This section uses several sources for exploring the question regarding responsible dissent from magisterial teaching. The first source is Avery Dulles's typology of dissent, which underscores the fact that dissent is considered a possibility resulting from conscience formation around particular issues.[12] Dulles's typology helps moral agents contemplate and discern what style, if any, dissent they will or might use to engage non-infallible (fallible) magisterial teaching.[13] Different purposes and places

---

[10] Karl Rahner explores in several articles what he calls gnoseological concupiscence. Gnoseological concupiscence refers to our inability to synthesize the vast knowledge that exists in the world. This calls for a recognition of the tension between what we do and do not know as well as the need for intellectual humility. See, for example, his articles "Faith between Rationality and Emotion," in *Theological Investigations* 16 (New York: Seabury, 1979), 125–44; "The Current Relationship between Philosophy and Theology," in *Theological Investigations* 13 (New York: Seabury, 1975), 61–79; and "Theology as Engaged in an Interdisciplinary Dialogue with the Sciences," in *Theological Investigations* 13 (New York: Seabury, 1975), 80–93.

[11] For a description of the advisory panel, see http://www.credo-economists.org/advisory-panel/. CREDO is the acronym for the Catholic Research Economists Discussion Organization.

[12] The reader is asked to recall that this type of conscience formation falls under the other headings of moral science, the process of practical judgment, or, as Gula also calls it, moral discernment.

[13] Avery Dulles, "Authority and Conscience: Two Needed Voices in the Church," *Church* 2, no. 3 (1986): 8–15; "Faith and Revelation" in *Systematic Theology: Roman Catholic*

for dissent compel reflection on different consequences and implications by the moral agent. The second source is a 1968 letter by the National Conference of Catholic Bishops.[14] Together, their work provides criteria for responsible dissent while also distinguishing dissent from an inability to live a teaching fully. In other words, a distinction exists between intellectual assent and the lived practice stemming from practical judgments about what is possible in the here and now.

Avery Dulles

One can find Avery Dulles's dissent typology in an article on faith and revelation. He describes revelation as the "process of God's self-disclosure" over time in history and "in an objective sense revelation denotes the fund or 'deposit' of knowledge, insights, and wisdom" from the process of God's self-disclosure.[15] The knowledge, insights, and wisdom found in Scripture and tradition "are transmitted to believers by education in the church, the living community of faith."[16] Because as humans we are finite, it is possible to agree to an incomplete, partially incorrect, or even fully incorrect formulation of revealed truth. Likewise, we might "reject a correct formulation" of revelation.[17] Therefore, we need the community, Scripture, and church doctrine, which help us understand revelation in an "objective sense." In a rich discussion of how revelation is transmitted

---

Perspectives, ed. Francis Schüssler Fiorenza and John P. Galvin, 2nd ed. (Minneapolis, MN: Augsburg Fortress Press, 2011), 79–108. Dissent is discussed on pages 105–6. The first edition of the book, *Systematic Theology* appeared as a two-volume work in 1991. I rely on the second, one-volume edition.

[14] The National Conference of Bishops was established in 1966 along with the United States Catholic Conference. The two groups merged in 2001, becoming the United States Conference of Catholic Bishops (USCCB). See the USCCB's website for a brief history at http://www.usccb.org/about/index.cfm. The bishops' letter raises questions regarding the authority of a letter versus other types of documents from groups of bishops. It also raises thorny questions regarding the validity of a statement when a new group of bishops might disagree with their predecessors. These questions are beyond the scope of this work.

[15] Dulles, "Faith and Revelation," 79–81. These are only two possible descriptions of revelation. Avery Dulles has written on various approaches to revelation in his book *Models of Revelation* (Maryknoll, NY: Orbis Books, 1992). The first edition of the book was published in 1983 by Doubleday & Company, Inc.

[16] Dulles, "Faith and Revelation," 81. Dulles is clear that God's revelation meets its fullness in Jesus Christ, yet God is not silent in our time; God remains active in God's self-communication. This would have implications for understanding that magisterial teaching as the witness to God's reveled truth might be incomplete in some instances.

[17] Ibid., 92.

and the value of tradition, Dulles accounts for how "authentic tradition is to be found not only in formal statements but also in the 'practice and life of the believing and praying Church' (DV 8)."[18] Formal statements include the creed and conciliar documents. The practice and life is where we concretely embody what we profess. It is here that diversity occurs, often leading to disagreement.

Drawing on both the First and Second Vatican Councils, Dulles delineates the role of the Magisterium to teach and proclaim sound doctrine as well as correct movements away from sound doctrine. After discussing the manner in which the Magisterium defines dogma and infallible teaching, Dulles writes "that the vast majority of the Church's official statements are not infallible. They are subject to correction in light of further evidence."[19] Even though much of the teaching is non-infallible, it remains authoritative, requires respect, and carries a "presumption of truth in its favor." This type of assent to potentially correctable statements is distinguished from the assent to core faith statements such as belief in the triune God. Dulles acknowledges that for various reasons a person may not be able to assent to a non-infallible teaching. One reason includes the possibility that in some cases the teaching could be wrong. According to him, it is only after trying to agree with the teaching—subjecting one's position to scrutiny, critique, and assessment—that one may consider options other than assent.[20] According to Dulles, the available options that relate to infallible teaching are submissive silence, private expression of nonacceptance, public expression of nonacceptance, and organized expression of nonacceptance.[21]

The first, submissive silence, is the most confidential and personally private. In the context of this discussion, "submissive" means agreeing to the teaching authority or expertise of the Magisterium. "Silence" means keeping doubt or questions about a teaching to oneself, a nondisclosure to any human being. In keeping one's dissent quiet, the believing person could be bringing his or her difficulties with and concerns about magisterial teaching to God in prayer.

Private expression of nonacceptance is slightly more open than submissive silence while remaining clearly more confidential and less public

[18] Ibid., 102.
[19] Ibid., 105.
[20] Ibid.
[21] Ibid., 106.

than either public expression of nonacceptance or organized expression of nonacceptance. Private expression of nonacceptance occurs when a moral agent speaks to one or several other people to receive help in evaluating challenges, identifying difficulties, and initiating clarification about a magisterial teaching. Private expression of nonacceptance could also take place during spiritual direction, which provides a venue for exploring one's questions and doubts in a safe setting within the context of one's relationship with God. Any private expression permits the individual to examine motives, beliefs, and value systems; gather information; research; consider; and reflect on the causes and warrants of their disagreement with magisterial teaching.

Dulles argues that private expression of nonacceptance can possibly set the stage for a change in magisterial teaching if change is necessary. Given that the Magisterium is the only body that can change or modify teaching, Dulles implicitly seems to presume access to the Magisterium when he claims that private expression of nonacceptance can influence teaching. Most Catholics do not have access to their bishop. Moreover, many Catholics have limited access to their priests who themselves may have limited contact with their bishops.[22]

While typically associated with individuals, submissive silence and private expression of nonacceptance as forms of dissent might and can extend to communities or groups of people as well. One can well imagine a religious community, a community of scholars, or a parish that disagrees with an official magisterial teaching. The religious community, community of scholars, or parish members may decide to remain silent, or they might internally begin a discussion and discernment process for thinking about their next course of action.[23] This could entail a confidential expression of dissent to their local bishop or archbishop. The tricky part of a communal stance is that it might not represent the views held by all members within a given community. Therefore, there may well be submissive silence or private expression of nonacceptance within a particular community related to a communal decision.

---

[22] This also presumes a bishop who is willing to listen to his flock, consider its insights, and not act or speak from unchecked assumptions.

[23] Anne Patrick provides examples of this occurring in her research on women's religious communities. See her *Conscience and Calling: Ethical Reflections on Catholic Women's Church Vocations* (New York and London: Bloomsbury, 2013), where she provides narrative examples throughout the text.

Whether individual or communal, submissive silence and private expression of non-acceptance as options for dissent contain the acknowledgment that magisterial teaching will not receive 100 percent assent by 100 percent of the faithful. On the one hand, by stressing a more confidential private approach to dissent, the presumption and appearance that magisterial teaching is correct is publically preserved and protected. On the other hand, especially with submissive silence, "silence" could be interpreted to mean assent or agreement with magisterial teaching. A person would need to accept this possible consequence. Furthermore, as already noted, depending on the forum where the more private discussion takes place, the moral agent who dissents might not affect or contribute to a possible change or clarification in magisterial teaching. Alternatively, the moral agent would need to accept that if any change in teaching took place it could occur slowly.[24]

The next two modes of dissent that Dulles delineates, public expression of nonacceptance and organized expression of nonacceptance, are definitely more public and open expressions of disagreement/dissent with magisterial teaching. People's motivations for publically expressing disagreement with magisterial teaching will vary. The public nature of dissent reaches a broader and larger audience. Public expression of nonacceptance, by the individual, can take many forms, for example, speeches, letters to the editor, or blog posts.[25] In the case of theologians, scholarship might be a form of public expression of nonacceptance.

Organized public expression of nonacceptance of teaching is a communal or group statement and would include statements or letters signed by multiple people, open-forum meetings, and possibly protests. Dulles argues that public expressions of nonacceptance, especially organized, cause harm. The harm includes weakening the community's witness, breaking the group's unity, and spreading "distrust in the hierarchical magisterium,"[26] and it raises the potential for scandal.

Both types of public expression of dissent are more concerning for the Magisterium because potential for breaking unity does exist. Even while the concern for unity can really be a call for uniformity, the person

---

[24] There is a discussion within some feminist literature about the distinction between private and public spaces. The private domain is never completely private due to our relationships.

[25] See Dulles, "Faith and Revelation," 106.

[26] Ibid.

or group publicly disagreeing needs to be aware of the potential harm to the broader Christian community. Therefore, anyone engaged in a public expression of dissent must consider the risk of misleading the faithful and the manner in which the expression of nonacceptance happens. Dulles's brief description of consequences of public expressions of nonacceptance presupposes their inevitability rather than their existence as potential consequences. Dulles appears more concerned with broader, ecclesial consequences. The individual or group could be sanctioned by the Magisterium. The individual or group could become estranged from family, their local faith community, or, in the case of scholars, the scholarly guild. The faithful, of all occupations, could also engage in hard, difficult conversations, debates, and encounters seeking a deeper understanding of truth.

Even with his concerns for the consequences of public dissent, Dulles does not think it is impermissible; rather, it must be an avenue rarely undertaken. Dulles writes that "public (especially organized) dissent requires special warrants—namely, that the dissenter be firmly convinced that the official teaching, if unopposed, would cause grave harm and that other, less destructive forms of dissent be unavailing."[27] While a good criterion, given the inaccessibility by many to their priests, let alone bishops, public organization might be seen by some of the faithful as one venue by which to be heard. Pope Francis's approach to the 2015 assembly of the synod on the Family, however, might be signaling the potential for a longer-term change in how the bishops listen to the members of their dioceses. The surveys he requested be sent out for feedback prior to the assembly indicate a potentially more open venue for gathering information about the broader church's experiences for the bishops to consider at their meetings. The collaboration on the newest encyclical also models a different method for discussing and teaching about the signs of the times.

Dulles, by using the term "faithful" in his dissent typology, appears to make no distinction premised on types of competency or roles within the church. Richard Gula, however, does make distinctions based on competency or roles within the church. Gula distinguishes between "organized scholarly dissent" and "organized popular dissent." Gula claims that organized popular dissent is "an effort to influence public opinion toward official teaching and to call for the official recognition of an alternative position." Given the dangers Gula sees because of organized

---

[27] Ibid.

popular dissent, including popular perspectives functioning as a rival to the Magisterium, he contends that the Magisterium "cannot tolerate this form of dissent in the ways that it tolerates the other forms."[28] This would apply to Catholics of all types.

According to Gula, organized scholarly dissent is tolerable. The example Gula provides is a scholarly professional conference called to engage a magisterial teaching and propose "a critical response" to the teaching. Gula argues that this scholarly professional theological activity remains "indispensable to the learning-teaching process in the church."[29] Given his argument, the possibility that all critical engagement with magisterial texts could be considered dissent exists and makes sense only if one uses a definition of dissent as disagreement, as outlined earlier from the Oxford English Dictionary. If dissent is seen as problematic, however, then Gula's argument lends itself to understanding many forms of theological inquiry as breaking unity with the Magisterium. This returns the risk of creeping infallibility and a diminishment of the theologian's role to buttressing and explaining magisterial teaching rather than inquiring about the validity of truth claims.

Given the difference Gula notes between organized scholarly and popular dissent, he further argues that dissent and the criteria for responsible dissent should be limited to "people trained in making sophisticated theological distinctions" or, stated differently, to "someone truly competent in the appropriate field." As a result, Gula contends, "the further one moves from internal to public, organized dissent, the greater the competence required."[30]

Gula's further delineations within the categories of dissent presented by Dulles are helpful for yielding useful rejoinders regarding roles within the church. Gula's caution about organized public dissent makes sense. If no tolerance for organized public dissent exists, however, a potential venue for speaking and being heard is sealed off. How does the Magisterium understand or know if the faithful assent to their teaching if there are no venues to gauge reception? Furthermore, if all Catholics choose submissive silence as their answer to disagreement with the Magisterium, how do we understand the role of the *sensus fidelium*?

---

[28] Gula, *Reason Informed by Faith*, 212.
[29] Ibid.
[30] Ibid., 208–9, 211.

Thus far, Dulles and Gula assume several things in the movement to "dissent." They expect that the person has undertaken a serious effort to assent to magisterial teaching. A rigorous examination of the teaching has been done. The person can articulate the reasons for dissent as well as reasons why the need for dissent overrides possible harmful consequences. The person recognizes that magisterial teaching holds a presumption of truth. The claim that the teaching holds the presumption of truth can be troubling because of historical examples when the church was plain wrong, for example, about slavery and the belief that women were inferior beings or defective males. Furthermore, the institutional church has been and can remain too embedded with the political powers of the times. So, even with the presumption that the teaching is true, if one has doubts and misgivings about a teaching, he or she can explore why the doubts exist. Hence the importance of the formation of conscience (the moral agent), as examined earlier. Finally, Dulles and Gula both acknowledge that since the majority of magisterial statements are non-infallible teachings, the teachings could be wrong and therefore may permit dissent (disagreement).[31]

Given that I live, work, and write in the United States, the guidance and instruction provided by the United States Bishops is where I turn next. The guidance comes from the 1968 group of US bishops.

The 1968 US Bishops' Letter

In November 1968, the US bishops issued a letter titled *Human Life in Our Day*.[32] The pastoral letter's focus "is precisely the doctrine and defense of life" written as a "response to the threat to life in certain problems of the family and war and peace."[33] Part 1 takes up the encyclical *Humanae Vitae*, looking at marriage, family, and birth control. Part 2 considers issues raised by the arms race, the international community's responsibility to promote peace and remove the threat of war, and conscientious objection to Vietnam and other wars.[34] The US bishops follow *Gaudium et Spes* in affirming that a concern for life encompasses a range of issues and that conscience works within a variety of spheres.

---

[31] See ibid., 207–12. Gula provides additional explanation of these points.

[32] National Conference of Catholic Bishops, *Human Life in Our Day: A Collective Pastoral Letter of the American Hierarchy* (Washington, DC: The Conference, 1968).

[33] Ibid., 5.

[34] Ibid., 30–45.

Their letter starts by describing the Christian family, along with the family's role, mission, and call to responsible parenthood. The bishops then turn to the encyclical *Humanae Vitae* where they cover the encyclical's content, the encyclical and conscience, and negative reactions to the encyclical. Several points are key before turning to what the 1968 US bishops say about dissent. They uphold and "proclaim" the doctrine in *Humanae Vitae* on contraception.[35] In the section on conscience, with references to Vatican II and Aquinas, they reiterate the idea that conscience operates in the realm of practical judgments, "not [as] a teacher of doctrine."[36] In other words, conscience does not teach or arrive at a teaching. Conscience makes determinations about the application of a teaching.

For example, a married couple could assent to the teaching on contraception while not always living the teaching because of a conscientious judgment. In these instances, the 1968 US bishops do not equate the use of contraceptives with dissent. Rather, they see the marital use of contraceptives as a failure to live up to the ideals encapsulated in magisterial teaching. The 1968 bishops acknowledge that "married couples faced with conflicting duties are often caught in agonizing crises of conscience" and that circumstances might mitigate moral culpability.[37] The bishops state that "they feel bound to remind Catholic married couples" that the married couples cannot "deny the objective evil of artificial contraception." Married couples who use contraception are counseled and encouraged to continue availing themselves of the sacraments of penance and Eucharist to receive strength, grace, and healing.[38]

The bishops also consider how a US citizen who is drafted could conscientiously object to the Vietnam war. They reference the tradition of evaluating whether a war is just, the Gospel message, and *Gaudium et Spes* for how a person could object to being drafted. They also say any reduction in war might result from the witness of the conscientious objectors. The bishops also say that the dangers and realities of war require "conversion" and the need for us to think about human life, the worth of humans, and our dignity with fresh recognition.[39] Furthermore, in both instances, the

---

[35] Ibid., 12.

[36] Ibid., 14.

[37] Ibid., 15–16. The quotation can be found on page 15. The bishops also state that neither they nor others can judge the good faith of these decisions of conscience; however, the faithful cannot be arbitrary in decisions of conscience.

[38] Ibid., 16.

[39] Ibid., 42–45. at 45.

bishops permit appeals to conscience as exercises in practical judgments. In one, the norm is upheld, while conscience renders with difficulty a different practical judgment. In the other, societal norms and laws are challenged due to conscientious objections to certain worldviews. If the 1968 bishops do not see either instance of a conscientious judgment as theological dissent, what constitutes theological dissent?

The 1968 bishops see dissent operating at the level of professional theological work. For them, dissent remains possible resulting from research and inquiry of thought on matters of fallible teaching. By recognizing licit and responsible dissent, the bishops implicitly condemn illicit and irresponsible dissent. They also create space for valid theological disagreement with fallible teaching. This valid theological disagreement requires norms, which the 1968 bishops provide in the section of their letter titled "Norms of Licit Theological Dissent."[40] The norms cover three general areas: the theologian's relationship with the Magisterium, responsibility in relationship to the whole Body of Christ, and intellectual concerns.

The norms pertaining to the theologian's relationship with the Magisterium require that the theologian retain "a presumption in favor of the Magisterium" because all teaching "remains binding" when addressed to the whole church, even if development, clarification, or revision might be needed. The scholar must distinguish between the degrees of authority of teachings since teachings do not carry the same weight, magnitude, or implication for the life of faith. Some teachings might be rooted in cultural constraints that no longer apply.[41]

In addition, the theologian in their dissent cannot impugn or question the teaching authority of the Magisterium. It is important to note that these norms allow a theologian to disagree or question the magisterial teaching but not the Magisterium's role as teacher of the faith. Unfortunately, the theologian's role as investigator into the validity of norms based on their theological foundations is too often seen as impugning the Magisterium's teaching authority or not presenting the teaching faithfully.

The norms involving intellectual pursuits rest on the premise that theological inquiry and research are important. It is when research leads a scholar to dissent that the norms become pertinent. Theological dissent must be well founded to account for the seriousness of the matter. Any alternative perspective is to be proposed "with prudence born of intellectual

---

[40] Ibid., 18–19.
[41] For a discussion of cultural constraints, see Gula, *Reason Informed by Faith*, 209.

grace and a Christian confidence that the truth is great and will prevail."[42] This concerns only matters of a non-infallible nature. Unfortunately, the 1968 bishops do not expound or develop what constitutes well-founded reasons for theological dissent.

The theological scholar must be aware of and respect the conscience of those who do not have his or her expertise or time for thoughtful, careful inquiry.[43] This requires awareness of the need for increasing competence when considering dissent. In other words, how does a theologian's scholarship affect those who do not have the requisite knowledge, skill set, or access to training to make decisions or judgments regarding particular teachings? Furthermore, the dissent should not cause scandal. The concern here is the unity of the church. Therefore, the theologian must be sensitive to division and aware of the dangers of breaking unity. Nonetheless, this criterion is exceedingly hard to meet since silence about a magisterial teaching can also create scandal. The next chapter explores this issue surrounding scandal in more detail.

The 1968 bishops observe that one sign of the times is "popular interest in theological debate." The popular interest in theological debate combined with the "realities of mass media" have the bishops recommending that they and theologians engage in "fruitful dialogue" to consider how to navigate "the ways in which theological dissent may be effectively expressed, in a manner consistent with pastoral solicitude."[44] The 1968 bishops seemed to expect and see a place for responsible theological dissent from theologians as well as the need to be in conversation about ways to discuss and express theological dissent. This almost fifty-year-old call to fruitful dialogue between bishops and theologians is more pressing today with the rapidly changing realities of twenty-first-century mass media. The 1968 bishops remind scholars that responsible dissent does not absolve them from faithfully presenting "authentic doctrine of the Church when one is performing a pastoral ministry in Her name."[45] In making a distinction here between the science of theology and pastoral ministry, they draw attention to the different roles and functions within the Body of Christ. Theological speculation and research is not the same as pastoral ministry, even as theology informs and effects pastoral ministry based

---

[42] *Human Life in Our Day*, 18.
[43] Ibid., 18–19.
[44] Ibid., 18.
[45] Ibid., 19.

on magisterial teaching. Furthermore, we are pressed to remember that dissent functions at the level of theological propositions. Conscience in this framework can yield practical judgments about living church teaching that do not necessarily equal theological dissent.

The criteria set forth by Dulles and Gula align, then, with the 1968 US bishops' norms for licit theological dissent. They show that theological dissent is not new. There is a place for theological disagreement. Some theologians have been silenced in the past and present, and others will be in the future. Other theologians have not been silenced, while in many instances the work of silenced theologians have later been rehabilitated in the church's intellectual tradition, history, and teaching. These facts requires theologians pondering dissent from magisterial teaching to discern the cost of both dissent and remaining silent. Both dissent from and assent to magisterial teaching have costs. Any assent to a teaching consists of both an affirmation (a yes to something) and a negation (a no to something else). The same holds true for dissent. It contains both a negation (a rejection of something) and an affirmation (an implicit yes to something else). Therefore, an individual or a community must always consider what they are affirming and negating. What values, beliefs, or commitments constitute the stronger pull toward either assent or dissent and why.[46]

Given the toxicity of many theological disputes today, additional dispositional criteria seem pertinent when thinking and talking about dissent. We must continue to see others as members of the Body of Christ. We must not treat others with malice or demonize those with whom we disagree. There cannot be a caricature of another's arguments or magisterial teaching. In other words, seeking truth requires giving other arguments, including magisterial teaching, a fair reading. Rather than seeing ourselves as theological adversaries, we must see ourselves as partners in a common endeavor, seeking truth for living the Gospel as disciples. This necessitates that we be honest about our mixed motivations as well as both strengths and the weaknesses in our positions. Likewise, it means recognizing the

---

[46] Margaret Farley explores in several of her writings the conflict moral agents experience when values, beliefs, and commitments conflict. While not directly addressing dissent or assent, her work is illuminating. See Margaret Farley, *Personal Commitments: Beginning, Keeping, Changing* (San Francisco: Harper and Row, 1986); and "Freedom and Desire," in *The Papers of the Henry Luce III Fellows in Theology*, ed. Matthew Zyniewicz (Atlanta, GA: Scholars Press, 1999), 57–73.

strengths and weaknesses in other positions. This would permit the theological and faith community to keep the pursuit of truth central.

Several questions emerge from this discussion regarding the validity of norms or criteria for responsible licit dissent within the tradition. If responsible dissent is the purview of theologians, does this mean the rest of the faithful are re-relegated to a passive mode of engagement with magisterial teaching? Do we diminish the Second Vatican Council's call for greater moral responsibility on the part of the whole Body of Christ? Furthermore, focusing on doctrinal assent or dissent does not help the people of God navigate differences in practical judgments that result in a plurality of practices within the ecclesial community. This is especially true when no careful distinction is made between doctrinal teaching concerning central tenets of the faith (what is to be believed) and teaching regarding morals (what is to be lived and practiced).

Lingering in the background and still influencing much of the thinking and activity about dissent (disagreement) is *Humanae Vitae*, promulgated almost fifty years ago. Back in 1987, John Mahoney shed light on why this encyclical has framed so many theological considerations when he wrote, "Above all, however, *Humanae Vitae* constituted the first major test for the post-conciliar church and for the various 'opening's which the Second Vatican Council had introduced to the Church's thinking and activity."[47] This test yielded many of the issues in ecclesiology and moral theology that plague us today. To understand the test and its effective history, some background is necessary.

Prior to the council, the question had arisen regarding the feasibility of changing the Roman Catholic Church's position on contraceptives. Many Catholics hoped that the council would change the teaching on the use of contraceptives.[48] Rather than permit the council to more definitively address methods of birth control in a conciliar document, however, Pope

---

[47] John Mahoney, *The Making of Moral Theology: A Study of the Roman Catholic Tradition* (Oxford: Clarendon Press, 1987), 300.

[48] The question regarding whether the Catholic Church's teaching on birth control will change is once again in the limelight. Many hope the assembly of the synod of Bishops on the Family called by Pope Francis will bring about development in Roman Catholic teaching. Even as the assembly is considering a range of concerns related to family life, attention to contraception demonstrates that although the teaching has remained constant (no chemical or prophylactic methods of birth control) since 1968, many Catholics hope that the teaching will change. The fact that many Catholics still follow what is happening in their church and hope for changes in teaching indicates that many, if not most, Catholics still

Paul VI exercised his papal authority and removed the discussion on con-traception from the conciliar agenda. Instead, Paul VI put together what has been called the Birth Control Commission to study the question.[49]

The commission members wrote two reports. One report favored changing the teaching. The other report favored maintaining the church's teaching. Paul VI's encyclical *Humanae Vitae*, published in 1968, drew on both reports. The encyclical is known as the birth control encyclical in many circles, even as it provides a vision of Christian marriage grounded in a renewed understanding of the unitive and procreative dimensions of marriage.[50] It receives its moniker as the birth control encyclical because in it Paul VI upheld the ban on all types of birth control labeled "artificial contraception." Paul VI affirmed Natural Family Planning (NFP) as an acceptable method of spacing or preventing pregnancies.

When Paul VI upheld the teaching prohibiting the use of chemical, technological, or prophylactic means of birth control, it sent ripples through the ecclesial community where many expected change. The posi-tive teaching regarding the validity of Natural Family Planning was seen

---

recognize and respect the teaching authority of the Magisterium. Engaged disagreement is different from apathy or outright disregard of most anything taught by the Magisterium.

[49] *Gaudium et Spes*, discussing birth regulation, says that Catholics "are forbidden to use methods disapproved of by the teaching authority of the church in its interpretation of the divine law" (51). The conciliar writers cite Pius XI's *Casti Connubii*, published in 1930, where he prohibits the use of methods that frustrate the conjugal act. In 1930, the most common method of birth control was the prophylactic (condom). *GS* also cites Pius XII's 1951 address to midwives where he states that making use of the infertile periods of a woman's cycle to regulate birth was permissible under certain circumstances. The pill or hormonal regulation as a form of birth control was not even possible until the mid-1950s. The conciliar members were aware that Paul VI put together a commission to study the question of the family, population, and birth regulation as they wrote *GS* 51. Thus, the questions raised at the Second Vatican Council regarding birth regulation were responding to various concerns regarding population control and recent developments in birth regu-lation. The literature on *Humanae Vitae* is vast and varied. For a variety of views, see this limited selection of material: Joseph A. Selling, *The Reaction to* Humanae Vitae: *A Study in Special and Fundamental Theology* (Ann Arbor, MI: University Microfilms International, 1979); Janet E. Smith, "The *Sensus Fidelium* and '*Humanae Vitae*,'" in *Called to Holiness and Communion: Vatican II on the Church* (Scranton, PA: University of Scranton Press, 2009), 291–319; William E. May, et al., *The Teaching of* Humanae Vitae: *A Defense* (San Francisco: Ignatius Press, 1988); Karl Rahner, "On the Encyclical *Humanae Vitae*," in *Theological Investigations*, vol. 11, trans. David Bourke (New York: Seabury, 1974), 263–87.

[50] For most of my students, the debates and fights that surround *Humanae Vitae*'s promulgation is history they study. They come to class, however, bearing the assumptions and prejudices from this history about the encyclical. Since most of them have never read the encyclical, they are inevitably surprised that it covers more than birth control.

as progress by some and insufficient by others.[51] For many, the question arose regarding what to do if one judged in conscience that a birth regulation method other than Natural Family Planning was a necessary practice for any number of moral reasons. Could a married couple in conscience make a decision contrary to magisterial teaching? The questions raised by married couples regarding birth control meant that theologians teaching in universities and parish priests working with their parishioners had questions to answer and research.[52]

Responses did and still do vary to these questions. Few, if any, theologians contested or contest that consideration of birth regulation (control) was and remains a moral concern. The fact that so many married Catholics, those most affected by the magisterial teaching, waited for, desired, and considered the papal teaching in 1968 speaks volumes about the seriousness with which couples considered how to live their marital sexuality. Despite public perception, this is still the case today. Yet, the early debates and their implications around *Humanae Vitae* reverberate almost fifty years after its publication.[53] In some circles, positions on birth control function as a litmus test of one's faithfulness and Catholicity, contradicting a richly textured approach to a moral life, morality, and

[51] Natural Family Planning (NFP) is not the same thing as what many remember as the rhythm method. Natural Family Planning has become more sophisticated over the years, using new scientific information to help explain the fertility cycle and make NFP's methods more effective. See http://www.usccb.org/issues-and-action/marriage-and-family/natural-family-planning/.

[52] The investigation and dismissal of theologian Charles Curran from his teaching responsibilities at The Catholic University of America is one instance of how the questions, possible answers, and magisterial responses stemming from *Humanae Vitae* played out. See, for example, Anne Patrick's analysis in *Liberating Conscience: Feminist Explorations in Catholic Moral Theology* (New York: Continuum, 1996), 108–18. See also, Curran and McCormick, *Dissent in the Church*, 357–539. These pages, in *Dissent in the Church*, contain various essays in a section titled "The Curran Case and Its Aftermath."

[53] In his analysis of the debates and controversies surrounding *Humanae Vitae*'s publication, John Mahoney discusses the effects on our understanding and consideration of conscience, dissent, magisterial authority, collegiality in the church, and the "function of reason, prophecy, and moral insight." See John Mahoney, "The Impact of *Humanae Vitae*," in *The Making of Moral Theology*, 259–301. For a recent book that places the conversation and debates about *Humane Vitae* in a broader context, looking at the social, political, and personal effects of violence, sex, and power, see Aline H. Kalbian, *Sex, Violence, and Justice: Contraception and the Catholic Church* (Washington, DC: Georgetown University Press, 2014).

discipleship within the tradition.[54] Questions about dissent, magisterial authority, the role of theologians, the voices of the faithful, where moral agency resides, among other issues, arose and were contested in the aftermath of *Humanae Vitae.*

Nevertheless, Mahoney also wondered back in 1987 if "out of this considerable disarray of moral theology, as part of the impact of *Humanae Vitae*, it may be that what was struggling to emerge was a deeper insight into the function of moral theology and a glimpse of theological pluralism behind the diversity of moral behavior."[55] If Mahoney is correct, can a way be found to hold both the validity of magisterial teaching regarding norms for behavior and a theological pluralism supporting a diversity of moral behavior stemming from various interpretations of the same norm?[56] More specifically, is a diversity of practices permitted within the Body of Christ?

Section 3: Disentangling Dissent and Practical Judgments toward Valid Theological Practices

As seen in the last section, conversations about responsible dissent take us only so far. Unanswered are the questions of whether a plurality of practices for living out norms and magisterial teaching automatically equates to dissent. Is it possible for us to understand a plurality of practices as pointing to various instantiations of a norm?

This section employs the work of two theologians to explore what might be happening when people of faith disagree with the ecclesial

---

[54] For example, Archbishop Oscar Romero was recently declared a martyr by Pope Francis for his opposition to political oppression that eventually led to his death. This announcement highlights that living a life of discipleship and a moral life requires more than following the teaching on contraception. Also, the effective history surrounding birth control coupled with the past decades' revelations about the extent of the sex abuse crisis contributes to the Magisterium's limited effectiveness in speaking authoritatively on other moral matters such as immigration, poverty, capital punishment, and war, among others.

[55] Mahoney, *The Making of Moral Theology*, 301.

[56] Julia Hanlon Rubio, in an article trying to get around the impasse about contraception, found that despite different contraceptive practices, common ground existed for understanding marital sexuality and the purposes of marriage among married couples. She does not take up the issue in the way I frame it here. Yet her article illuminates the possibility for considering how common ideals, beliefs, and commitments actually can yield different practices in concrete situations. See Julie Hanlon Rubio, "Beyond the Liberal/Conservative Divide on Contraception: The Wisdom of Practitioners of Natural Family Planning and Artificial Birth Control," *Horizons* 32, no. 2 (September 1, 2005): 270–94.

teaching body, the Magisterium, regarding practices stemming from practical judgments. Thomas Kopfensteiner applies various aspects from the philosophical schools of metaphor and hermeneutics to argue for a metaphorical structure to normativity.[57] Normativity means the guiding standards, usually articulated but sometimes unarticulated, that structure a community's life. His conception of normativity as metaphorical permits the norm to stand while addressing new situations in new contexts. Theologian and philosopher Anthony J. Godzieba uses music theory to argue that identity and difference, unity and diversity, can be held together in the church. It is this claim that holds promise for recasting questions around dissent.[58] More specifically, his work has implications for comprehending divergent applications of the normative moral standards within the community while recognizing that only some may ultimately be judged good.

Thomas Kopfensteiner

As noted above, Thomas Kopfensteiner argues for a metaphorical structure to normativity using the work of philosophers of metaphor. Paul Ricoeur has several insights that he argues are particularly "relevant for moral reflection." Kopfensteiner states:

> First is the appreciation of metaphor as a revelatory mode of discourse, revealing "a proposed world, a world I may inhabit and wherein I can project my ownmost possibilities." Second is the creative and imaginative role of metaphor, whereby a new epistemic access to the world is achieved when significant features of the world are carried over, appropriated, and transformed in light of another.[59]

In other words, the norm reveals something about the world or reality I live in that I recognize, a world in which I can imagine possibilities for living my life. Metaphor's creative and imaginative role reveals new knowledge about the world. The new knowledge occurs because various aspects of the world become realigned and understood differently in relationship to

---

[57] Thomas R. Kopfensteiner, "The Metaphorical Structure of Normativity," *Theological Studies* 58, no. 2 (June 1, 1997): 331–46.

[58] Anthony J. Godzieba, "'. . . And Followed Him on the Way' (Mk 10:52): Identity, Difference, and the Play of Discipleship," *CTSA Proceedings* 69 (2014): 1–22.

[59] Kopfensteiner, "The Metaphorical Structure of Normativity," 335–36. The Ricoeur quote that Kopfensteiner cites is from Paul Ricoeur, *Essays in Biblical Interpretation*, ed. Lewis Mudge (Philadelphia: Fortress, 1980), 102.

each other when described poetically or metaphorically. Stated differently, metaphors both reveal and conceal something about the reality or truth they are describing. By their poetic construction metaphors can help us see things we did not see before. In this way, metaphors reveal. Their meaning is never exhausted, however, and metaphors remain open to new interpretations or insights about the world. Therefore, the metaphors are always incomplete or conceal insights about the world.

Kopfensteiner's concern in making the case that a metaphorical structure to normativity exists stems from his analysis that some conceptions of natural law are too static, reifying some norms' meaning, and thus rendering those norms ineffective in new situations. Kopfensteiner seeks a way to retain natural law's validity (and norms) while also finding a way for the norms to be relevant in new situations. In his approach, normative standards establish limits and reveal in their formulation insights into a community's expectations of freedom (possibilities for living life well in response to God) and behavior. Like metaphors, however, normative claims have a concealing feature. There is an element of indeterminacy to them. Furthermore, because normative statements conceal, they also require interpretation. As a result, "moral reasoning has an active, imaginative, and a creative role in fashioning human goods in the service of the ideology of human fulfillment."[60] In other words, we do not just passively receive the norms. We must arrive at, understand, and apply a norm in various situations in our lives within the confines of how we understand human fulfillment. The Christian understands human fulfillment within the call to discipleship and ultimate union with God.

In summary, a metaphorical structure to normativity means that the norm's meaning is always unfolding. The norm reveals and illuminates particular applications. As such, the norm structures our sense of meaning, our worldview, and behaviors in particular ways. At the same time, the norm can be said to conceal the fullness of its meaning. The possibility of new applications of the norm exists because not all situations for employing the norm have been encountered. New eras or situations possibly require new applications of the norm. In this way, we see that the norm's meaning is not exhaustive. Notice that the norm persists continuing to structure and shape a worldview along with possibilities for acting, even as the sphere of application and its meaning expand.

---

[60] Kopfensteiner, "The Metaphorical Structure of Normativity," 339.

Anthony Godzieba

Using a variety of sources Anthony Godzieba argues that "a *performance hermeneutic* is the most adequate way to discern the truth and the underlying logic of the Christian tradition, which is an ensemble of practices, beliefs, and reflections."[61] In other words, we comprehend the Christian tradition by living it, by practicing it, and, in so doing, we know more fully what it is we profess. In the living of the Christian tradition, we are also engaging in an interpretative activity, incarnating the Gospel message anew in different times and places. While Godzieba's goal is to provide an explanation for how unity and diversity coexist in the church, I believe his work has implications for moral theology.

Godzieba uses Bach's *Goldberg Variations* as an example of how there can be variation and unity at the same time within Christianity. Godzieba details how Bach has a foundational bass line interpreted and appearing in over "thirty *different* melodies." The melodies differ but build and follow the "harmonic logic of the bass line." Godzieba uses this fact to argue that "The New Testament's christological claim and its call to discipleship have the same function as the *Goldbergs'* bass line: they provide the unifying background shaping impetus to the varied lived experiences of Christian life throughout the centuries."[62] What this means is that while we recall the origins of Christianity by attending to the practices of Jesus of Nazareth we must incarnate those practices again since we live in a different time and place.

Continuing the musical analysis, Godzieba argues that Christianity is like music. It is not enough to have the musical score (propositions); the score must be played (practices, performances, behaviors) in time and space. Because of varied places, times, and audiences, different performances of the same score exist. Likewise, with Christianity, propositions by themselves are not enough. Christianity must be lived in time and space, and thus, how we live (perform) and interpret the tradition "discloses the past's future possibilities to be discerned, actualized, made effective, and savored."[63] Therefore, both context and temporality matter for comprehending Christian discipleship.

[61] Godzieba, "'. . . And Followed Him on the Way,'" 7.
[62] Ibid., 16.
[63] Ibid., 8.

Like music that is always positioned in a particular era, responding to that era's concerns, discipleship is lived in particular places in particular historical periods. Music is also played out over time; it must be performed.[64] Likewise, "embodied discipleship is constituted and developed individually and communally only over real time."[65] We live our discipleship; we "perform" on a daily basis, minute by minute, our discipleship. This means that our understanding of the tradition, its practices, and what discipleship means are limited by our "temporal horizon." We cannot see all the "performances" of Christian discipleship; nor can we see the future contours or situations whereby we will be asked to live, "perform," our discipleship. By way of example, we can see the way our local parish celebrates Eucharist. We do not see all the various ways other parishes celebrate the Eucharist, or the ways the Eucharist has been celebrated over the centuries. Variations in eucharistic practices exist.

What we eventually realize is that there exists an authentic diversity of how discipleship is lived over time, grounded in a tradition that "never loses sight of its origins in the practices of Jesus of Nazareth and his followers." Moreover, through the diversity present in tradition, the means exist for new or altered "performances" or practices in the future, grounded in and dependent on the past.[66] Unity and diversity can coexist since they are part of the same reality of discipleship. The Scriptures capture this unity and diversity in the gospels and elsewhere.

Godzieba's arguments for unity and diversity within the church have implications for moral theology. Moral norms or standards for behavior must be rooted in the practices of Jesus and his followers. While the practices remain the same, however, their instantiation might vary in different times and places. For example, people of every era must seek justice, but justice depends on what injustices exist in different eras. Hospitality, even as it is a key Benedictine practice, looks different in various Benedictine communities.

---

[64] Ibid., 17.

[65] Ibid., 18. Godzieba's comprehension of this real time has a certain nonlinear dimensionality to it. Theologically embodied discipleship understood as practices and behaviors of the church means that the church inhabits past, present, and future concurrently. Any performance includes the past, how the past is implemented in the present, with an eschatological dimension to it. The same can be said for moral behavior (practices). They build on the past, require appropriation in the present, and point toward a more just future because of their incompleteness due to our finitude.

[66] Ibid., 17.

Godzieba's work, when applied to moral theology, means we can have a bass line operating in the background that shapes and structures a variety of normative interpretations of what discipleship and good moral living look like. The bass line is the universal norm that structures and supports a worldview, shaping possibilities for acting and living a life of discipleship. Examples of a bass line would be "pray without ceasing." The variations in musical scores supported by the bass line interpret, give texture to, nuance, and embody what it means to pray in practice. While variations or types of prayer exist, they remain prayer.

Possible Applications

We see Kopfensteiner's and Godzieba's frameworks at play when considering the normative concept of human dignity. The belief that human dignity resides in the human person's being created in the image and likeness of God is a foundational Christian claim (norm or bass line). The actual practice of treating all human persons with dignity, however, has varied over time (interpretations and variations). In the United States we did not always see or treat people of color as full human beings; at one point in our history they were classified as two-thirds human beings. Women were not always given the same rights as men. As a result, human dignity as a norm for structuring our encounters with each other has not been fully realized at all times in history. Only over time did the United States come, at least in theory, to recognize that "all men are created equal" includes all men and women of varying colors, backgrounds, and countries. The norm's meaning was expanded in light of new insights and analysis of experience. It was determined over time that some variations on the norm, those that functioned to oppress and exclude, were not valid interpretations of the bass line. Therefore, we see that applications and interpretations of norms are subject to criticism and their validity evaluated.

The frameworks could also be applied to *Humanae Vitae*'s teaching on contraception. This specific teaching is based on the teaching that marriage is both unitive and procreative. Using the insights from a metaphorical structure of normativity, we see that the more general norm—marriage is unitive and procreative—reveals something about marriage. Yet the norm conceals specifics about what unitive and procreative means. Thus, the norm requires interpretation and a practical judgment about how a marriage is to be unitive and procreative.

The teaching on contraception makes a statement about how to live marital unity and procreativity. In this example, disagreement revolves around the specifics of living the unitive and procreative dimensions of marriage. There is no dispute about the underlying claim of marriage's unitive and procreative goods. The disagreement revolves around varying interpretations about how to apply and live a more general norm. This would be a matter of varying practical judgments.

Using the same example but applying Godzieba's performance hermeneutic to the teaching on contraception reveals that the foundational claim about the unitive and procreative goods of marriage operating in the background, the bass line if you will, is often ignored. The varied performances (interpretations) of this bass line (how to live the unitive and procreative aspects of marriage) receive most or all of the attention in one specific area. When considering varying practices limiting pregnancy, a performance hermeneutic challenges the moral theologian to view these practices not as necessarily violating the norm but as possible viable variations. Godzieba's performance hermeneutic approach allows for time, time to reflect and see the fruits of the lived reality of the norm's interpretation. Our judgments regarding the validity of various interpretations can be more informed when we take time to properly assess the effects of those interpretations. This requires honest, frank conversations with people living various practices built on listening and learning from others.

Drawing attention back to the bass line about marriage as unitive and procreative and its interpretation in various scores permits a reimagining of how to live marriage in practice. Julie Hanlon Rubio models what practices support the fullness of a narrative about marriage in her work on marital and family ethics. Moving beyond marital sexual ethics, she explores and examines practices around eating, tithing, serving, and praying in the context of family and marital ethics.[67] In doing so, she provides new possibilities for envisioning family and marital life as a context for embodying Christian discipleship focused on practices (praying, eating, tithing, and service) that shape family life and engagement with the world.

Together Kopfensteiner and Godzieba provide possible pathways for conceiving different applications of norms, or different interpretations of truth claims, without falling into a binary framework pitting individual

---

[67] Julie Hanlon Rubio, *Family Ethics: Practices for Christians* (Washington, DC: Georgetown University Press, 2010).

consciences against magisterial authority. They offer the possibility of maintaining common commitments to universal norms while protecting the need to continue dialogue regarding the application of those norms in people's practices.

Their work helps us see that several alternative possibilities exist to one operative framework that labels all disagreement with magisterial teaching about practical matters dissent, whereby dissent in this instance means an unfaithful Catholic. The first alternative is that differing practices and applications or interpretations of a norm (or teaching) indicate an adaptation to new situations. The second alternative is that different interpretations of the norm do not necessarily negate the norm itself or even overturn prior interpretations. It could be that multiple interpretations and practices might need to sit alongside each other as authentic truth instantiations of the norm or teaching. The third alternative is that time is needed to separate the wheat from the weeds in order to discern what constitutes authentic practices or practical judgments.

The analysis about new possibilities for acting recalls various New Testament passages where Jesus, his disciples, and the early church upheld, nuanced, interpreted differently, ignored, or reappropriated various teachings regarding behavior. While a more detailed scriptural analysis cannot be undertaken at the moment, a few examples will suffice. Jesus ate with various groups of people who were considered unfit to dine with. He had intellectual exchanges with the Sadducees and Pharisees, giving us a way of looking at the role of intellectual engagement with the tradition. The woman with the hemorrhage reached out, touched Jesus, a man, and broke taboos about cleanliness. Jesus was taken aback; he noted someone touched him uninvited, and still he healed her. The Acts of the Apostles provides us with martyrs, beheadings, healing in front of the synagogue, as well as the preaching at the acropolis using Greek philosophy to try to persuade the Gentiles that Jesus was Lord. These stories in Acts shed light on what living in the Holy Spirit might bring forth. Responding the Holy Spirit's call to proclaim the Gospel in word and deed might bring personal death, healing, and new life on earth, or even the need to adapt the Gospel message for a new audience.

Conclusion

My purpose for this chapter was to rethink dissent. In so doing, my hope was to provide theological space and rationale to remove the polarizing reaction to and use of the term. Additionally, I hoped to distinguish dissent about core beliefs of the faith, and foundational principles of the faith community for morality, from disagreements regarding practical judgments for action, behaviors, and practices. In order to facilitate a more common understanding of dissent, definitions for the term "dissent" were given. This was followed by an examination of Cardinal Avery Dulles and the 1968 US bishops on dissent.

Six key insights emerged in this chapter. One, that dissent has historically had an appropriate place within the community of moral deliberation within the ecclesial body. Two, the term "dissent" does not adequately capture what occurs at the nexus of magisterial teaching and practical judgments by the faithful regarding how to live and interpret magisterial teaching in all situations. Three, that to properly understand the relationship between magisterial teaching and the faithful's interpretation requires new frameworks for analysis. Four, interpretations of the more general norm are often matters of practical judgments regarding practices and not disparagement of the Magisterium's teaching authority; nor are they necessarily dissent from ecclesial teaching. Five, divergent and plural practices might be valid applications of more general norms. The underlying more general norm holds, even as different applications arise. Thus, time is required for ongoing reflection, analysis, and dialogue about which practices are valid interpretations of the norm.

Finally, theological dissent is not to be undertaken lightly. If one dissents from ecclesial teaching, then the type of dissent must be considered. Each type—submissive silence, private expression of nonacceptance, public expression of nonacceptance, and organized expression of nonacceptance—has strengths and limitations. In addition to dissent type, various criteria for dissent must be met. This means that dissenting must be based on more than a feeling or unreflected-upon experience. The moral agent must undergo a discernment and decision-making process before dissenting. Included in the criteria for dissent was the criterion to avoid or minimize scandal. This concern to avoid or minimize scandal requires more examination in light of the call to live out our relationship with God, as Christian disciples. Discipleship has certain practices that would be scandalous to others who do not share the Christian worldview. Moreover, any concern for scandal must grapple with the scandal of the cross and its implications for Christian discipleship and practices. This is the task of the next chapter.

Chapter 5

Scandal, Discipleship, and the Cross

Introduction

The discussion in chapter 4 raised concern about scandal as a potential outcome of dissent. Scandal needs to be placed within a larger context than as a deal breaker for quieting disagreement with magisterial teaching. Scandal needs to be put in the broader context of the Christian faith and, more specifically, the scandal of the cross and Christian discipleship. The scandal of the cross and Christian discipleship are connected. Conscience formation ultimately leads to action, thus understanding the demands of Christian discipleship under the scandal of the cross shapes our grasp of what influences, informs, and fosters conscience formation and subsequent action.

How we conceive the scandalous cross remains important because we can cause scandal by our omissions, what we fail to do, as well as by our commissions, what we do. Can we ever avoid causing scandal? Do we bear responsibility if others are scandalized? If so, what responsibility do we bear? If not, how do we account for the reality that others might be scandalized and account for that scandal in a reasonable way, honoring our own commitments and living with integrity from values that support and reflect the good, true, and beautiful? How is a theological notion of scandal different from, yet informed by, a sociological definition of scandal?[1]

Theologically, if one lives a life of deepening relationship with the living triune God, scandal can never be fully avoided. It is an integral part of Christian discipleship. Does our reaction to events/actions as scandalous

---

[1] Angela Senander addresses some of these questions in her book *Scandal: The Catholic Church and Public Life* (Collegeville, MN: Liturgical Press, 2012).

accurately reflect the event or action as scandalous? Is the scandal due to wrongful, sinful behavior, or do we label an event or action scandalous because it challenges our worldview? While she does not call the behavior scandalous, Irene Nowell's description of Jonah's reaction to God raises this last question for me. Nowell states that the story of Jonah is "about the greatness of God's compassion." Jonah is unhappy with his success as a prophet and God's graciousness and mercy (Jonah 4:2). Nowell points out that we do not know "if Jonah's heart was softened." As a result, "we are . . . left with the challenge to pick up where Jonah left off. Can we forgive our enemies, even the worst ones? Can we allow God to forgive them?"[2]

The greatness of God's compassion is all too frequently greeted as scandalous rather than met with a grateful relief. If we can find God's compassion scandalous, then maybe this indicates that we must more carefully examine how we use the term "scandal." Do we claim scandal authentically? Alternatively, is the term "scandal" standing as a means of silencing voices or maintaining the status quo? Is it both? Do we claim we are scandalized because we are angry, frustrated, feeling left out, challenged, or unwilling to change, therefore, by talking about scandal we deflect the need for internal examination and reflection? Before saying we are scandalized or charging someone with scandal, a proper understanding of scandal is important in order to use the term authentically. Scandal, when understood biblically, can mean presenting a vision of discipleship, a worldview, that is challenging, a stumbling block.

Section 1 begins the process of dissecting the idea of scandal. A consideration of what scandal is and what it is not will be undertaken. This section relies on Angela Senander's work on scandal in both its sociological and theological manifestations. Senander connects scandal to discipleship. It is clear that discipleship requires more than a profession of Jesus Christ as Lord. Section 2 then looks at practices of Christian discipleship. Terrence Tilley's work on discipleship practices provides resources for considering contemporary practices of discipleship faithful to the early radical witness of what it means to be a disciple of Jesus. Section 3 takes up the obstacle of the cross. The cross can be domesticated, losing the force of its first-century scandalous nature. When this happens, modern Christians can over-romanticize or underestimate the radical nature of first-century disciples who claimed they followed Jesus

---

[2] Irene Nowell, "Within the Word: Jonah," *Give Us This Day* (October 2013): 75.

Christ, the one who was crucified. Alternatively, as Acts 10:39 describes it, "They put him to death by hanging him on a tree." James Cone's work *The Cross and the Lynching Tree* goes after this domestication by connecting Jesus' crucifixion with the black American experience of the lynching tree. Cone's critique of white Christianity's inability, for the most part, to see the scandal of the cross concretely shows that Christians so often misappropriate the Gospel message. How we live our Christianity and appropriate its symbols matters because distorted discipleship causes scandal. Reengagement with the scandal of the cross and Scriptures challenges and functions as a call to conversion for a complacent, distorted, and partial life of discipleship.

Section 1: Considering Scandal from Sociological and Theological Perspectives

Angela Senander, drawing on sociology analysis, states that scandal has four important features. It requires an act, an agent, an announcer, and an audience.[3] While the four features of a scandal can be used to analyze scandal in both secular and religious institutions, I will use a religious context for my example.

The act is the single event, or a compilation of events that taken together are spoken of as one act. For example, during the fall of 2013 a Minnesota paper, *The Star Tribune*, ran a series of articles about clergy sexual misconduct in the Archdiocese of Minneapolis–St. Paul. One question that arose was whether the archdiocesan officials covered up recent clergy sexual misconduct.[4] The action named "cover-up" is actually comprised of a series of prior actions contributing to the consideration of a single action, a cover-up.

Scandal can occur because of a person's inaction (act of omission) as well as their action (act of commission). The ability of inaction to cause scandal is evidenced in the multilayered reality of the sexual abuse crisis in the Roman Catholic Church. There is the initial scandal of abuse by

---

[3] Senander, *Scandal*, 7–14. Senander uses biblical examples when defining the features. She then applies them to the clergy sex abuse crisis more broadly construed. I localized the example by using the Archdiocese of Minneapolis–St. Paul, Minnesota.

[4] See *Star Tribune* coverage about the Archdiocese of Minneapolis–St. Paul from mid-September through October 2013. The *Star Tribune* continues to report on clergy sexual misconduct and the role of archdiocesan administrators and had a series of articles in June 2015 on the latest developments.

numerous priests, which are direct actions. Then there is the seeming inaction of those in charge when they failed to report the abuse to civil authorities or to strip priests of their functions and duties. Yet, this inaction is also an action of sorts, since there is a choice to act in a different manner. Another example of scandal is described by Bishop Oscar Cantú, who has in the past called cutting funding to the food stamp program a moral scandal. In so doing, he challenges us to see that scandalous actions can also occur outside the realm of sexuality.

The agent is the person who acts. In the case of scandal that is the result of a series of actions over time, there might actually be multiple agents. There were multiple agents in the recent case in Minneapolis–St. Paul where the actions of the archbishop, his vicar, and other bishops were called into question. This is, of course, in addition to the original actors, the priests who abused their parishioners. Furthermore, those who were abused became agents when they chose to reveal what had happened to them. The act of telling their story, while not scandalous, revealed the behavior that the community deemed scandalous.

The third and fourth features of scandal, an announcer and an audience, matter for determining if the community recognizes and acknowledges scandal. The announcer and an audience matter because if no one knows (no announcer) then there is no communal scandal. Several reasons exist for the lack of an announcer. In the one instance, no one witnessed the event that would be considered scandalous. In other instances, someone witnesses the event, but they are quiet for some reason. Therefore, a potential announcer of the scandal to the community exists. The witness or potential announcer could also be a victim. In this instance, the witness is privately scandalized, but the wider community is not yet scandalized. Since the action or series of actions have occurred, however, the potential for scandal still endures. The communal scandal can occur when the witness or victim to the potentially scandalous events speaks up. This was the case in Minneapolis–St. Paul when Jennifer Haselberger decided that she needed to go outside the church structures and report clergy sexual misconduct to the police. Both local and national media picked up and reported her actions.

The fourth feature of a scandal is the audience. If there is no audience or no one cares, then there is no scandal. Someone needs to pay attention to the actions committed by others; a person or a community needs to care and want a different vision for life, transparency, punishment, or an injustice corrected for it to matter that actions are deemed scandalous. By caring, I mean that people are deeply troubled, disturbed, and possibly angered by the action or series of actions. The scandal shakes the person's or community's worldview. When people are troubled this moves them to talk about the event, discuss the need for change, maybe consider leaving an institution or withholding donations, or possibly advocate for transformation within structures. In the case of the Minneapolis–St. Paul archdiocese, the newspaper editors and reporters were both audience and announcer. The editors and reporters were initially the audience by listening and being concerned by the news of a potential cover-up, at least enough to determine the events should be reported. In reporting the events, the *Star Tribune* became the announcer of the event(s) deemed scandalous by members of the Catholic and the broader Minnesota communities (the audience).

Theological Scandal

At its root, the concern with scandal is the desire not to destroy the faith of another, not to harm the faith of another, or not to cause another to stray, falling from the path of spiritual growth. This concern is different from dismay or perceived scandal when someone wears different types of clothing from the norm, or transgresses socio-economic boundaries and class structures. If manifestations of different cultural norms cause scandal while not directly related to the center of the faith, then education of the community must ensue. At times, however, we may be living the Gospel message, thinking about others, meaning no harm, and still others are scandalized. Are we responsible for this scandal and what do we do to avoid paralysis and inaction for fear of causing scandal?

Thomas Aquinas is helpful in sketching a beginning answer to these questions, since he distinguishes between different types of scandal.[5] This is where categories and delineations can be extremely helpful. Direct scandal occurs when we intend to tempt another to sin.[6] Using a daily example, say we know someone overeats and their food of choice is potato chips. We know they are trying to break the habit of eating potato chips, yet we invite them over and provide only seven types of potato chips for

---

[5] Senander, *Scandal*, 14–18. Senander notes that while Aquinas's explanation of scandal is philosophical, he is using biblical sources and is therefore faithful to the biblical notion of scandal as an obstacle or stumbling block. See Thomas Aquinas, *Summa Theologica* II–II, q. 43.

[6] Senander, *Scandal*, 16. For what follows, in addition to Senander's work, see Aquinas, *Summa Theologica* II–II, q. 43.

food, wanting them to eat as many chips as possible. We intend to tempt them to sin and commit a form of gluttony. If we bait a sibling, friend, or colleague to act in an unhelpful manner, we are tempting the other to sin in a different way, thus engaging in direct active scandal.

Accidental scandal "refers to wrong or apparently wrong actions that could unintentionally influence another to sin."[7] In other words, our wrong actions, whether we intend them to or not, can possibly create obstacles for others. We might unintentionally or indirectly through our actions cause another person to act poorly, respond poorly in a situation, or have doubt about their faith. We do not mean to create an obstacle; we might not consider the effect of our action or behavior on others.[8] In other cases, we are not acting sinfully, but others perceive our actions as sinful, and this could cause an obstacle for them.[9] Furthermore, Aquinas considers what he calls passive scandal, where good actions are obstacles because of ignorance of others. Senander argues that Aquinas "is clear that truth should not be sacrificed in an effort to avoid the scandal of the weak."[10] Education helps minimize this type of scandal. Teachers, ministers, pastoral associates, theologians, and even bishops in different ways run the risk of this type of passive scandal. This happens when actions are not wrong and do not harm the other person's relationship with God, but due to ignorance the actions, for example, of a minister or pastoral associate might be obstacles to someone else's faith.

Nevertheless, whether direct or indirect, scandal occurs because humans are in relationships with each other. In both types of scandal, there are two or more persons exercising freedom. Thus, while the obstacle is the occasion for sin, it does not make the other person sin.[11] The other person still gets to respond to the obstacle; they have to take responsibility for their actions. "In other words, a person strong in faith will not succumb to the obstacle created by the other."[12] Responsibility for the obstacle lies with the one who put the obstacle out there. Responsibility for succumbing to the obstacle and sinning resides with the person who succumbed. We do not get to blame others for our actions or reactions.[13]

---

[7] Ibid.
[8] Ibid., 16–17.
[9] Ibid.
[10] Ibid., 17.
[11] Ibid.
[12] Ibid.
[13] Ibid., 17–18.

Culpability matters for both the person who puts an obstacle out there (directly or indirectly) and the person responding to the obstacle.[14] There might, however, be mitigating factors that lessen the culpability of both the scandalized and the person causing the perceived or real scandal. A mitigating factor for the person causing the perceived or real scandal is a belief that others know as much as he or she does about a given theological area. In this instance, behavior or statements aligned with teaching can cause unintentional harm. The harm exists, but not because it is willed. For the person scandalized, sometimes unconscious reactions to past events triggered by current events influence present actions or perceptions of the actions of others. As noted, people are still responsible for their actions, even if they have to understand and probe the actions or responses they do not fully understand and only later come to realize that the past was influencing the present without them being aware of it. This, then, is why ongoing reflection, prayer, and consideration of our day matters. Not to beat oneself up, or to engage in self-flagellation, but to better understand and come to a greater appreciation of the depth of ourselves and our responses, so that we can act better in the future. Moreover, Senander notes that when considering our interactions with others we need to be careful that we do not ascribe motives, perceptions, or attitudes toward teachings onto another. She writes, "One's own fears and emotions can affect our perception and interpretation of another's attitude."[15] We must let others speak for themselves and to their motivations for acting.

While looking at scandal in the manner above focuses on action, action connects to faith. Therefore, Senander also argues that "the biblical understanding of scandal as a stumbling block to faith invites reflection on the meaning of faith."[16] She identifies and discusses four obstacles to faith: language, understandings of God, persecution, and law.[17]

The first stumbling block to faith is how language functions. We must express our experience of God using language. Since language changes and meanings evolve, this affects our capacity and ability to convey God's revelation. For example, "man" used to mean "humanity." Yet for many women it means one-half of humanity. Thus, in the twenty-first century, "man" or "men" is often read as referencing only one-half of the human

---

[14] Ibid., 17.
[15] Ibid., 22.
[16] Ibid., 29.
[17] Ibid., 39–46.

race. There are other words used to convey a group comprised of women and men, such as "people," "human beings," or "the people of God." Exclusively male language for human beings or for God can then become an obstacle for many women and men in the context of faith.[18] For example, in the case of abuse at the hands of one's male parent or an authority figure, the abused person might have trouble relating to the image of God as either parent or a male figure, particularly if the images used are seen as set in stone. The victim might have trouble relating to the image of God as Father. This is particularly problematic when alternative images for God are not permitted, especially since God is beyond all description. Any image for God that humans arrive at, or description of who God is, does not do justice to the One who is "I am."[19]

The second stumbling block to faith is our understanding of God. Senander argues that this stumbling block often occurs in the midst of suffering. Similar to Job, suffering happens to us or our friends, and we, like Job's friends, try to find reasons that God would inflict suffering on us.[20] On the one hand, we question and believe we must have done something. On the other hand, we find it hard to believe in a God who "permits" suffering. As a result, our perceptions of God have to change. Our sufferings challenge particular theological viewpoints we hold about God. Otherwise, we have to live in a particular theological tension.

Sendander further argues, "The incarnation and crucifixion are even more profound challenges to the ideas of God, particularly God's omnipotence."[21] Senander focuses on why the incarnation and crucifixion would have been challenging in Jesus' time, but why might the incarnation and crucifixion be a challenge for us today? For many it is hard to imagine or believe that the almighty God would come down to earth and become a baby, a male human being born of a woman. Children, especially newborns, are completely dependent on others. Babies cannot feed themselves, cannot change themselves, and cannot keep themselves dressed appropriately for the weather. Thus, babies come into this world completely vulnerable, at the mercy of others, trusting that their needs will be met. Furthermore, babies' and infants' ability to communicate

---

[18] Ibid., 39–41.

[19] For one extended study regarding language for God, see Elizabeth A. Johnson, *She Who Is: The Mystery of God in Feminist Theological Discourse* (New York: Crossroad, 1992).

[20] Senander, *Scandal*, 41–42.

[21] Ibid., 42.

with those of us who have verbal language as our primary mode of communication is limited. They cry, laugh, and fuss to convey meaning and their needs. Babies are not simple passive creatures. That God would be born as Jesus, a vulnerable baby who needed his diaper changed; who needed to be fed, washed, held; who probably cried and was fussy as well as laughed can become a stumbling block for some believers. A newborn baby, as messiah, as God, does not fit the image of an almighty God, king and savior. Thus, the incarnation of God as a baby, an infant, upturns and unsettles ideas of how God would save and how God would and did come into the world. This is no God who descends from heaven a fully grown human being. God entered a violent, unjust world as an impoverished, vulnerable infant and trusted that creation would take care of him, hoping that all would be well. God loved humanity enough and gave us freedom to believe the incomprehensible.

Fast forward to the crucifixion: this could be a stumbling block as well. In biblical times, this is because the God who was to come, the savior, was believed by many to be a warrior king, one who would lead the Israelites into battle and reclaim the land against the Romans and all other occupiers. Thus, for Jesus to be crucified and to suffer the death of a criminal was seen as a sign of defeat. This is witnessed to in the gospels when Jesus is ridiculed as he hangs on the cross—he saved others but cannot save himself. King of the Jews, beaten, scorned, laughed at, deserted by many of his closest followers. For us today, would we want to follow the one who is laughed at, ridiculed, the non-cool person, the one who seems powerless in the face of the ruling class, or those with the most sway and influence?

Humans have a desire to follow those who appear strong as a means of protecting themselves. Following the "weak" might mean having to take a stand ourselves, being the focus of the same treatment as those we follow. Is this not the reason Peter denies Jesus—to avoid the same ridicule, beatings, scorning? He wants to know what happens, he wants to be with Jesus, yet does not want to pay the cost. Peter redeems himself later by weeping and realizing what he has done. He returns to the other disciples and apostles willing to take up the cross of following Jesus. Judas, on the other hand, collaborates with the societal power structure and betrays Jesus. When Judas realizes what he has done, he kills himself. These two men show two possible responses to when we hit a stumbling block in our faith or act in a manner that we regret. We can, like Peter, repent and trust the redemptive power of God's forgiveness, as well as the forgiveness of our communities. On the other hand, like Judas, who has remorse, we can despair. We can withdraw from God and our communities, not seeking redemption and forgiveness, but choosing instead self-destructive behavior.

Therefore, we have choices even when we turn away from what we know to be true, good, and worthwhile when we are afraid of the consequences, of being belittled, scorned, and laughed at by other human beings. With Judas, we can isolate ourselves, not seeking reconciliation or forgiveness. Or with Peter, we can turn back to the One who loves us, the One who called us in the first place, and the One who will forgive us. In so doing, we can also be welcomed back into the community of believers. In these ways, the incarnation and the crucifixion are stumbling blocks. They are, however, blocks that cause us to stumble but not fall, never to get up. By stumbling we temporarily get off course, something makes us question our direction, and we correct as needed. Therefore, obstacles or scandals can become a source of grace too.

The resurrection is the final element of Jesus' life that poses a stumbling block for some. The idea that Jesus was raised from the dead is too much to believe. Thomas's story in John's gospel is seen as the classic example of one who does not believe (John 20:24-29). Thomas is not present when Jesus appears to the other disciples and apostles. When he is told about Jesus' appearance, Thomas says he will not believe until he can see Jesus and touch his wounds. Jesus appears to Thomas, and Thomas is able to see and touch Jesus' wounds. Jesus' response is this: "Have you believed because you have seen me? Blessed are those who have not seen and yet have come to believe" (John 20:29).

This scriptural narrative is typically interpreted as a statement about faith not requiring visible proof but trusting the testimony of the apostles and disciples. Thus, the need to see, touch, and have proof for faith to blossom is seen as a stumbling block. I would like to propose, however, a possible alternative reading. It could be that Thomas might believe his fellow companions but wants to see for himself that the Jesus who appears has had his wounds healed. It is possible that Thomas had a more complete grasp of the cost of discipleship. He wanted to see the cost of Jesus' crucifixion, the wounds. Maybe Thomas understood that the scars, the wounds he wanted to touch, remain as a reminder of the cost and beauty (resurrection, new life) that comes from following the covenant and one's call. Thomas touches the wounds. As far as we know, aside from the women and men who dressed and prepared Jesus' body for burial, Thomas is the only one willing to enter the experience of Jesus, by touch.

Thus, it is possible Thomas understood the spiritual, emotional, and embodied reality of the cost of discipleship. Thomas possibly doubted not from disbelief but out of a wish to confirm the resurrection in order to gather strength for the ongoing journey of discipleship. Perhaps what some see as an obstacle others see as a source of strength.

The third stumbling block that Angela Senander points to is the persecution of Christians and the early church martyrs.[22] Today, in many parts of the world, Christians find it hard to consider dying for what we believe. This is even as the twentieth and twenty-first century provide many examples of Christians dying for their faith. The news in 2014 and 2015 has been filled with stories of Christians and believers of other religious traditions in the Middle East and elsewhere being persecuted and killed for their faith. Martyrs today continue to die for what they believe in, for following the Gospel call, and for living counter-cultural messages that challenge the status quo and advocate for dignity and justice wherever it is needed.

The fourth stumbling block that Senander identifies is the law, civil and ecclesiastical. She looks at laws in a variety of contexts. When is a law unjust and when might it need to be changed? When can we cooperate with laws (civil) that are counter to Catholic teaching and belief? She provides no specific answers here.[23]

While obstacles to faith exist and the desire to avoid scandal remains valuable, they cannot prevent us from acting. Senander writes:

> To move beyond this scandal, the community needs to continually seek to effectively communicate God's revelation in a given historical and cultural context. An absolute avoidance of scandal associated with language and ideas about God would result in a lack of evangelization. When faith is reduced to teaching and when dissent from any teaching becomes a scandal, one will miss the invitation of the Holy Spirit to communicate God's reign in new ways. The virtue of humility and a life of prayer in a community of faith equip one to take steps beyond the scandal of the limits of language and ideas, as inadequate as those steps might be.[24]

In other words, discipleship requires actions, not just a profession of faith. Failure to act means ignoring the Holy Spirit who continues to assist humans in communicating what God's reign looks like in new eras

---

[22] Ibid., 43–45.
[23] Ibid., 45–46.
[24] Ibid., 46.

and in new ways. Humility and prayer centered in a faith community are virtues as correctives to scandal caused by language and ideas. Humility and prayer help disciples move beyond stasis and paralysis to action.

Wanting to avoid both the appearance of scandal and the suffering that arises from scandal is normal. Avoiding scandal that arises from sin makes sense. Avoiding scandal that stems from living a life of Christian discipleship neuters the Gospel message, rendering it nothing more than another slogan. When the natural and normal desire to avoid scandal stifles our willingness to live a life of discipleship due to the cost, then a fear or concern for scandal becomes a form of idolatry. Reacquainting ourselves with some practices of Christian discipleship focused more on living our love of God and neighbor could reinvigorate our lives of discipleship. Scandal, while still an important consideration, contextualized by discipleship would require us to attend to whether scandal results from sin or from responding appropriately to grace.

Section 2: Discipleship

Following a similar methodology in other chapters of this book, in this section I am not going to provide a survey of the contemporary scholarship on discipleship. Nor am I going to survey contemporary scholarship in the area of Christology. Therefore, the reader will not receive an analysis of current debates with implications for the church's intellectual heritage. Rather, I chose one particular author who looks at how the New Testament records various practices that shaped and embodied responses to Jesus' teachings, life, death, and resurrection. This is followed by attention to selected passages of Scripture to see what they say about discipleship and the cross. The purpose is to begin an initial exploration of what a life of Christian discipleship that considers responses practices of discipleship, not our intellectual assent to the creed, might mean for understanding the contours of a moral life.

The Disciples' Jesus

In his book *The Disciples' Jesus*, Terrence Tilley argues that the practices of Jesus and the early Jesus movement form the foundation for what it means to be a disciple of Jesus Christ.[25] My purposes in using the book

---

[25] Terrence W. Tilley, *The Disciples' Jesus: Christology as Reconciling Practice* (Maryknoll, NY: Orbis, 2008).

are not to engage his Christology by determining its merits and its flaws. Rather, I want to engage his argument and consider its implications for understanding discipleship as a component of Christian morality. As I have argued elsewhere in this text, moral theology has frequently focused on action separate from being. Moral theology is too often seen as a set of rules to be followed rather than fostering the development of virtues and providing proper perspectives and the formation of right relationships with God, self, and others. Therefore, Tilley's argument that Christology begins in practices is informative and illuminating for considering how discipleship affects, shapes, and informs what actions spring from a properly formed conscience.

What Tilley offers in his assessment of certain practices by Jesus and the early Jesus movement, although not an inclusive list, is a group of foundational practices. Tilley in turn discusses exorcising and healing,[26] teaching,[27] forgiveness,[28] and table fellowship.[29] These foundational practices provide the contours and criteria for assessing other individual or group actions. Focusing on foundational practices shifts the question both for judging actions and for assessing the judgments of conscience. Therefore, this means that we can no longer simply ask, "Is this action right or wrong?" Rather, we must ask, "Does this action or judgment of conscience fit as part of a larger practice furthering God's reign or does it further the reign of those opposed to God? Do I perceive and envision correctly so that this action/practice implements and lives into God's reign?" Stated differently, we ask, "Does my action foster healing, reconciliation, forgiveness, inclusion, and/or justice?"

The language of right or wrong has built into it an assumption that "right" equals an appropriation of God's reign and "wrong" has built into it an assumption that we do not see God's reign rightly. The language of right and wrong is helpful. Contemporary moral theologians have argued, however, that a further classification is necessary to connect our actions and our motivations. Distinctions are made between right actions with wrong motivations and wrong actions with correct motivations. The insight by James Keenan and others that actions and motivations might not match is similar to Tilley's argument that one can say the right thing

---

[26] Ibid., 137–49.
[27] Ibid., 150–64.
[28] Ibid., 165–74.
[29] Ibid., 175–87.

and not understand what one is saying. The words are right, but the agent does not comprehend or have a depth of knowledge that recognizes the ramifications of his or her statement. Stated differently, saying the right thing does not mean one has the right vision or perception about the meanings of one's words.[30] Conversion to God's vision requires both proper statements and proper visioning, which in turn leads to particular practices and actions that instantiate the reign of God. Practices also lead to a deepened understanding and an embodied knowledge of what the reign of God entails. For example, a person can understand something about prayer by reading what other people have written about prayer. The practice of praying, however, yields a different form of knowledge and understanding about prayer.

Tilley argues that both doctrine and practice are necessary for Christian faith. Christology is not just about belief in propositions or the creeds, the doctrine by Christians. Christology also requires of the disciple a set of lived practices. Discipleship is more than assenting to the *what* of one's beliefs; *how* one is a disciple is important too. Attention to the *how* of discipleship connects the discipline of Christology to moral theology.

Transferring Tilley's insight regarding the distinction between "what" and "how" of christological claims to moral theology means that living a moral life requires more than assenting to propositions about moral behavior. The propositions are important, but they are often proposed in the negative, in "do not do" statements. The result is that Christians often think that they are living a moral life by not doing prohibited actions. At best, this is a minimum threshold for discipleship. On the other hand, virtue theory argues for a set of positive actions or dispositions that foster growth in the moral life and life of discipleship. The virtues require practices, which help foster growth. Therefore, Tilley, with his emphasis on a practical Christology, challenges the moral theologian and the disciple to consider how their actions and practices incarnate and illuminate the reign of God. Rather than focus on behaviors to avoid, focus shifts to modeling Jesus' reconciling behavior and practices. Like Christology, moral teaching is more than just the *what* that is taught; moral teaching includes a *how*, a set of practices for what is taught.[31]

---

[30] Tilley discusses this in more depth with his examination of Peter at Caesarea Philippi. See ibid., 78–95.

[31] See William C. Spohn, *Go and Do Likewise: Jesus and Ethics* (New York: Continuum, 1999), 27–49. He examines the connection among virtues, practices, and discipleship in this section of his book.

Discipleship requires practices that promote the full human flourishing of all human beings by continuing the practices of Jesus that fostered the reign of God. Practices "that lead to the reconciliation of humans with themselves, each other, and God are the practices of reconciliation, the practices that realize God's reign, the practices that empower all to flourish together."[32] While Tilley discusses exorcising and healing, teaching, forgiveness, and table fellowship, he does not want to limit us to these practices. We must account for how the twenty-first century is different from the time of Jesus and the early church. Therefore, we must be in continuity with the past, faithful to the Gospel while valuing new or renewed practices. Two quick examples: Jesus had a practice of withdrawing to pray. The contemporary version of withdrawing would not be to a physical desert. Rather, we would need to withdraw to the desert of no electronic devices, silencing our constant connectivity to sit in silence to hear the still, small voice of God. Second, events of communal oppression require us to explore what healing, forgiveness, and reconciliation look like today. Using the American history of lynching as an example, the ideas of practices of reconciliation would require more than just white Americans asking for forgiveness of their black and brown brothers and sisters. The practices of reconciliation, healing, and forgiveness require the continued hard work of identifying the false perceptions and idols that permitted lynching to happen in the first place. A practice of reconciliation requires ongoing resistance to racism and oppression in all its insidious manifestations.

Scriptural Considerations

The purpose of this section is to use certain scriptural passages as a brief look and meditation on how Scripture captures various responses to God and the call to discipleship. Obviously, the selection is limited and partial with more that could be said. Given that Scripture forms and shapes us and is authoritative for discipleship, however, some reflection is warranted.

The morning canticle, Zechariah's canticle, when one prays the Liturgy of the Hours, comes from Luke's gospel. This canticle prayed consistently tutors the person in a summary of what God has done and will do by setting the people free and sending a savior. Furthermore, this canticle from

---

[32] Tilley, *The Disciples' Jesus*, 244.

Luke's gospel records the event of Zechariah, John the Baptist's father, being filled with the Holy Spirit and speaking a prophecy regarding his son. Zechariah's canticle blesses Israel's God, who has raised up a savior from the house of David (Luke 1:68-69), explaining what the Lord God has done. The canticle also outlines the role John will play in salvation history. John will be the prophet of the Most High and will prepare the way of the Lord (Luke 1:76). Given that the ongoing, eschatological reality of salvation history, that humans still oppress each other, turn away from God, and sin, we can ask ourselves, how do we model John today? Do we, as John did, with our actions, dispositions, practices, and words prepare the way of the Lord? Luke indicates that part of this preparation is the forgiveness of sins.

Mark's gospel gives testament to John's practice of forgiving sins. John proclaims repentance of sins by baptism (Mark 1:4). While many people were being baptized by John and confessing their sins (Mark 1:5), John the Baptist draws attention to Jesus and proclaims, "The one who is more powerful than I is coming after me; I am not worthy to stoop down and untie the thong of his sandals. I have baptized you with water, but he will baptize you with the Holy Spirit" (Mark 1:7-8). John brought knowledge of salvation by the forgiveness of sins in baptism, and Jesus brings the baptism of the Holy Spirit. Jesus' baptism by John had the clouds opening up and the Holy Spirit descending upon him; Jesus was then driven into the desert. Therefore, we see that at the very beginning of Jesus' ministry he had to choose God or certain temptations put before him. Jesus chose God; God was the center and foundation of Jesus' work and ministry. For us, the narrative challenges us to realize that baptism is not enough, being forgiven for our sins is not enough. Rather, we must continually choose God over the various temptations that pull us away from God. It is not just following Jesus Christ that fosters right living; following the promptings of the Holy Spirit, given by Jesus Christ, is also paramount.

Scripture records how the Holy Spirit is given to the community. We read in Acts 2:38, "Peter said to them, 'Repent, and be baptized every one of you in the name of Jesus Christ so that your sins may be forgiven; and you will receive the gift of the Holy Spirit.'" The forgiveness of sins is connected here with the gift of the Holy Spirit. Discipleship, then, means living as a follower of Jesus Christ and living in the Holy Spirit. If Jesus is to baptize with the Holy Spirit, then this is to show us what it means to live in intimate relationship with God.

Therefore, if we are to be disciples of Jesus Christ, discipleship starts with a relationship with the living God, grounded in a faith tradition, yet deeply personal and intimate. This relationship forms the foundation from which one works, lives, moves, decides, and breathes. John's baptism and Jesus' forgiveness of sins show us what it means to live in freedom, which in the Scriptures means following God, choosing life, not death.

In addition to baptism, however, Jesus' crucifixion has also been interpreted as atonement for human sinfulness, and Jesus has been seen as the suffering servant. In Isaiah 53:3-5 we read, "He was despised and rejected by others; a man of suffering and acquainted with infirmity. . . . Surely he has born our infirmities and carried our disease; yet we accounted him stricken, struck down by God and afflicted. But he was wounded for our transgressions, crushed for our iniquities; upon him was the punishment that made us whole, and by his bruises we are healed." Isaiah 53 continues in verses 10-11: "It was the will of the LORD to crush him with pain. When you make his life an offering for sin, he shall see his offspring and shall prolong his days; through him the will of the LORD shall prosper. Out of his anguish he shall see light; he shall find satisfaction through his knowledge. The righteous one, my servant, shall make many righteous, and he shall bear their iniquities." Finally, we read in verse 12 that "because he poured out himself to death, and was numbered with the transgressors; yet he bore the sin of many, and made intercession for the transgressors." The image of the suffering servant applied to Jesus has scriptural weight.

The early Christians, in trying to figure out who Jesus was and answer the question of the meaning of the cross, would have used the Scriptures they knew and that were part of their prayer life. Isaiah's description of the suffering servant would have been part of the canon, shaping and influencing the interpretation of the cross. By Anselm's time in the early Middle Ages, with his cultural and historical framework of serfdom and the concept that someone more powerful needed to make acceptable reparations for debt, the idea of atonement made sense in a different way than it did in the first centuries of Christianity.

Atonement models of salvation grounded in the paschal mystery are one reasonable interpretation of Jesus' death on the cross. Jesus' death on the cross can be seen as preordained, as necessary for the forgiveness of sins and to reconcile humanity to God.[33] Believing that Jesus' death on the

---

[33] Atonement theories influence how the incarnation is viewed, so much so that in the Middle Ages some theologians argued that the incarnation was required because of the first sin by Adam and subsequent sins of the rest of humanity. Others argued that the incarnation would have happened anyway because of God's love for the world and

cross was preordained and necessary in a cosmic sense in order to reconcile humanity back to God leads to one conception of the moral life. Believing that Jesus' death on the cross was an outcome of his behavior in staying true to the covenant and his relationship with God leads, however, to another.

When considering the paschal mystery as resulting from Jesus' faithfulness to God, then the cross becomes the symbol of a life lived from the depths of the intimate relationship with God, in the pursuit of overturning oppressive power structures and living in solidarity with the ones most harmed by the world's injustice. It can be argued that the crucifixion results from the choices Jesus made to follow God and live from the covenantal relationship. Margaret Farley makes the case that the cross is about relationships holding and life coming from situations that seem deadly and hopeless. With James Cone and other liberationist theologians we can say that the cross is a logical outcome of following Jesus Christ, the one who lived from a relationship with the Lord God, as opposed to following the prevailing norms of the day. While death by a cross was scandalous, Jesus' death on a cross shows that scandal can result from a living relationship with God that challenges unjust structures. As such, discipleship means doing as Jesus did. This means putting the relationship with God and others first, not the pursuits of personal gain. Jesus showed us what consideration about our identity looks like. In one of his discourses with his disciples Jesus asked, "Who do you say that I am?" (Mark 8:29; Luke 20:29). The responses varied, and they reflect outsider expectations of who Jesus was, not the reality of who he was. Only when Peter hit upon Jesus' own sense of self-identity did Jesus respond. As a result, we learn from Jesus to own our identity; this is who I am, not who someone else thinks I am. Relationality and self-knowledge, then, form the basis of ethics.

Discipleship Practices, Scandal, and Ongoing Formation

Taking seriously that scandal has various forms is helpful when thinking about discipleship practices. Some forms of scandal are problematic because they lead to sinfulness. Other types of scandal result from discipleship, from following the one who was nailed to a tree and who lived a set of reconciling practices. Jesus healed and preached compassion, love,

---

God's creation. A theoretical debate, to be sure, but there are different visions of God and humanity within this debate.

forgiveness, and hospitality. As disciples we are meant to follow Jesus, living life in the Spirit, choosing life over death, health over illness, justice over injustice, reconciliation over retribution.

The prophets begin to tell us that, rather than burnt offerings and temple offerings of various sorts as means of reconciling with God, God prefers other visible manifestations that we are repentant of our sins. The prophets exhort their listeners to act for justice; be merciful; walk humbly with God (Micah); beat swords into plowshares (Isaiah); care for the widow, orphan, and poor; return from their whoring ways and live again in a covenantal relationship with God. The prophets claim that God is pleased by our care of the poor, the aliens in our midst, the widows and orphans. In light of the prophets' exhortations, Jesus' death on the cross can be seen as a result of his living commitment to the covenant of YHWH, to embodying the depths of his relationship with God, and to living out his sense of identity. Jesus did not live his life based on people's expectations; rather, he lived from the heart of his relationship with God.

To state these ideas differently: God has already forgiven our sins, a gift freely given. Therefore, the cross need not be about repayment or sacrifice to God as an offering. There is no longer a need for sacrifice of offerings to appease God. Jesus, on the other hand, marks the forgiveness of sins by healing. In some cases, he even notes that broken relationships and disease are not the result of sin at all. He heals these folks as well. Jesus does not require changed behavior to issue invitations to be in deeper relationships with God; in fact, it is the invitation to a deeper, fuller life that becomes the catalyst for change. The tax collector Zacchaeus wanted to see who Jesus was so badly he climbed a tree. Jesus saw him and invited himself to Zacchaeus' house. In response to Jesus, Zacchaeus resolves to give away some of his possessions to the poor and repay anything exhorted from others. Jesus then notes that salvation has come to Zacchaeus' house in two ways: first, because Zacchaeus is also a descendent of Abraham and, second, because "the Son of Man has come to seek out and save the lost" (Luke 19:1-10). Zacchaeus, in attending to the poor, returns to one of the tenants of the covenant with YHWH as laid out by the prophets. Jesus, through invitation and seeing the goodness in Zacchaeus, was able to bring him back into the fold.

The gospels record, as Tilley notes, the practices of the early communities who drew inspiration from Jesus, so much so that they continued his ministry after his death on the cross. The cross, as a symbol of Christian discipleship, is both a scandal resulting from a yes to God's call and a challenge to scandal stemming from a no or a blind misappropriation of the demands of discipleship. Intellectualizing the cross can lead to horrific practices that malform the individual moral agent, corrupt communities, scandalize other people, and are an affront to human dignity. James Cone's recent work provides a salient example of how the cross can be both misemployed and utilized to critique structures of oppression and injustice.

Section 3: Scandal of the Cross and Scandalous Witness

James Cone, African Methodist Episcopal minister and black theologian, gave the Saturday morning plenary address at the January 2013 Society of Christian Ethics meeting. While the address was about his 2011 book *The Cross and the Lynching Tree*,[34] in his opening remarks, Cone mentioned that he had been invited to speak to the society in the early 1970s. This was shortly after his first two books had come out: *Black Theology and Black Power* (1969) and *A Black Theology of Liberation* (1970). He mentioned the lively conversation after he addressed the society that first time and remarked that the society took over forty years to ask him back to speak. I took his point to be, in light of his recent book, *The Cross and the Lynching Tree*, that white and black Christianity, and ethicists in particular, still have not grappled with our intertwined legacy stemming from slavery and structural injustice and sinfulness. Furthermore, Cone's remarks illustrate how entrenched distortions of the gospel can influence our perceptions, behaviors, theology, and scholarship.

White theologian and ethicist Gloria Albrecht gave a response where she thanked Cone and stated she was not going to address his remarks directly. Instead, she addressed her fellow white colleagues in the society, laying out what she saw as the implications of Cone's address for the work of theological ethicists. Her response challenged white ethicists to listen to the oppressed, the marginalized, and those who suffer all manner of injustice. It is by listening that our veils of blindness can be pierced. We must be willing to learn from others and not presume the correctness of our theology or position.[35] The subject of the address and the response at the 2013 Society of Christian Ethics meeting challenges (1) privatized

---

[34] James H. Cone, *The Cross and the Lynching Tree* (Maryknoll, NY: Orbis Books, 2011, paperback 2013).

[35] These few paragraphs came from my conference notes and subsequent reflections on Cone's address and Albrecht's response.

notions of discipleship withdrawn from engagement with the world and (2) how even active, engaged Christians can have areas where they are morally blind. Lynching was taking place in the United States while the Second Vatican Council was meeting, and yet, in a search of *Gaudium et Spes*, the term or reference to lynching cannot be found. So in the list of specific injustices to resist as a manifestation to love God and neighbor injustices are overlooked. While it could be argued that lynching is covered in the idea that any action, behavior, or structure that harms human dignity is to be resisted this might not be sufficient. Black Catholic priest and theological ethicist Bryan Massingale has noted how very few American Catholic theologians wrote about the civil rights movement as it was happening. If the civil rights movement was not an area of theological study or engagement for most Catholic theologians, it makes sense that those same theologians would not engage the causes for the movement. Thus, Cone, as an AME Christian, with his scholarship on lynching showcases how Christianity as an institution and its theologians, with their own areas of blindness, need ongoing conversion. What exactly does Cone say about the connection between lynching, the cross, and discipleship?

In *The Cross and the Lynching Tree*, Cone grapples with the terror-inducing history of lynching in the United States, particularly as it affected black Americans.[36] He makes a compelling case for connecting the cross and Jesus' crucifixion to the lynching of Americans by Americans. He writes,

> The cross and the lynching tree are separated by nearly 2,000 years. One is the universal symbol of Christian faith; the other is the quintessential symbol of black oppression in America. Though both are symbols of death, one represents a message of hope and salvation, while the other signifies negation of that message by white supremacy. Despite the obvious similarities between Jesus' death on a cross and the death of thousands of black men and women strung up to

[36] For other theological treatments of lynching, see Angela Sims, *Ethical Complications of Lynching: Ida B. Wells's Interrogation of American Terror* (New York: Palgrave MacMillan, 2010); and "Nooses in Public Spaces: A Womanist Critique of Lynching—A 21st Century Ethical Dilemma," *The Journal of the Society of Christian Ethics* 29, no. 2 (Fall/Winter 2009): 81–95. Both 2014 and the early part of 2015 saw numerous media outlets reporting on recent scholarship by historians, legal scholars, theologians, and others on the effects of lynching. Furthermore, there are groups advocating for memorials that mark lynching sites and the people who were lynched. The hope is that by making this lynching tradition more publically present, the country can come to grips with its past and heal for the future.

die on a lamppost or tree, relatively few people . . . have explored the symbolic connections.[37]

He explores, researches, and answers the question of how black Americans, like his parents, survived and resisted the lynching terror, married, raised children, loved, lived meaningful lives, and, for his parents and others, did not hate. His answer: faith. Blacks used faith to survive and resist even though whites used the cross and faith against them. They have faith in the cross because God is with Jesus on the cross. Likewise, God is with them because they are on the cross too. Personally, the cross helped Cone "deal with the brutal legacy of the lynching tree, and the lynching tree helped [him] to understand the tragic meaning of the cross."[38] In confronting the legacy of what whites did to blacks through lynching, and how the families of black victims resisted, coped, and fought a system of terror Cone re-enlivens the scandal of the cross. The cross stands as an indictment against all forms of terror and injustice. Yet for many Christians this is not the case.

Given the disconnect Cone sees between the cross and the history of lynching in the United States, he cites Dietrich Bonhoeffer and argues that the cross has become a form of "cheap grace." Agreeing with Ignacio Ellacuría, Jesuit and Salvadoran martyr, Cone argues that the cross has become disconnected from "any reference to the ongoing suffering and oppression of human beings . . . 'the crucified peoples of history.'"[39]

Following various womanist theologians, Cone further argues that the cross resulted from Jesus' "solidarity with the oppressed." Therefore, we do not suffer because Jesus suffered on the cross. Rather, we see in the cross God's presence with and affirmation of Jesus' solidarity with the

---

[37] Cone, *The Cross and the Lynching Tree*, xiii. Cone uses the work of black poets, novelists, musicians, and historians; newspaper accounts; and various other sources to lay out the ways lynching not only affected but was resisted, talked about, and not forgotten by the black American community. In his research, he turned to the poets and the activists who talk about the people he loves, since academic theologians do not always address the issues most concerning him.

[38] Ibid., xviii.

[39] Ibid., xiv. There are many theologians who are attending to the cross in their theological analysis of current events, however. Shawnee Daniels Sykes is examining the meaning of public shrines memorializing deaths in Milwaukee and how these shrines make use of religious symbols. Nancy Pineda-Madrid also looks at how crosses function as a sign of resistance by the women of Ciudad Juárez. See her book, *Suffering and Salvation in Ciudad Juárez* (Minneapolis, MN: Augsburg Fortress, 2011).

oppressed. The cross is central because of the hope for liberation and God's ongoing solidarity with the marginalized, oppressed, and terrorized.[40] Furthermore, the cross becomes a challenge to Christians, which Cone states along these lines: "If you worship someone nailed to a tree, you might end up on a tree yourself; we need to speak for those who cannot speak."[41]

Herein lies the paradox of the cross. Christians recognize it as a symbol of our salvation. Yet, too often we forget that Jesus' crucifixion at the hands of the Romans was a form of public torture and humiliation. It was a punishment for criminals. God upturns this worldview, bringing forth life from death. Suffering does not have the last word. God redeems. God, through Jesus' crucifixion and resurrection, critiques injustice and oppressive power. This critique by God supplies hope; God has the final word. God sees and affirms human dignity, even where other humans do not.[42] Yet, when the cross becomes detached from the crucified peoples of the world—detached from its challenge to resist oppression, to resist domination, to resist violence that is meant to silence and control—then the cross has become a form of cheap grace. This is the result when Christians sentimentalize the cross, when it becomes a non-challenging symbol, an easy way to be saved.

For too many Christians the cross has become about individual salvation, rather than a call and challenging invitation to resist oppression and injustice, to live God's message of justice and shalom like Jesus. As a result, Cone writes: "When American Christians realize that they can meet Jesus only in the crucified bodies in our midst, they will encounter the real scandal of the cross."[43] The cross is a paradoxical symbol that upturns the power of the world, not just in the first century, but again today. Hope comes by way of defeat; suffering does not have the last word; Jesus' cross represents God's transcendent presence, eschatological hope today.

---

[40] Cone, *The Cross and the Lynching Tree*, 149–51. He mentions Delores Williams and Shawn Copeland in particular.

[41] My notes from Cone's 2013 address to the Society of Christian Ethics. In the subsequent question-and-answer session he also said that ethics needs to talk about the ugly. In other words, ethics deals with right living and if we are going to talk about right living and right relationships, ethicists need to talk about the ugliness of the human condition that needs conversion and God's salvific presence.

[42] Cone, *The Cross and the Lynching Tree*, 2–3, 155–66.

[43] Ibid., 158.

Returning to the Society of Christian Ethics meeting with which I began this section, respondent Gloria Albrecht posed three things to her fellow theological ethicists that January morning in 2013.[44] Her comments provide a helpful way forward for all of us in various capacities as we seek to form ourselves as disciples, seeking healing from our blindness. First, she advocated that we see Cone's remarks (and scholarship) as an invitation to see how those on the margins see us. She said it is a gift to have those on the margins speak to us honestly. We need to listen to what they have to say without defending ourselves. This creates a space to hear how the past affects the present and shows a willingness to engage in the hard work of conversion.

Second, Albrecht argued that we need to think about the implications of what is said to us from the margins for understanding faith. If we do not as white Christians account for the black Christian experience, are we possibly standing outside of Christian identity? Do we not need to integrate our faith by attending to the experiences of all? While this conversation was cast in a black/white paradigm, the insights hold true for anyone who speaks from the margins. Thus, in the United States how do we as Christians engage our sisters and brothers in the faith from other cultural backgrounds that are not Western Europeans? What would it mean to actually incorporate and appropriate insights into worship, prayer, theology, and ministry from our Catholic sisters and brothers whose ethnic backgrounds and religious patrimony spring from Vietnam, Mexico, Korea, Ecuador, Nigeria, or Kenya to name a few? To be clear, no one is advocating replacing one interpretation or experience of Christianity for another. The challenge is to account for the plurality of experiences and insights in developing a theological vision and articulation of the faith that continually gives rise to practices of authentic discipleship.

Third, Albrecht asked how in the academy theologians use our power to deconstruct our theology. We need to ask, what do we teach? What is it about white Christian theology that allows and permits us not to see justice as the core of the Gospel?[45] Moving outside of the academy,

---

[44] The three ideas that Gloria Albrecht posed are not unique. Theologians and scholars have been working in various ways on the ideas she presents. She pulled various streams of theological scholarship together, however, and, in so doing, highlighted the implications of scholarship for a lived life of discipleship and implications for the faith community.

[45] The three points about Gloria Albrecht's response to Cone's work are from my notes and fleshed out by my own reflections. Regarding this last thought, attention has been and continues to be given to pedagogical concerns regarding how to teach theology that addresses the injustice of racism.

how might these insights influence how you interact at your place of work? What might our parish programming look like if it accounted for the diversity within our midst and risked moving away from a Western European paradigm for music, for example?

Liberation theologians with their attention to marginalized and oppressed peoples have challenged Christians on these questions too. Since much liberation theology comes from the global south, however, it becomes easy for some people to discount the insights or realities described by liberation theology. Cone, by connecting the cross to the lynching tree, brings home to the United States the question of solidarity with the oppressed, retrieving dangerous memories, and making the invisible visible within our own cultural location. In so doing, he places the cross with its paradox at the heart of Christian identity and discipleship. Cone's work provides, I believe, the next step when considering scandal by placing scandal in the context of Christian discipleship. How is scandal reconceived if we, as Christians, take to heart his insight that if "we worship someone nailed to a tree, we might end up on a tree ourselves." What would it mean to embrace one's core belief in the paschal mystery, letting the crucifixion and resurrection affect and form us in how we make decisions for actions in the world? Can we move from a God who saves me as an individual to a vision where we act scandalously, upsetting the status quo, resisting oppression, standing in solidarity with the oppressed, giving up our own privileged status, and thereby providing a challenging witness for others? Can we let the paschal mystery help us see: What thoughts do we have about the "other" that need conversion? How have our hearts been hardened? Where does God need to work in our individual and communal lives? Who is the guest within and outside our communities of faith that we need to offer hospitality to and welcome as Christ? Cone's challenge and these questions require us to consider our Christian practices of discipleship rather than only the statements we profess as a matter of belief. The symbols of our faith function in our speech, theologizing, and practices.[46]

---

[46] For more on the idea that the symbols of our faith function, see Elizabeth A. Johnson's study of the symbol of God in her book *She Who Is: The Mystery of God in Feminist Theological Discourse* (New York: Crossroad Publishing Co., 1992; 10th anniversary ed., 2002).

Conclusion

Given that avoidance of scandal was a criterion when considering theological dissent, I began this chapter with an exploration of various types of scandal. This clarified that some concern with scandal by the faithful when acting is warranted. Other types of scandal, however, are unavoidable in a life of Christian discipleship. Cone's scholarship connecting the symbolism of the cross with the historical events of lynching puts in sharp relief how a moral theology premised on assent to teaching without consideration of practices and living a life of discipleship can lead to malformation and the fostering of oppression. Discipleship requires an embodied engagement in the world and practices that foster the reign of God. Therefore, conscience formation requires schooling in a life of virtue, prayer, and other practices that help the disciple take on the mind of Christ. Since practices and their effects are seen over time, it is the sum of a person's life that testifies to their success or failure as a disciple of the living God.

Discipleship prompts us to recall that an encounter with the living God, an embodied experience with the historical person of Jesus or the resurrected Christ, and the outpouring of the Holy Spirit undergirds Christian action. It is hoped that the encounter nurtures a new being, one grounded in relationship with the triune God, the Scriptures, and practices of Christian community. Practices of Christian discipleship embody the values and commitments we profess to believe. Therefore, discipleship requires acknowledging that ultimately, even when abiding by magisterial teaching, we must take individual and communal responsibility for our decisions, our actions, and their effects on all of our relationships. Recalling our discipleship helps keep the moral agent and moral community's focus on facilitating and fostering right relationships, fighting for God's justice, and embodying the call to promote God's vision for health, life, peace, and wholeness on earth.

Even when emphasizing discipleship, questions about whether an action is right or wrong retain validity. Yet, other questions more explicitly concerned with relationality and moral formation become more relevant when considering discipleship. These additional questions include: Who are we as disciples? What does it mean to live a life of holiness? How did I/we respond to God today? Where did I/we fail to respond to God today? Am I/Are we growing in holiness? How does this action or potential action deepen my relationship with God and others? Are my intentions, my inner life, supporting an outward life of discipleship? Questions like these can function as the horizon by which we evaluate and contemplate the rightness, wrongness, gracefulness, or sinfulness of our actions as thoughts, words, and deeds attentive to their effects on others. Subsequently, we potentially bridge the all too frequent disconnect between piety, worship, and our moral life. In other words, discipleship has demands, obligations, and responsibilities for action in the world besides worshiping God and professing Jesus as Lord.

Discipleship means living in authentic freedom, choosing life, not death, on a daily basis, in matters large and small, even in the face of adversity. The disciple should not be turned inward, concerned primarily with his or her own salvation and ledger of right and wrong behaviors. Instead, the disciple turns outward, helping make manifest God's loving presence in the world by living the life advocated by Jesus and practiced by his early disciples. A disciple lives in the Spirit, attending to the Spirit's movements, calling forth goodness, righteousness, and life, despite difficulties or persecution. A disciple fosters kindness, mercy, compassion, love, hope, justice, and a sense of welcome and belonging among all because we are the beloved ones of God. A life of discipleship entails trusting that the One who has called those before us (Moses, Sarah, Miriam, Hagar, Abraham, Rachel, Isaac, Judith, Mary Magdalene, Phoebe, Peter, Paul, and myriad others) calls us not because of our perfections but because we have gifts to contribute to the community.

Therefore, considering conscience within the context of the call to discipleship pushes the moral agent to consider concerns beyond hot-button issues, a minimalist ethic, or an emphasis on what I can or cannot do. On the one hand, this in no way negates the task of moral theology in considering the formulation of norms, figuring out first principles, and applying them to specific cases and the categorization of right and wrong behavior. On the other hand, the need exists to develop the insight that conscience also aids us in navigating the in-between spaces, the mixed spaces, the ambiguous, dawn/dusk times of our lives. For it is in the shadows of the dawn and dusk times that we see different colors, different possibilities for being, for living, for creating, for cooperating with God. We need to attend differently at these times of day and pay more attention.

It is similar with conscience: it directs our considerations more carefully to the interplay of grace and sin, helping us see that the shadows can hold the beginnings of new life, that the dawn and dusk focus our attention on what the night hides and the daylight permits us to overlook. Conscience directs us—if we stop, look, attend, breathe, pause, peer thoughtfully, and mindfully enter into the shadows—to the colors, the possibilities, the new life that can emerge from living in and engaging ambiguity, uncertainty, and, yes, even areas of conflict. Therefore, conscience's judgments require proper seeing, watchfulness, a willingness to revise, patience, and wisdom as a means for discussing human cooperation with grace in the nitty-gritty of finite existence as we grow as disciples. In other words, as a theological category, conscience illuminates the concern about shaping a discerning disciple attuned to the life-giving practices of the community, aided by the critique and movements of the Spirit given by Christ.

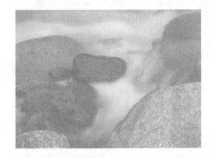

Conclusion

Thank you for journeying with me in this consideration of conscience, its formation, and its connection to discipleship. The book's genesis was my experience with people's desire to know what the church taught about conscience, what went into formation, how to navigate instances where their consciences differed from magisterial teaching or pronouncements and concerns about scandal when acting from their conscience. Underlying these desires, I heard people wrestling with how to live their lives of Christian discipleship. Therefore, these concerns structured the book's outline and research.

Chapter 1 started by examining definitions of conscience in the documents of the Second Vatican Council. This examination was followed by an exploration of how those definitions were understood in magisterial documents following the Second Vatican Council. A textual analysis briefly compared and contrasted how different documents use prior statements on conscience and demonstrated that magisterial documents pull from various corners within the tradition's intellectual history to describe conscience. As an exercise in ecclesial hermeneutics it shows why tensions arise when speaking about and trying to understand what it means to form one's conscience. This tension embedded in magisterial documents means that the magisterial documents themselves do not reify our understanding of conscience. Rather, they provide guidance when pursuing a description of the phenomenon of judging, acting, discerning, perceiving, and schooling ourselves in the moral life.

Chapter 2 continued the hermeneutical exercise by exploring how conscience has been defined and debated while outlining its evolution as an intellectual category throughout the centuries, starting with the biblical tradition. This included the move to consider conscience not as a faculty among other faculties but rather as a term that captures the reality that the human person needs formation and full development as a moral agent. Several post–Vatican II theologians reveal the ongoing need to clarify and describe how people in their moral lives experience and understand conscience. This development entails considering the person "wholly considered." This requires that formation and growth in the moral life attend to the human being's intellectual, social, emotional, affective, bodily, and spiritual dimensions. The will to act well and out of a commitment to covenantal values occurs when reason, affections, body, and spirit are attuned to and shaped by God's vision of wholeness. Therefore, I agree with Anne Patrick's call to consider, at least for a time, using the language of the formation of the moral agent rather than the formation of conscience. We need to remember that conscience functions as a metaphor for the whole person and their formation.

Chapter 3 considered the myriad ways by which communities shape and form us for good or ill. I developed how conscience (the moral agent's) formation has been understood and described new insights for forming our consciences (ourselves) as a key feature of our moral agency. This exploration looked at the process for developing moral awareness, ongoing discernment, decision making, and moral action, including the need for ongoing reflection after acting.

Chapter 4 took up the notion of dissent from magisterial teaching and examined how to navigate the reality that the teaching office and authority in the church (bishops, cardinals, and pope) is comprised of finite, contingent human beings that can error in fallible matters. The usefulness of the term "dissent" was taken up, and it was argued that certain types of dissent are not permitted since core beliefs regarding faith cannot be disputed. Dissent as a category fails, however, when matters concern a more practical, embodied enacting of faith. Therefore, it is imperative for the people of God to determine whether the issue at stake is a central tenet of the faith, disputes about what constitutes fundamental norms and principles (for example, care for the earth), or matters of practical judgments. This is especially crucial in matters of practical judgment, since what at first glance appears to be dissent might in fact be a plurality of practices arising from varying interpretations of the same teaching. Time, conversation, and discernment help determine which practices faithfully embody the scriptural good news and are valid interpretations or applications of an ecclesial norm or principle. Furthermore, a judgment of conscience disagreeing with magisterial teaching on fallible matters might be the Holy Spirit working in and through the faithful. Dissent as disagreement about practical judgments and practices can function as a corrective of bias and blindness, drawing attention to where we as a community of believers fail to live out and up to the Gospel values. As a result, dissent can function to highlight where the light needs to shine, yeast needs kneading in, and salt needs pouring in order for the kingdom of God to be brought forth.

Since dissent can cause scandal, chapter 5 began by exploring scandal and the reality that, since Christianity was founded on a scandal, scandal cannot always be avoided. In many instances scandal results from authentic discipleship. I then briefly took up the question of discipleship, what it is and how we can think about it today. Drawing on contemporary works, I argued that discipleship is not merely a belief that one is saved; it entails more than simply a profession of faith but requires living out the Gospel. We must turn to what Jesus did and model his behavior. The implications of this shift were explored by examining a select work by James Cone and his challenge to consider how the cross has, at times, been used to oppress rather than free. His explication of the racism in Christianity raises serious questions that affirm and support seeing conscience formation as the formation of the moral agent in his or her totality—intellect, spirit, affections, body—so that we can serve God with our whole heart, mind, and soul.

Using the language of conscience again, following one's conscience, at times, might entail conflict between external hierarchical authority and individual judgments. This conflict, when it occurs, cannot be the result of personal whims or uncritical obedience to earthly authority because the call to discipleship encourages us to remember that judgments of conscience remain at their core a graced response to God's presence in our lives. Following one's conscience in many instances will require challenging the status quo or fighting unjust structures.

Given that communities can both form us well and be the source of our malformation, each person must also enter into a relationship with the triune God, challenging themselves with God's grace to excise, resist, or tamp down impulses that lead to death. Discipleship, as a following of the incarnate Word, requires embodied actions that heal, bring forth life, and sustain each other in the quest for justice that acknowledges the human dignity and worth of everyone. As individuals and communities, we must be willing to change, realizing that the conversion of our hearts of stone is ongoing. Thus, we must be willing to continually place ourselves into the hands of the God who holds us in her mercy and continually shapes us into human persons living in freedom in order to be more authentic messengers of the Good News in thought, word, and practice.

Realizing that conscience's judgments encompass more than assessments regarding an individual action's "rightness or wrongness" means recognizing that considering conscience profoundly implies considerations about relationality. One criterion for evaluating the accuracy and validity of conscience's judgments will be the fruitfulness resulting from those judgments and the moral agent's growth in virtue or holiness as a disciple. As a result, conscience's judgments need assessment before and after action. Therefore, ongoing examination of conscience (our emotions, thoughts, reactions, and motivations) is vital.

As a practice, the examination of conscience should not be reserved for the sacrament of reconciliation. It also is a prayer exercise. For example, the Ignatian and Benedictine spiritual traditions, albeit in different ways, utilize an examination of conscience to foster growth in holiness, attention to the workings of grace, identification of sinful behavior, and consideration about one's overall response to God's invitation to do and seek goodness, truth, wisdom, and holiness. Practices of "examination of conscience" require the moral agent's attention to patterns of behavior (actions) as well as motivations, intentions, and effects. The moral agent and communities ideally grasp that small ideas, patterns, and behaviors can either blossom into larger flaws, vices, and sins or strengthen the virtues, character traits, and gifts already present; additionally, practices can either diminish or foster an intimacy with God and others. Placing an examination of conscience within a sacramental, prayerful, or specific spiritual framework as opposed to a juridical context helps shift emphasis from an analysis that isolates action from a moral agent's spiritual growth to an analysis that respects the dynamic, ongoing interaction between moral formation, relationships, behavior, and discipleship.

The work of the formation of conscience (the moral agent) is ongoing. It entails attention to Scripture, prayer, ecclesial teachings, the living tradition of the church, and communities of accountability. Formation is a life-long perennial task that requires continual conversion as we attempt to live more authentically as Christian disciples. May we remember that our conversion is not dependent only on our own work but rather rests more on our willingness to respond to the triune God's self-communication and to be shaped by this relationship.

Select Bibliography

Aquinas, Thomas. *Summa Theologiae.*

Billy, Dennis J., and James Keating. *Conscience and Prayer: The Spirit of Catholic Moral Theology.* Collegeville, MN: Liturgical Press, 2001.

Böckle, Franz, and Jacques-Marie Pohier, eds. *Moral Formation and Christianity.* New York: Crossroad Book, Seabury Press, 1978.

Bourdeau, F., and A. Danet. *Introduction to the Law of Christ.* New York: Paulist Press, 1966.

Bretzke, James T. *A Morally Complex World: Engaging Contemporary Moral Theology.* Collegeville, MN: Liturgical Press, 2004.

Brough, Sonia, ed. "Erfahrung," and "Erlebnis," *Langenscheidt New College German Dictionary.* New York: Langenscheidt, 1995.

Bryant, M. Darrol, and Christopher Lamb, eds. *Religious Conversion: Contemporary Practices and Controversies.* New York: Cassell, 1999.

Cahalan, Kathleen A. *Formed in the Image of Christ: The Sacramental-Moral Theology of Bernard Häring.* Collegeville, MN: Liturgical Press, 2004.

Cahill, Lisa Sowle. *Global Justice, Christology and Christian Ethics.* New York: Cambridge University Press, 2013.

Callahan, Sidney. *Called to Happiness: Where Faith and Psychology Meet.* Maryknoll, NY: Orbis Press, 2011.

———. *In Good Conscience: Reason and Emotion in Moral Decision-Making.* San Francisco: HarperCollins, 1991.

———. "The Role of Emotion in Ethical Decision Making." *Hastings Center Report* (June/July 1988): 9–14.

The Catechism of the Catholic Church. 2nd rev. ed. Vatican City, Rome: Libreria Editrice Vaticana, 1994, 1997.

Cates, Diana Fritz. *Aquinas on the Emotions: A Religious-Ethical Inquiry.* Washington, DC: Georgetown University Press, 2009.

Chan, Lucas. *Biblical Ethics in the 21st Century: Developments, Emerging Consensus, and Future Directions.* New York: Paulist Press, 2013.

Clague, Julie. "Moral Theology and Doctrinal Change." In *Moral Theology for the Twenty-First Century: Essays in Celebration of Kevin Kelly,* edited by Bernard Hoose, Julie Clague, and Gerard Mannion, 67–79. London: T&T Clark, 2008.

Clifford, Catherine E. "The Ecumenical Context of *Dignitatis humanae*: Forty Years after Vatican II." *Science Et Esprit* 59, no. 2–3 (May 1, 2007): 387–403.

Colberg, Kristin. "The Hermeneutics of Vatican II: Reception, Authority, and the Debate over the Council's Interpretation." *Horizons* 38, no. 2 (September 1, 2011): 230–52.

Cone, James H. *The Cross and the Lynching Tree.* Maryknoll, NY: Orbis Books, 2011.

Conn, Walter E. *Conscience and Conversion in Newman: A Developmental Study of Self in John Henry Newman.* Milwaukee: Marquette University Press, 2010.

Coornhert, Dirk Volkertszoon, and Gerrit Voogt. *Synod on the Freedom of Conscience: A Thorough Examination during the Gathering Held in the Year 1582 in the City of Freetown.* Amsterdam: Amsterdam University Press, 2008.

Curran, Charles E. "Conscience in the Light of the Catholic Moral Tradition." In *Catholic Moral Tradition Today: A Synthesis.* Washington, DC: Georgetown University Press, 1999.

———, ed. *Conscience.* Readings in Moral Theology, no. 14. New York: Paulist Press, 2004.

D'Arcy, Eric. *Conscience and Its Right to Freedom.* London: Sheed & Ward, 1961.

Delhaye, Philippe. *The Christian Conscience.* Translated by Charles Underhill Quinn. New York: Desclee Company, 1968.

———. *La Conscience Morale du Chrétien.* Belgium: Desclée & Co, 1964.

Demmer, Klaus. *Living the Truth: A Theory of Action.* Translated by Brian McNeil. Washington, DC: Georgetown University Press, 2010.

———. "Sittlich Handeln aus Erfahrung." *Gregorianum* 59 (1978): 661–90.

Doak, Mary. "Resisting the Eclipse of *Dignitatis humanae*." *Horizons* 33, no. 1 (March 1, 2006): 33–53.

Dougherty, M. V. *Moral Dilemmas in Medieval Thought: From Gratian to Aquinas.* Cambridge: Cambridge University Press, 2011.

Dulles, Avery. "Faith and Revelation." In *Systematic Theology: Roman Catholic Perspectives,* edited by Francis Schüssler Fiorenza and John P. Gavin, vol. 1, 89–128. Minneapolis: Fortress Press, 1991.

———. *The Reshaping of Catholicism: Current Challenges in the Theology of the Church.* New York: Harper and Row, 1988.

Dumm, Demetrius. *Cherish Christ above All: The Bible in the Rule of Benedict.* Latrobe, PA: Archabbey Publications, 2002, 2008; originally Mahwah, NJ: Paulist Press, 1996.

Elsbernd, Mary. "The Reinterpretation of *Gaudium et Spes* in *Veritatis Splendor.*" *Horizons* 29, no. 2 (2002): 225–39.

Evans, Bernard F. *Vote Catholic? Beyond the Political Din.* Collegeville, MN: Liturgical Press, 2008.

Faggioli, Massimo. *Vatican II: The Battle for Meaning.* New York: Paulist Press, 2012.

Farley, Margaret A. "Freedom and Desire." In *The Papers of the Henry Luce III Fellows in Theology*, ed. Matthew Zyniewicz, 57–73. Atlanta, GA: Scholars Press, 1999.

———. *Personal Commitments: Beginning, Keeping, Changing*. San Francisco: Harper & Row, 1986.

Flannery, Austin, ed. *Vatican Council II: The Basic Sixteen Documents*. Collegeville, MN: Liturgical Press, 2014.

Fuchs, Josef. *Christian Ethics in a Secular Arena*. Washington, DC: Georgetown University Press, 1984.

Gadamer, Hans-Georg. *Truth and Method*. 2nd rev. ed. Translated by Joel Weinsheimer and Donald G. Marshall. New York: Continuum, 1995.

Gaillardetz, Richard R. *By What Authority? A Primer on Scripture, the Magisterium, and the Sense of the Faithful*. Collegeville, MN: Liturgical Press, 2003.

———. *Teaching with Authority: A Theology of the Magisterium in the Church*. Collegeville, MN: Liturgical Press, 1997.

Gathercole, S. J. "A Law unto Themselves: The Gentiles in Romans 2.14-15 Revisited." *Journal for The Study of the New Testament* 85 (2002): 27–49.

Gilley, Sheridan. "Life and Writings." In *The Cambridge Companion to John Henry Newman*, edited by Ian Ker and Terrence Merrigan, 1–28. Cambridge: Cambridge University Press, 2009.

Gilleman, Gérard. *The Primacy of Charity in Moral Theology*. Translated by William F. Ryan and André Vachon. Westminster, MD: The Newman Press, 1959.

Godman, Peter. *Paradoxes of Conscience in the High Middle Ages: Abelard, Heloise, and the Archpoet*. Cambridge Studies in Medieval Literature. New York and Cambridge: Cambridge University Press, 2009.

Godzieba, Anthony J. "'. . . And Followed Him on the Way' (Mk 10:52): Identity, Difference, and the Play of Discipleship." *CTSA Proceedings* 69 (2014): 1–22.

Greene, Robert A. "Synderesis, the Spark of Conscience, in the English Renaissance." *Journal of the History of Ideas* 52, no. 2 (April–June 1991): 195–219.

Griffin, Leslie. "Commentary on *Dignitatis humanae* (Declaration on Religious Freedom)." In *Modern Catholic Social Teaching*, edited by Kenneth R. Himes, 244–65. Washington, DC: Georgetown University Press, 2004.

Gula, Richard M. "Conscience." In *Christian Ethics: An Introduction*, edited by Bernard Hoose, 110–22. Collegeville, MN: Liturgical Press, 1998.

———. *Moral Discernment*. New York: Paulist Press, 1997.

———. *Reason Informed by Faith*. Mahwah, NJ: Paulist Press, 1989.

Häring, Bernard. *Das Gesetz Chrisit* (Freiburg: Verlag Wewel, 1954); *The Law of Christ*. Translated by Edwin Kaiser. Westminster, MD: The Newman Press, 1961.

———. *Dare to Be Christian: Developing a Social Conscience*. Liguori, MO: Liguori Publications, 1983.

———. *Embattled Witness: Memories of a Time of War*. New York: Seabury Press, 1976.

————. *Free and Faithful in Christ.* New York: Crossroad, 1978–1981.

————. *My Hope for the Church: Critical Engagement for the Twenty-First Century.* Liguori, MO: Liguori Publications, 1999.

————. *Road to Renewal: Perspectives of Vatican II.* New York: Paulist Press, 1966.

Harrison, Beverly Wildung. "The Power of Anger in the Work of Love." *Union Seminary Quarterly Review* 36 (1981): 41–57.

Hass, John M., ed. *Crisis of Conscience.* New York: Crossroad Herder, 1996.

Heft, James L., and John O'Malley, eds. *After Vatican II: Trajectories and Hermeneutics.* Grand Rapids, MI: William B. Eerdmans Publishing Company, 2012.

Hein, Rudolf B. "Conscience: Dictator or Guide?—Meta-Ethical and Biographical Reflections in the Light of a Humanist Concept of Conscience." In *Moral Theology for the Twenty-First Century: Essays in Celebration of Kevin Kelly,* edited by Bernard Hoose, Julie Clague, and Gerard Mannion, 34–50. London: T&T Clark, 2008.

Himes, Kenneth R. "The Formation of Conscience: The Sin of Sloth and the Significance of Spirituality." In *Spirituality and Moral Theology: Essays from a Pastoral Perspective,* edited by James Keating, 59–80. New York: Paulist Press, 2000.

Hittinger, Russell. "The Declaration on Religious Liberty, *Dignitatis humanae.*" In *Vatican II: Renewal within Tradition.* New York: Oxford University Press, 2008.

Hogan, Linda. *Confronting the Truth: Conscience in the Catholic Tradition.* New York: Paulist Press, 2000.

Hollenbach, David. "Commentary on *Gaudium et Spes.*" In *Modern Catholic Social Teaching: Commentaries and Interpretations,* edited by Kenneth R. Himes, 261–91. Washington, DC: Georgetown University Press, 2005.

Hoose, Bernard. *Proportionalism: The American Debate and Its European Roots.* Washington, DC: Georgetown University Press, 1987.

Hughes, Gerard J. "Conscience." In *The Cambridge Companion to John Henry Newman,* edited by Ian Ker and Terrence Merrigan, 189–220. Cambridge: Cambridge University Press, 2009.

Johnson, Elizabeth A. *She Who Is: The Mystery of God in a Feminist Theological Discourse.* New York: Crossroad, 1992.

Johnstone, Brian V. "Erroneous Conscience in *Veritatis Splendor* and the Theological Tradition." In *The Splendor of Accuracy: An Examination of the Assertions Made by* Veritatis Splendor, edited by Joseph A. Selling and Jan Jans, 114–35. Grand Rapids, MI: William B. Eerdmans Publishing Co., 1995.

Kaufman, Philip S. *Why You Can Disagree and Remain a Faithful Catholic.* Rev. ed. New York: Crossroad, 1995.

Keenan, James F. *A History of Catholic Moral Theology in the Twentieth Century: From Confession Sins to Liberating Consciences.* New York: Continuum, 2010.

Ker, Ian, and Terrence Merrigan, eds. *The Cambridge Companion to John Henry Newman.* Cambridge: Cambridge University Press, 2009.

Kopfensteiner, Thomas R. "The Metaphorical Structure of Normativity." *Theological Studies* 58, no. 2 (June 1, 1997): 331–46.

Lamb, Matthew, and Matthew Levering, eds. *Vatican II: Renewal within Tradition.* Oxford: Oxford University Press, 2008.

Madges, William ed. *Vatican II: Forty Years Later.* Maryknoll, NY: Orbis, 2006.

Mahoney, John. *The Making of Moral Theology: A Study of the Roman Catholic Tradition.* Oxford: Clarendon Press, 1987.

Marinelli, Anthony J. *Conscience and Catholic Faith.* New York: Paulist Press, 1991.

May, William E., et al. *The Teaching of* Humanae Vitae: *A Defense.* San Francisco: Ignatius Press, 1988.

McCool, Gerald A. *Nineteenth-Century Scholasticism: The Search for a Unitary Method.* New York: Fordham University Press, 1989.

———. *Unity to Pluralism: The Internal Evolution of Thomism.* New York: Fordham University Press, 1989; reprint 1977.

Mealey, Ann Marie. "The Bioethical Conscience." In *An Irish Reader in Moral Theology: The Legacy of the Last Fifty Years,* vol. 3, edited by Enda McDonagh and Vincent McNamara, 46–56. Dublin: Columba Press, 2013.

Merrigan, Terrence. "Conscience and Selfhood: Thomas More, John Henry Newman, and the Crisis of the Postmodern Subject." *Theological Studies* 73, no. 4 (December 2012): 841–69.

Murray, John Courtney. "The 'Declaration on Religious Freedom.'" In *Change in Official Catholic Moral Teachings.* New York/Mahwah, NJ: Paulist Press, 2003.

National Conference of Catholic Bishops. *Human Life in Our Day: A Collective Pastoral Letter of the American Hierarchy Issued November 15, 1968.* Huntington, IN: Our Sunday Visitor, 1968.

Newman, John Henry. *A Letter Addressed to His Grace the Duke of Norfolk on the Occasion of Mr. Gladstone's Recent Expostulation.* 4th ed. London: B.M. Pickering, 1875.

———. "Sermon 17: The Testimony of Conscience." In *Parochial and Plain Sermons,* vol. 5, 237–53. Waterloo, London: Rivingtons, 1882.

O'Malley, John W. *What Happened at Vatican II.* Cambridge, MA, and London: The Belknap Press of Harvard University Press, 2008.

Orsy, Ladislas. "The Divine Dignity of Human Persons in *Dignitatis Humanae.*" *Theological Studies* 75, no. 1 (March, 2014): 8–22.

Patrick, Anne E. *Conscience and Calling: Ethical Reflections on Catholic Women's Church Vocations.* London: Bloomsbury T&T Clark, 2013.

———. *Liberating Conscience: Feminist Explorations in Catholic Moral Theology.* New York: Continuum, 1996.

———. *Women, Conscience, and the Creative Process.* 2009 Madeleva Lecture in Spirituality. New York: Paulist Press, 2011.

Piñeda-Madrid, Nancy. *Suffering and Salvation in Ciudad Juárez*. Minneapolis, MN: Augsburg Fortress, 2011.

Pohl, Christine D. *Making Room: Recovering Hospitality as a Christian Tradition*. Grand Rapids, MI: Eerdmans Publishing Company, 1999.

Pope Leo XIII, *Aeterni Patris* (On the Restoration of Christian Philosophy), 1879. http://www.vatican.va/holy_father/leo_xiii/encyclicals/documents/hf_l-xiii_enc_04081879_aeterni-patris_en.html.

Potts, Timothy. *Conscience in Medieval Philosophy*. New York: Cambridge University Press, 1980.

———. "Conscience." In *Cambridge History of Later Medieval Philosophy: From the Recovery of Aristotle to the Disintegration of Scholasticism, 1100–1600*, edited by Norman Kretzmann, Anthony Kenny, and Jan Pinborg, 687–704. New York: Cambridge University Press, 1982.

Rahner, Karl. "On the Question of a Formal Existential Ethics." In *Theological Investigations*, vol. 2, translated by Karl-H. Kruger, 217–34. Baltimore, MD: Helicon Press, 1963.

———. *The Trinity*. Translated by Joseph Donceel. New York: Crossroad Herder, 1998, 1970.

Ratzinger, Cardinal Joseph. *On Conscience*. San Francisco: Ignatius Press, 2007.

Rubio, Julie Hanlon. "Beyond the Liberal/Conservative Divide on Contraception: The Wisdom of Practitioners of Natural Family Planning and Artificial Birth Control." *Horizons* 32, no. 2 (September 1, 2005): 270–94.

———. *Family Ethics: Practices for Christians*. Washington, DC: Georgetown University Press, 2010.

Schindler, David L. "Freedom, Truth, and Human Dignity: An Interpretation of *Dignitatis humanae* on the Right to Religious Liberty." *Communio* 40, no. 2–3 (2013): 208–316.

Selling, Joseph A., and Jan Jans, eds. *The Splendor of Accuracy: An Examination of the Assertions Made by* Veritatis Splendor. Grand Rapids, MI: William B. Eerdmans Publishing Co., 1994.

Senander, Angela. *Scandal: The Catholic Church and Public Life*. Collegeville, MN: Liturgical Press, 2012.

Shin, Joyce. "Accommodating the Other's Conscience: Saint Paul's Approach to Religious Tolerance." *Journal of the Society of Christian Ethics* 1 (2008): 1–23.

Sims, Angela. *Ethical Complications of Lynching: Ida B. Wells's Interrogation of American Terror*. New York: Palgrave MacMillan, 2010.

———. "Nooses in Public Spaces: A Womanist Critique of Lynching—A 21st Century Ethical Dilemma." *The Journal of the Society of Christian Ethics* 29, no. 2 (Fall/Winter 2009): 81–95.

Smith, Janet E. "The *Sensus Fidelium* and '*Humanae Vitae*.'" In *Called to Holiness and Communion: Vatican II on the Church*, 291–319. Scranton, PA: University of Scranton Press, 2009.

Smith, Robert J. *Conscience and Catholicism: The Nature and Function of Conscience in Contemporary Roman Catholic Moral Theology.* Lanham, MD: University Press of America, 1998.

Smith, Russell E., ed. *Catholic Conscience Foundation and Formation.* Proceedings of the Tenth Bishops' Workshop, Dallas, Texas. Braintree, MA: The Pope John XXIII Center, 1991.

Spohn, William C. *Go and Do Likewise: Jesus and Ethics.* New York: Continuum, 1999.

Sullivan, Francis A. *Creative Fidelity: Weighing and Interpreting Documents of the Magisterium.* Eugene, OR: Wipf and Stock Publishers, 2003. Previously published New York: Paulist Press, 1996.

Thompson, Daniel Speed. *The Language of Dissent: Edward Schillebeeckx on the Crisis of Authority in the Catholic Church.* Notre Dame, IN: University of Notre Dame Press, 2003.

Tilley, Terrence W. *The Disciples' Jesus: Christology as Reconciling Practice.* Maryknoll, NY: Orbis Books, 2008.

Tillmann, Franz. *The Master Calls: A Handbook of Morals for the Layman.* Translated by Gregory J. Roettger. Baltimore: Helicon Press, 1960.

Tracy, David. *The Analogical Imagination: Christian Theology and the Culture of Pluralism.* New York: Crossroad, 1981.

———. *Plurality and Ambiguity: Hermeneutics, Religion, and Hope.* Chicago: The University of Chicago Press, 1987.

Vacek, Edward C. "Discipleship and the Moral Life: Conscience Formation." *Catechist* (January 2003): 54–58.

———. *Love, Human and Divine: The Heart of Christian Ethics.* Washington, DC: Georgetown University Press, 1994.

Wadell, Paul J. *Happiness and the Christian Moral Life.* Lanham, MD: Sheed and Ward, 2008.

Weaver, Darlene Fozard. "Vatican II and Moral Theology." In *After Vatican II: Trajectories and Hermeneutics,* edited by James L. Heft and John O'Malley, 23–42. Grand Rapids, MI: William B. Eerdmans, 2012.

Williams, Thomas D. *Knowing Right from Wrong: A Christian Guide to Conscience.* New York: Faith Words, a division of Hachette Book Group, 2008.

Index of Subjects

Index of Names